Lessons Learned from Popular Culture

Lessons Learned from Popular Culture

Tim Delaney and Tim Madigan

Published by State University of New York Press, Albany

For information, contact State University of New York Press, Albany, NY
www.sunypress.edu

Production, Eileen Nizer
Marketing, Anne M. Valentine

Library of Congress Cataloging-in-Publication Data

Names: Delaney, Tim. | Madigan, Tim.
Title: Lessons learned from popular culture / Tim Delaney and Tim Madigan.
Description: Albany : State University of New York Press, 2016. | Includes
  bibliographical references and index.
Identifiers: LCCN 2015036579 | ISBN 9781438461458 (hardcover : alk. paper) |
  ISBN 9781438461465 (pbk. : alk. paper) | ISBN 9781438461472 (e-book)
Subjects: LCSH: Mass media and culture—United States. | Popular culture—
  United States.
Classification: LCC P94.65.U6 D47 2016 | DDC 306.0973—dc23
LC record available at http://lccn.loc.gov/2015036579

10 9 8 7 6 5 4 3 2 1

Contents

Contents

Preface

The world of popular culture not only entertains us and reflects our cultural values and norms, it provides valuable life lessons. *Lessons Learned from Popular Culture* is filled with a number of "short stories" from the world of popular culture, each of which concludes with a "Lesson Learned" offering from the authors. The "Lesson Learned" concept serves as a brief, generally one-sentence "moral of the story" type of explanation for each popular culture story. In other words, what we hope the reader learned from the story. We do, however, encourage readers to come up with their own lessons learned following each story and compare them to ours and their friends'. Because this is a book on popular culture and written to be as entertaining as it is informative, the authors' "lessons" tend to be brief—like a "Final Thought" to wrap up the story. People who are good storytellers do this in everyday life; that is to say, they tell a story to their friends or family members and then offer a final thought, like a punch line designed to make people laugh, smile, or think about what was just said. In this regard, the "Lesson Learned" statements provide the reader with an opportunity to reflect on the story told. It's like a ribbon on a present.

The lessons provided by the authors are generally meant to be funny and at times a bit sarcastic as well. For example, the "Lesson Learned" about the *Sharknado* craze provided at the end of chapter 1—"Never underestimate the public's willingness to suspend reality!"—is clearly meant as an attempt to be sarcastically funny, as the concept of a "Sharknado" is rather silly, but the public often enjoys silly forms of popular culture. Other "Lesson Learned" statements attempt to provide readers with a "food for thought" type of scenario with deeper sociological and/or philosophical undertones. For example, at the conclusion of the first story in chapter 2 ("If Apes Evolved Instead of Humans"), the "Lesson Learned"—"As the 'Law of Unanticipated Consequences' warns, the testing of experimental drugs on apes may alter the natural evolutionary process"—involves a deeper message on such topics as experimental drug testing on animals, genetic research, the evolutionary process, and the "Law of Unanticipated Consequences" itself. It is the hope of the authors that readers may actually take the time to look up the "Law of Unanticipated Consequences" for themselves, if they wish to learn more about this topic.

The idea of learning life lessons from popular culture is not a new one. In fact, representatives of popular culture themselves often attempt to provide a life lesson. Consider, for example, the 2014 season finale of *The Simpsons* ("Yellow Badge of Cowardge") when Homer Simpson states, "If the *Expendables* movies taught us anything, people do their best after they're old and forgotten." Homer's statement manages to both slam the *Expendables* movies because of their perceived lack of quality, while also offering hope that if Sylvester Stallone, Dolph Lundren, and Steve Austin can keep on making action films when they're eligible for AARP membership, then there's hope for all of us.

During his May 21, 2014, opening monologue of *The Jimmy Kimmel Show*, Kimmel described the incredible journey of *Dancing with the Stars* contestant Amy Purdy. Purdy was competing under a seemingly insurmountable handicap as she had lost both her legs as a teenager after contracting meningitis (Griffith 2014). Purdy and her dance partner Derek Hough reached the finals of the dancing contest but lost to Meryl Davis, a gold medal Olympian ice dancing skater and her *Dancing with the Stars* partner Maksim Chmerkovskiy. The results led Kimmel to offer this life lesson: "Even if you lose both of your legs, if you work hard and believe in yourself, you can *almost* achieve your dreams." Clearly, this sarcastic attempt at humor was designed to applaud people who attempt to overcome challenges while implying that nevertheless, in most cases, people should maintain realistic goals and aspirations.

In their "Lesson Learned" statements, the authors utilize the same approach as the Homer Simpsons and Jimmy Kimmels of the world; that is to say, we will provide a lesson at the end of each story and leave it at that. It is up to the reader to figure out the meaning of the statement. In most cases, the meaning of the lesson should be quite clear, while in other cases, figuring out the meaning behind the authors' words involves a hermeneutic approach. Hermeneutics is a special approach to the understanding and interpretation of published writings, with its goal to understand both the basic structure of the text as well as the thinking of the author (Pressler and Dasilva 1996; Delaney 2014). When utilizing a hermeneutic interpretation of published writings the reader comes to understand, for example, that seemingly vague and generalized statements may have a specific meaning to the author.

Perhaps the most noteworthy examples of popular culture offering life lessons come from fairy tales. Fairy tales, short stories that in our culture typically feature characters taken from European folklore, provide the concept of: "the moral of the story" (via their "happy endings") at the end of each short story. Little Red Riding Hood learned a lesson about the dangers of talking to strangers, and the Three Bears not to leave their doors open to thieving little girls. Each of the stories presented in this book concludes with the authors offering a lesson learned based on their insights from their observations and participation in popular culture.

The authors hope you will enjoy *Lessons Learned from Popular Culture* and come to view popular culture itself in a slightly different manner, as it has cultural value beyond its initial entertainment face value. Popular culture is a good means to confront, in a harmless way, the many issues that can otherwise overwhelm us. Perhaps the main lesson to learn is that life would be pretty dull without the diversions and attractions that popular culture provides to us all.

Acknowledgments

The authors would like to thank the anonymous reviewers of the early drafts of this publication; we appreciate your input. We would also like to thank Michael Rinella and Rafael Chaiken of SUNY Press for your assistance throughout the review and acquisitions process. In addition, we'd like to thank Eileen Nizer, our Production Editor, and the anonymous copyeditor, for all their hard work.

As Ambassadors of Popular Culture, both authors would like to acknowledge all the different genres of popular culture.

Tim Delaney is thankful for Christina and all others who have contributed to the world of popular culture.

Tim Madigan would like to give a shout out to the late Steve Allen, first host of *the Tonight Show*, who inspired his ongoing love for popular culture with a zany twist.

About the Authors

Tim Delaney is a professor and department chair of sociology at the State University of New York at Oswego. He earned his BS in sociology from SUNY Brockport, MA degree in sociology from California State University Dominquez Hills, and a PhD in sociology from the University of

Nevada Las Vegas. Delaney has published fifteen books, numerous book chapters, journal and encyclopedia articles, and has been published in five continents. Professor Delaney is listed as a "Media Expert" and regularly grants interviews with newspapers and radio programs primarily across the United States and Canada. He has also appeared on a number of local TV entertainment and news programs.

Tim Madigan is associate professor of philosophy and director of the Irish Studies program at St. John Fisher College in Rochester, New York. He earned his PhD degree in philosophy from the State University of New York at Buffalo, as well as his MA and BA degrees from the same institution. A frequent lecturer on topics relating to applied ethics, philosophy and popular culture, and the ethics of belief, Madigan has given presentations at several institutions of learning throughout the United States and abroad. He is the president of the Bertrand Russell Society, the former president of the Northeast Popular Culture Association, and former board member of the Popular Culture/American Culture Association.

1

An Introduction to Popular Culture

The term *popular culture* holds different meanings depending on who is defining it. It is a generic, or conceptual, term that can be defined in a variety of (sometimes conflicting) ways depending on the context of use. Popular culture is generally recognized as the vernacular or people's culture that dominates any society at a given point in time. As Brummett (1991) explains, popular culture involves the aspects of social life that are most actively involved in by the public. As the "culture of the people," popular culture is determined by the daily interactions between people and their everyday activities. Styles of dress, the use of slang, greeting rituals, and the foods that people eat are all examples of the various influences on popular culture. Popular culture is also influenced by such social forces as the mass media and the many forms of entertainment, such as sports, music, film, and television. Popular culture serves an inclusionary role in society as it unites the masses on ideals of acceptable forms of behavior.

There is no universally accepted definition of popular culture. However, there are a number of generally agreed-upon elements that comprise popular culture. For example, popular culture encompasses the most immediate and contemporary elements in our lives. These elements are often subject to rapid change, especially in a highly technological world in which people are brought closer and closer by the omnipresent mass media. Certain standards and commonly held beliefs are reflected in pop culture. Because of its commonality, pop culture both reflects and influences people's everyday life (Petracca and Sorapure 1998). Furthermore, certain brands of products (e.g., the Apple logo, the Nike "swoosh," or the McDonald's "golden arches") can attain iconic status with the populace. However, iconic brands, like other aspects of popular culture, may rise and fall (Holt 2004). With these fundamental aspects in mind, popular culture may be defined as the items (products) and forms of expression and identity that are frequently encountered or widely accepted, commonly liked or approved, and that are characteristic of a particular society at a given time. Ray Browne, founder of the Popular Culture Association, offers a similar definition: "Popular culture consists of the aspects of attitudes, behaviors, beliefs, customs, and tastes that define the people of any society. Popular culture is, in the historic use of term, the *culture of the people*" (Browne 2005:24).

Popular culture is a vehicle that allows large heterogeneous masses of people to identify collectively with others. Along with forging a sense of identity that binds individuals to the greater society, consuming the various popular items of culture often enhances an individual's level of prestige as well. Further, popular culture, unlike folk or high culture, provides individuals with a chance to impact, modify, or even change the prevailing sentiments and norms of behavior.

Popular culture is usually defined in such a way as to distinguish it from folk or high culture. In some ways, folk culture is similar to popular culture because of the mass participation involved with both. Folk culture, however, represents the "traditional" way of doing things; consequently, it is much more static than popular culture and is not as amendable to change. Folk culture represents a simpler lifestyle that is generally conservative, largely self-sufficient, cohesive, and often characteristic of rural life. Individualism is generally discouraged. Group members are expected to conform to traditional modes of behavior adopted by the greater community. Folk culture is local in orientation and noncommercial. Because of this, popular culture often represents an intrusion and challenge to the tradition of folk culture. Conversely, folk culture rarely intrudes upon popular culture. There are times when certain elements of folk culture (e.g., Turkish rugs, Mexican blankets, and Irish fairy tales) find their way into the world of popular culture. Generally, when the folk culture items that were appropriated by the popular culture become marketed, the original folk culture item(s) gradually disappears from its original form. In short, folk culture is looking for stability for its societal members, whereas the popular culture is generally looking for something new, or fresh. That is why popular culture often has an air of being ephemeral or fleeting, and why references to recent popular works often date quickly, while references to folk cultures are usually immediately understood. Popular culture is a dynamic, unstable field. Once-beloved cultural icons can become tomorrow's forgotten figures.

In the words of the Irish wit Oscar Wilde (a high culture figure much referred to in popular culture), "[I]t is only the modern that ever becomes old-fashioned."

A key characteristic of popular culture is its accessibility to the masses. It is, after all, the culture of the people. High culture, on the other hand, is not mass produced nor meant for mass consumption. High culture belongs to the socially elite. (Note: This does not mean that social elites do not participate in popular culture or that members of the masses do not participate in high culture.) High culture (e.g., the arts, opera, theatre, and intellectual superiority) is associated with the upper socioeconomic classes. Cultural items of high culture often require extensive experience, training, or reflection to be appreciated. These items seldom cross over to the domain of popular culture. Consequently, popular culture is generally looked upon as being superficial, especially when compared to the sophistication of high culture. And conversely, popular culture often pokes fun at high culture, as can be seen, for instance, in the frequent opera parodies of the Warner Brothers' *Bugs Bunny* cartoons or jokes about modern art in episodes of *The Simpsons*.

There are numerous sources of popular culture. As implied above, a primary source of popular culture is the mass media, especially popular music, film, television, radio, video games, book publications, and the Internet. In addition, advancements in communication systems allow for the rapid transmission of ideas by word of mouth; especially via cell phones. Shows such as *American Idol* have for years provided viewers with a phone number so that they may vote for their favorite contestant. Newer reality shows have given viewers more options than phone voting for a favorite contestant. As explained by Brian Anthony Hernandez (2011), *The Voice* has allowed viewers to vote by buying the contestants' songs on iTunes. Over the years, *The X Factor* has allowed viewers to vote via phone calls, texts, Twitter direct message–enabled voting, access to the show's website, and via The Xtra Factor App. *Project Runway* lets fans use Twitter hashtags to vote for a fan favorite every episode. The combining of sources (such as television and communications) of popular culture represents a novel way of increasing public interest and further fuels the mass production of certain commodities.

Popular culture is also influenced by professional entities that provide the public with information and facts about the world. These sources of pop culture include the news media, scientific and scholarly publications, organizations like the Popular Culture/American Culture Association, and "expert" opinions from people considered an "authority" in their field. For example, a news station reporting on a specific topic (e.g., the effects of playing violent video games on youths) will seek someone who is an "expert" in that field (e.g., a noted philosopher or sociologist that has published in this area) so that they can be interviewed as part of the news broadcast. This production strategy is a useful way of influencing the public and may shape their collective opinions on a particular subject. At the very least, it provides a starting point for public discourse and differing opinions. Generally, news stations allow viewers to call or e-mail their opinions—which may be shared with the public—on the topic at hand.

Examples of popular culture come from a wide array of genres, and each of the chapters from 2 through 12 in this book cover these different topics. Sports, television, and social media, for example, are among the most widely consumed examples of popular culture. Sports are enjoyed by males and females of all ages, races/ethnicities, and regardless of social class. In fact, in 2012, six in ten Americans reported being sports fans; this is a dramatic increase from fifty years earlier, when just 30 percent of Americans considered themselves sports fans (Beneke and Remillard 2014). Sports are popular throughout the world and some sporting events, such as the World Cup and the Olympics, are consumed by a collective world viewing community numbering in the billions. As Delaney and Madigan (2015) explain, sports are pervasive in most societies and represent a major part of many people's lives. The pervasiveness of sports is evidenced by the large amount of print coverage dedicated to sports, talk radio shows, local and national television coverage, electronic media coverage (e.g., games available online), attendance figures, sports-related movies and videos, and the hundreds of millions of websites found online via a Google search. Showing allegiance to a sports team as a means of self-identification is a common behavior of many people. Further, cheering for a sports team or a favorite athlete is a way that any individual can become a part of popular culture. Feeling elation when one's team wins, or devastation when it loses—known respectively as "Basking in Reflected Glory" (BIRGing) or "Cutting Off Reflected Failure" (CORFing)—are real emotions felt on a mass level (Delaney and Madigan 2015).

Many people watch numerous hours of television every day. (Note: As we shall see in chapter 3, however, most of the people watching TV are aging and younger adults are not watching nearly as much.) Some people watch so much television that they resemble TV's Homer Simpson's "couch potato" persona. With the vast array of television programs available on cable or satellite combined with high density, large screen, viewing capacity, is it any wonder we watch as much television as we do?

Television brings us news, weather, sports, and entertainment. It is such a prevalent aspect of contemporary culture that it is difficult to imagine life without it. There are those who believe that television is responsible for the "dumbing down" of society. Critics are especially concerned that children watch too much television and that the couch potato syndrome has contributed to the growing epidemic rate of childhood obesity.

The globally popular *The Simpsons* show provides us with an interesting perspective on television. While doing time in prison, "Sideshow Bob" became a critic of television. Although he was once a regular on "The Krusty the Clown Show," Bob has become obsessed by television's harmful effect on society. In the "Sideshow Bob's Last Gleaming" episode (#3F08), Bob argues that everyone's life would be much richer if TV were done away with. As a result, he devises a scheme to detonate a nuclear bomb unless all television is abolished in Springfield. Unable to locate Bob, who has escaped from prison, Springfield's city officials meet to discuss Bob's demands of abolishing television. A panicky Krusty the Clown proclaims, "Would it really be worth living in a world without television? I think the survivors would envy the dead." Although there are people who agree with Sideshow Bob's perspective on television, millions of people, who make up part of the popular culture world, would more likely agree with Krusty that living in a world without television is not really living. And while the life lesson here may be similar to that offered by Krusty the Clown—Do we really want to live in a world without television?—we offer this life lesson: It is more difficult to imagine a world without popular culture.

We do know that today millions of people are ignoring television and finding entertainment value in streaming shows on much smaller screens, such as computer, smart phone, and iWatch screens. The introduction of electronic technology, or social media, fuels our thirst for instantaneous information. Social media provides us with live streaming, and live streaming can give us sports information, television programming, and much, much more in the palms of our hands. Social media also gives us social networking sites and devices such as Facebook, Twitter, Instagram, and so on, so that we can communicate with one another in the cyber world. We will discuss the popularity of social media in chapter 4.

In the following chapters, the authors have divided popular culture into specific categories, or genres, consisting of: movies; television; social media; music; radio; cartoons and comics; books; fads, fashion, technology, and trends; comedians, celebrities, and other ambassadors of popular culture; sports; and virtual reality. The authors will share six "short stories" relevant to each category of popular culture and offer a "lesson learned" at the conclusion of each. The "lesson learned" concept was described in the Preface but it is worth repeating here that it serves as a brief, generally one-sentence "moral of the story" type of explanation for each popular culture story told, thus providing a brief synthesis and evaluation of what we hope the reader learned from the story.

It should also be noted that, as demonstrated with our earlier example of reality TV talent shows that incorporate audience voting via such methods as phoning, texting, tweeting, and using an app, there are many occasions when a story centered on one genre of popular culture overlaps with other venues, creating a true popular culture phenomenon. Thus, we define a *popular culture phenomenon* as any instance when an aspect of one form of pop culture crosses over to at least six other genres of popular culture. Such is the case with the *Sharknado* made-for-TV movie franchise. If you've never heard of *Sharknado* you are not a true consumer of popular culture, as this B-style movie propelled the Syfy Channel (former known as the Sci-Fi Channel) to its highest level of movie viewership. The attention this movie franchise garnered from so many other popular culture venues is astounding.

For the unacquainted, the *Sharknado* movie franchise began in July 2013 with the first movie, simply titled *Sharknado*. The *Sharknado* films star Ian Ziering (as Finley "Fin" Shepard) and Tara Reid (as April Wexler, Fin's ex-wife), both of whom as actors were nearly forgotten by Hollywood. In the first *Sharknado* movie, an abnormal hurricane sucks up a seemingly infinite number of sharks from the ocean and drops them from the sky over Los Angeles onto the horrified citizens below. With an estimated budget of just $1 million, *Sharknado* was never expected to draw the attention of the Academy of Motion Pictures Arts and Sciences. Instead, Syfy hoped to gain some interest and entertain a viewing audience that enjoys campy B movies about sharks and natural disasters. *Sharknado* garnered 1.4 million viewers in its initial airing (Villarreal 2014).

Surprisingly, however, the absurdity of *Sharknado* caught the attention of more than just the viewers who turn to Syfy looking for low budget entertainment (one of the authors of this book especially enjoys the Saturday B movie offerings of Syfy); it drew reactions from many people in the media. Howard Stern, for example, discussed the movie on his radio show and seemed to marvel at its silliness. *Sharknado* was trending on social media. Other popular culture commentators and word of mouth led to the re-airing of *Sharknado*, which drew an additional half-million viewers (*Deadline* 2013). Regal Cinemas and NCM Fathom Events decided to show *Sharknado* for one night in limited release, where it took in nearly $200,000 in box office receipts (*Deadline* 2013). While viewership numbers such as these are considered low for networks and movie production companies, the Syfy Channel was delighted; so much so that they decided to film a second installment.

A year after the first movie originally aired, Syfy released *Sharknado 2: The Second One*. The ridiculousness of this sequel is revealed in the title of the film itself; after all, if you have the number 2 in the title, you don't need to also say "The Second One." But such is life with B movies. Embracing *Sharknado* for what it really is, the plot of this film was similar to the first, only this shark-infested storm wreaks havoc in New York City instead of Los Angeles. Once again Fin and April must save the day. This tongue-in-cheek horror film is actually quite entertaining, and one cannot help but laugh at its suspension of reality. *Sharknado* 2 is filled with cheesy one-liners too. For example, after having her hand bitten off by a shark, April (Tara Reid) states, "He had a scar. It's like he knew who I was." Martin Brody (played by Mark McGrath), perhaps underscoring the *Sharknado* films B-movie quality, proclaims in one scene, "You know what you just did, don't you? Jumped the shark." "Jumping the Shark" is a term used to describe the episode aired when a TV show has run out of viable plot lines and adds something odd to the show, more or less signifying that it's near demise. The expression was first popularized when *Happy Days* had its iconic character Fonzie ride his motorcycle over a pit of sharks. Critics proclaimed the show dead at that point because the quality of the show had gone down, and, since then, when a show has long ago reached its peak and desperately attempts to add continued life, it is said to have "jumped the shark." When a movie franchise is all about sharks and killing thousands of them that fall from the sky, it has "jumped the shark" from its very inception. And yet, like watching a train wreck, the viewing audience cannot turn away.

The beauty of the *Sharknado* films also resides in the realization that the stars themselves recognize the films for what they are. As Tara Reid explains, "*Sharknado* was a fun, silly movie that we made—we knew it was ridiculous. The second one is still ridiculous. But this one has a heart. It's not like I did *Titanic*, or I'm up for an Academy Award" (Lansky 2014).

The limited plot line that does exist involves Fin and April flying to New York City to help promote April's book *How to Survive a Sharknado and Other Unnatural Disasters*, based on their experiences with the Los Angeles Sharknado. Outside of NYC, their plane flies through a storm that includes, you guessed it, sharks. Sharks enter the plane, killing passengers and crew, including both pilots (one of whom, in an amusing bit of casting, is played by Robert Hays of *Airplane!* fame). As Fin takes over control of the cockpit, April tries to shoot and kill a shark but the shark bites off her hand. Fin eventually lands the plane safely in New York. At the airport, Fin and April try to warn the media of the incoming storm filled with sharks but no one believes their story. Shortly thereafter, Fin takes a cab, driven by Ben (Judd Hirsch of *Taxi* fame) to Citi Field in an attempt to warn some of his friends. Just as they are leaving the baseball stadium the storm strikes. Seeking to avoid the sharks and urban flooding, Fin and his friends get on the subway. They grab a number of items to use as weapons. One of passengers proclaims, "No one messes with a Mets fan on the 7 Train." Immediately afterward, a shark breaks through the back of the train car and swallows the Mets fan, thereby negating his claim.

Fin and April and some of their friends make it back to Manhattan to reunite and have one final standoff with the sharks. Spoiler alert: Fin and April survive. Of course, they had to survive or how else could they star in *Sharknado 3*? And in fact, in the following summer of 2015 *Sharknado 3: Oh Hell No!* appeared, with Fin and April again saving the day.

Sharknado 2 drew 3.9 million viewers the first night it aired, of which 1.6 million were between ages eighteen and forty-nine, the most coveted group for advertisers to target. The ratings represent Syfy's best for an original telepic. The media awareness for *Sharknado 2* far exceeded the original, helping to boost viewership for the encore airings to nearly ten million over six airings (Villarreal 2014). The media attention given to this film is what makes it a popular culture phenomenon. Nearly every genre of popular culture reported on *Sharknado 2*, including talk show hosts, morning and evening news shows, DJs on AM, FM, and Satellite radio, ESPN reporters (because of the Mets tie-in), comedians, political cartoons, and social network sites. Name any type of popular culture genre and the *Sharknado* crossover was likely to have occurred. Here are a few specific examples of the *Sharknado* influence on popular culture:

- Nielsen estimates that 5.5 million people saw one or more of 581,000 tweets posted during the airing. "At one point, the film held all top 10 trending topics in the United States" (*The Post-Standard* 2014).

- Jon Stewart on *The Daily Show* (July 31, 2014) referred to the inept U.S. Congress as the *Sharknado 2* of government.

- A political cartoon in *The Citizen* (August 5, 2014) depicted an exasperated President Obama reading a newspaper with the headline—"House Approves Lawsuit against Obama"—with sharks (the word "lawyer" on each of them) swimming toward him. The political cartoon was captioned *Sharknado 3*.

- Like the first *Sharknado* made-for-TV movie, *Sharknado 2* was released on the big screen (August 21, 2014). This time, however, it was shown at twice as many theatres (more than four hundred) as the first one.

- The numerous cameos of celebrities assured the crossover appeal of *Sharknado* from TV movie to other popular culture genres. Among the cameos: Kelly Ripa, Michael Strahan, and Michael Gelman from *Live! With Kelly and Michael*; Al Roker and Matt Lauer from the *Today Show*; Wil Wheaton; Anne Wheaton; Daymond John; Stephanie Abrams; Andy Dick; Kelly Osbourne; Billy Ray Cyrus; and Perez Hilton.

- On July 20, 2014, "Sharknado: The Video Game" was released (available as an app).

- The book that Tara Reid's character was to promote in the film, *How to Survive a Sharknado and Other Unnatural Disasters*, was released through Three Rivers Press on July 8, 2014. So a fictional book became a "real" book thanks to pop culture demand.

- There is a Tara Reid perfume inspired by Sharknado as well and it is simply called "Shark."

As the examples above of the crossover appeal of *Sharknado2* illustrate, this B movie has indeed become a popular culture phenomenon. With the release of *Sharknado 3: Oh Hell No!* in July 2015 we saw an even greater crossover effect, to the point where we can introduce the concept of a "Super Pop Culture Phenomenon," since it connected with *all* of the categories of popular culture discussed in this book. This time, our heroes have to save the day in Orlando, Florida, Washington, D.C., and the entire East Coast of America. Reflecting its popularity, a number of stars and celebrities are added to the cast—some who just make cameo appearances. Among those joining Ziering and Reid are Frankie Muniz, Bo Derek, David Hasselhoff, Kendra Wilkinson, Rick Fox, Mark Cuban, Jerry Springer, Penn and Teller, and Michael Bolton. Cuban, billionaire owner of the Dallas Mavericks and star of the popular TV show *Shark Tank*, portrays the President of the United States, who bestows a medal on Fin for his heroic work, and tells him, "They used to call me a shark."

With scenes that include sharks at the nation's capital's major monuments (e.g., a shark lands in the lap of Abraham Lincoln), the absurdity of the *Sharknado* franchise lives on. Once again, all areas of popular culture are connected with. Sports star Brad Keselowski solemnly intones the third installment's subtitle when a shark lands on him from the sky at a NASCAR race in Daytona Beach. Many of the commercials shown throughout directly referred to *Sharknado* itself, increasing the self-referential silliness. Other pop culture connections included "Archie vs. Sharknado," a comic book tie-in with the venerable eternal teenager Archie Andrews saving his gang from a shark attack, and a cameo from Ian Ziering in another SyFy production, the equally silly *Lavalantula*, in which Fin states he has no time to fight the lava-spewing giant tarantulas attacking Los Angeles because he's too busy fighting sharks. There's even a catchy theme song at the beginning, with suitably cheery lyrics and animation. The ratings were down for *Sharknado 3*, with an estimated 2.9 million viewers, but it was still the number one cable program for its time slot, and doubled the audience for 2013's *Sharknado 1*. And like the first two, it was a trending sensation. Given *Sharknado 3*'s cliffhanger ending and absurd final scenario—sharks in space—a fourth installment is inevitable. Resistance to *Sharknado* is futile.

The low budget, sequel-friendly *Sharknado* franchise provides a cheesy brand of entertainment that appeals to many and allows itself to become a punch line for so many others in the world of popular culture. It also provides us with our first opportunity to provide a lesson learned, and because of its tie-in with so many other aspects of popular culture it is difficult to limit ourselves to just one. As will be the case throughout the book, readers may come up with their own ideas as to the lesson learned by the short stories described.

Lesson Learned: Never underestimate the public's willingness to suspend reality.

2

Movies and Popular Culture

People have been enjoying motion pictures for generations now. First there were the silent black and white films, originally developed in the late 1890s by pioneers such as Thomas Edison, the Lumière Brothers, Edwin Porter, and D. W. Griffith. For the first time ever, it was possible to watch locomotives in action, famous individuals like President Teddy Roosevelt or author Mark Twain moving about, and scenes such as the launching of the *Titanic* unfold. The original such "movies" were short, with basic plots. The first screen comedy, for instance, is usually said to be *Fred Ott's Sneeze*, a five-second depiction of one of Edison's assistants taking a pinch of snuff and reacting accordingly, filmed in 1894. While it was a big hit at the time, audiences soon demanded longer and rather more sophisticated entertainment. Initially, these were often filmed recreations of the acts of popular Vaudeville actors at the time, but soon a new type of celebrity—the motion picture "star"—arose. People such as Charlie Chaplin, Douglas Fairbanks Jr., Mary Pickford, John Barrymore, Gloria Swanson, and Erich von Stroheim became famous for holding an audience's attention through the use of their facial expressions, exaggerated movements, and intimate knowledge of how cameras captured their essential character.

While silent films were wildly popular throughout the world, the necessarily artificial aspect of not having sound was off-putting to many. Indeed, while the films themselves were silent, almost always there was some sort of musical accompaniment that highlighted what was occurring on the screen. Still, this wasn't sufficient, and the desire for "talkies" became a quest for movie producers. Thanks to the work of people like Thomas Case (from Auburn, New York) and Thomas Edison, sound was eventually added to film and by 1927 the age of silent movies came to an end, marked by the spectacular success of that year's hit movie, *The Jazz Singer*, starring the great Al Jolson. While a few performers, such as Charlie Chaplin, tried for a time to continue to make silent movies, by the early 1930s the talking film was here to stay.

But that still wasn't sufficient for those who wanted movies to better reflect real life. Black and white film, while it could be aesthetically rich, was looked upon by many as a deficient medium, and companies like Eastman Kodak in Rochester, New York, experimented with various techniques to make color film. It was a long and complex process, and while the means to make such films were available by the 1930s (as fans of the 1939 *The Wizard of Oz* can attest, when Dorothy leaves black and white Kansas to follow the Yellow Brick Road), the costs involved were high, which is why most films up until the late 1950s were still made in black and white. But the era of Technicolor would soon arrive, as motion picture producers needed a way to combat a new rival, namely television. The sizes of screens were increased as well, and for a time 3-D movies were all the rage. While it was a passing fad in the late 1950s, 3-D has recently made a reappearance, as today's motion picture producers vie to get viewers into the theaters and away from their latest rival, streaming videos.

We don't only watch the films on the screen when going to the movie theater, we also consume a great amount of food. For many people, munching on snacks while watching a movie is a given, and this is true whether we are at home or at a movie theatre. As for moviegoers, it should come as no surprise that the favorite snack food consumed is popcorn. According to the National Association of Concessionaires, with 176 million orders, popcorn purchases far exceed other snack favorites of moviegoers, including sweets (100 million orders), 36 million orders of nachos, and 12 million hot dogs (Scott 2014b). A number of theaters now serve alcohol in a further attempt to draw people to the "big screen."

All of these various advancements in motion picture technology have improved the quality of films and have kept us entertained through the ages; and yet, one has to wonder what the next big advancement on the silver screen will be. As the Statler Brothers once put it in popular song: "The movies are great medicine/Thank you, Thomas Edison/For giving us the best years of our lives."

The six stories in this chapter discuss six diverse movies, including one, *The Simpsons Movie*, that is based on America's favorite animated family, who take on a pro-environmental stand; another, *Apocalypse Now*, a Vietnam War film with one-line quotes that remain a part of popular culture lexicon today; and four movies that allow the viewer an opportunity to suspend reality. In addition to *Apocalypse Now*, all of these films have produced catchphrases or subject matter that have stood the test of time, and that is one among many reasons why we chose each of them for inclusion in this chapter. Certainly, our first story, the *Planet of the Apes* series, has one of the most enduring movie quotes of all time—"Take your stinking paws off me, you damn dirty ape!" The movie theme idea of human hubris is also prevalent in the entire *Apes* series.

If Apes Evolved Instead of Humans:
"Take your stinking paws off me, you damn dirty ape!"

It took humans quite a while before they were advanced enough to create films, but through the process of evolution, humans climbed to the top of the species ladder. But what if our distant relatives the apes had evolved instead? What would become of humans, and what would become of the planet Earth? Although it would be conjecture to imagine a planet where apes ruled over the other species, the world of popular culture offers such a scenario via the *Planet of the Apes* film series.

The first *Planet of the Apes* film was released in 1968 and starred such film stars as Charlton Heston, Roddy McDowall, Maurice Evans, Kim Hunter, and Linda Harrison. The original *Apes* series includes five films—all released by 20th Century Fox—made between 1968 and 1973. A remake of the original conception of *The Planet of the Apes* was released in 2001 (starring Mark Wahlberg) and a conceptually different version of the film was released in 2011 (*Rise of the Planet of Apes*, starring James Franco). The rebooted version of the *Apes* franchise was followed by the sequel, *Dawn of the Planet of the Apes* (2014).

The first *Apes* film (which was based on the 1963 science fiction novel *La Planète des Singes* by French author Pierre Boulle) was both a commercial and critical success as its uniqueness entertained audiences and pleased film critics alike. Having traveled through time to the year AD 3978, a crew of Earthling astronauts has crash-landed on a planet that seems desolate. One of the surviving astronauts performs a soil test that determines that the soil is incapable of sustaining life. Nonetheless, the crew realizes that they must discover what else the planet has to offer if they are to survive.

After crossing a desert, the astronauts find an area of land that has both plant life and a source of fresh drinking water. They also discover a number of humans who appear to be grazing on corn from a nearby cornfield. Much to the surprise of the astronauts, the humans are suddenly attacked by gorillas on horseback that possess firearms and nets. The gorillas capture some of the humans and kill those who attempt to flee. One astronaut, Dodge (Jeff Burton), is killed, while Taylor (Charlton Heston) and Landon (Robert Gunner) are captured. Taylor, who was shot in the throat during the gorilla attack on humans, has temporarily lost his ability to speak. This will become a significant plot point later on.

Taylor and Landon are separated but both are taken to Ape City, where Taylor is shocked to learn that apes have evolved to the point where they have cultivated a thriving society, and where humans are enslaved, tortured, and experimented on by ape scientists. We learn later that the apes have conducted a lobotomy on Landon, making him catatonic. Taylor, who is locked in a cage with Nova (Linda Harrison), a pretty human woman, notices a distinctly caste-based society, divided according to ascribed characteristics: the gorillas, because of their strength and lack of advanced intelligence, serve as police, military, hunters, and workers; the orangutans serve as administrators, politicians, lawyers, and religious leaders; and the chimpanzees, the most evolved of the apes, serve as scientists and intellectuals. This caste and class distinction serves as a social commentary on human societies wherein different humans have different functions and are evaluated differently based on their social position.

To illustrate the differences within the evolutionary process on this planet, the apes are capable of speech, intellectual pursuits, the creation of a god(s) and spiritual belief, and so on, while the humans are mute creatures who seem more like deer (a dazed look on their faces) or sheep (blindly following the commands of their captors) in their overall intellectual development. Having been wounded in the throat, Taylor is assumed to be such a typical mute creature.

Taylor is assigned to be studied by scientists—Zira (Kim Hunter), an animal psychologist, and her fiancé, Cornelius (Roddy McDowall), an archaeologist. At one point, Taylor manages to escape captivity, and with his throat healed from the earlier gunshot wound, he utters the famous phrase—"Take your stinking paws off me, you damn dirty ape!"—upon his recapture. The apes are shocked to learn that a human can speak. The rulers of Ape City recognize the potential harm Taylor could cause to their society. With the help of Zira and Cornelius, Taylor again manages to escape and flees Ape City. Taylor, Nova, and his ape sympathizers head toward the "Forbidden Zone." The ruling apes, who know the truth about the past history of their planet, attempt to kill Taylor. Taylor reaches the

Forbidden Zone and finds evidence of a past, technologically advanced human society predating simian domination of the mysterious planet.

Dr. Zaius, the ruler of Ape City, admits that he has always known that human civilization existed long before apes took over control of the planet. He lectures Taylor that the desolate Forbidden Zone was once a paradise but humans destroyed the environment. Over the course of the next couple of thousand years, the apes evolved to the top of the food chain and humans devolved. Dr. Zaius states, "The Forbidden Zone was once a paradise, but [man] made a desert of it—ages ago." Dr. Zaius allows Taylor and Nova to ride away on horseback.

Taylor and Nova follow the shoreline and eventually discover the secret of the planet when they find the top portion of the Statue of Liberty, indicating that this environmentally compromised planet was Earth. It dawns on Taylor that humans destroyed the environment while he and his crew were traveling for thousands of light years. Heston delivers the famous and chilling last lines: "Oh my God. I'm back. I'm home. All this time, it was. . . . We finally really did it. (*Screams*): You maniacs! You blew it all up! Ah, damn you! God damn you all to hell!"

In this and the subsequent four other original *Apes* movies, along with the 2001 remake, we see that the social fabric of advanced society is not much different when controlled by apes than it is when controlled by humans. In these films, the apes inherited a planet with an environment compromised by human neglect. And while their living environment appears to thrive, perhaps because of the lack of any evidence of the use of fossil fuels, areas of the planet—identified as the "Forbidden Zone"—remain compromised.

Starting with *Rise of the Planet of the Apes*, a different scenario leads to the emergence of intelligent apes. In this series of *Apes* films, a chimpanzee named Caesar gains humanlike intelligence and emotions via an experimental drug. Caesar was also raised like a human child by the drug's creator, Will Rodman (James Franco), and a primatologist, Caroline Aranha (Freida Pinto). After a succession of events, Caesar is taken away from his human caretakers, his human source of love and nurturing, and imprisoned in an ape sanctuary in San Bruno.

In the sanctuary, the apes are treated poorly by their human keepers. Furthermore, Caesar is not treated well by the other apes. His sense of loss from missing his human friends eventually transforms into resentment. He gives his fellow apes the same drug that he has been injected with over the years. Before long, Caesar forms a simian army that breaks out of the sanctuary and heads toward a forest. *Rise of the Planet of the Apes* concludes with a battle scene between humans and apes that foreshadows what will happen in *Dawn of the Planet of Apes*. In *Dawn*, the genetically evolved apes, still led by Caesar, go to war with the humans who survived a deadly virus unleashed a decade earlier. Attempts to broker peace fail and the two "evolved" species fight for supremacy.

In these film portrayals of intelligent apes, we are led to believe that while their development as the master species is characterized by many of the same social ills (e.g., class distinction, elitism, and speciesism) as human-led societies, they also seem less reliant on the extraction, production, and consumption of fossil fuels. As a result, their ecosystems remain healthy but as potentially vulnerable to worldly and celestial sources of environmental destruction as our current human-led societies.

Lesson Learned: As the "Law of Unanticipated Consequences" warns, the testing of experimental drugs on apes may alter the natural evolutionary process.

The Simpsons Movie:
Sure We Lost a Glacier, but We Gained a Lake

As usual, when *The Simpsons* address a major social cause, such as environmentalism, they do so through the "Lisa" character. Lisa represents the segment of the American public that is concerned about human behavior that causes harm to humanity and/or the environment, and those who attempt to mobilize others to action in order to address social issues. She loves the idea of stimulating collective action that leads to the creation of a social movement designed to improve society. Lisa recognizes that often one needs to sound an alarm in order to fuel action.

In *The Simpsons Movie*, Lisa attempts to warn the residents of Springfield about the increasing water pollution in Springfield Lake. She gives a speech titled "An Irritating Truth" (in homage to Al Gore's documentary film *An Inconvenient Truth*) about the lake's water quality. The local newspaper describes Lisa as "pushy kid" who is nagging the town. The beauty of *The Simpsons* is that it demonstrates opposing viewpoints on major social issues through a variety of regular characters. The rebellious troublemaker Bart Simpson symbolizes people who are apolitical or otherwise disengaged from social issues. Marge Simpson, the wife of Homer and nurturing mother of Bart, Lisa, and Maggie, who often mediates family disagreements, represents the moderate position on social issues expressing concern about environmental issues but little personal involvement. Homer Simpson represents the conservative perspective and expresses his belief that global warming is nothing but a bunch of "hot air"—pun intended. For example, in the "O Brother, Where Bart Thou?" episode (first air date December 13, 2009) Homer and Lisa hear a weather report announcing that a huge snowstorm will hit Springfield:

> HOMER: Gee, Lisa, looks like tomorrow, I'll be shoveling ten feet of global warming.
>
> LISA: Global warming can cause weather at both extremes, hot and cold.
>
> HOMER: I see. So you're saying warming makes it colder. Well, aren't you the queen of crazy land! Everything's the opposite of everything. (*Homer dances, twirling and waving his arms*).

Lisa mutters to herself at her father's antics. No matter how clearly she explains it to her father, like other doubters he cannot figure out how global warming (and, more applicable, climate change) really works. Homer is not the only *Simpsons* character that expresses doubt in the legitimacy of global warming as a real problem. In a much earlier episode of *The Simpsons* ("Mr. Plow," original air date November 19, 1992), news anchor Kent Brockman states, "Could this record-breaking heat wave be the result of the dreaded greenhouse effect? Well, if seventy-degree days in the middle of winter are the 'price' of car pollution, you'll forgive me if I keep my old Pontiac." Although many people who live in the Midwest, and especially the Northeast, might share Brockman's outlook on global warming during winter months, those of us (including both authors of this book) who live near the Great Lakes recognize that warmer lake temperatures result in significantly higher amounts of snowfall because of lake effect snow. Lake effect snow takes place when cold air from the Arctic blows across the warmer lake water, which results in heavy snowfalls in a short period of time. People like Homer have a hard time coming to grips with this reality—that warmer temperatures can cause higher snow totals for specific regional areas.

After Lisa's initial failed attempts at warning the residents of Springfield about the water pollution in Lake Springfield, she meets a park ranger who denies the existence of climate change. Lisa is amazed by this. She asks about the melting glaciers. She explains that glaciers are nature's alarm clock and proclaims that it's time for humanity to wake up and face environmental reality.

> PARK RANGER: Young lady, the federal government's position on global warming is that it does not exist. This glacier's doing just fine.

> LISA: No, it isn't. It's a lump of slush. Look at it!

> (*Lisa falls in a pool of meltwater created by the disintegrating glacier.*)

> LISA: Help, I'm sinking in the lake!

> PARK RANGER: You mean, you're walking on the glacier!

The message conveyed in this verbal exchange is designed to highlight the federal government's frequent reluctance to acknowledge climate change and establish specific restrictions designed to slow the growing damage to the earth's environment.

The *Simpsons* references made here are a mere sampling of the many examples of environment-themed episodes that have aired over the years. *The Simpsons Movie*, the first of the projected multiple *Simpsons* movies to be made, had a heavy dose of environmental sermonizing, although it is accomplished while maintaining the film's commitment to entertainment and humor.

Lesson Learned: While lakes are nice, we should not trade them for glaciers.

Apocalypse Now:
Loving the Smell of Napalm in the Morning

There is an old adage—often attributed to Union Civil War General William Tecumseh Sherman—that "War is Hell." Anyone who has fought in a war or lived in, or near, a war zone can attest to the validity of such a statement. The world of popular culture is certainly aware of the hellish aspects of war, and the countless films made about war are often reflective of the many horrors associated with it. There are war films, including *Apocalypse Now*, that acknowledge the negative environmental impact of waging war.

Apocalypse Now is a 1979 film set during the Vietnam War, directed and produced by Francis Ford Coppola and starring Marlon Brando, Robert Duvall, and Martin Sheen. *Apocalypse Now* received a number of awards and nominations for awards and was selected for preservation by the National Film Registry (Library of Congress 2011). The film follows the assignment of Captain Benjamin L. Willard (Sheen), a veteran U.S. Army special operations officer who has been serving in Vietnam for three years, who has been ordered to follow the Nung River into the remote Cambodian jungle and assassinate rogue U.S. Army Special Forces Colonel Walter E. Kurtz (Brando). Col. Kurtz has apparently gone insane and has established his own quasi-kingdom equipped with his own army of Montagnard (indigenous mountain people) troops inside Cambodia, a nation that at the time was neutral in the Vietnam War. Captain Willard is escorted up the Nung River by Lieutenant Colonel William "Bill" Kilgore (Duvall), who commands a squadron of attack helicopters and is himself of questionable sanity. Reaching Colonel Kurtz will prove challenging due to the thick rainforest along the river's path.

The Vietnam War was unique for American forces, as the battles generally took place in areas of dense forest. Distinguishing noncombatant civilians from combatants was difficult. As a result, the "rules of engagement" were blurry and often violated. For example, in its effort to fight enemy troops, the U.S. military opted to spray huge amounts of deadly toxic chemicals into the jungle and its thick vegetation. Among the more common toxins sprayed in Southeast Asia were Agent Orange and napalm. Some of the many dangers associated with Agent Orange include the environment and the endangerment of a number of animal and plant species, as well as a wide variety of health problems to humans (including U.S. military personnel, enemy troops, and innocent civilians) exposed to the deadly toxins. For example, a number of veterans who were crew members on C-123 Provider aircraft—the U.S. Air Force (USAF) used C-123 aircraft to spray Agent Orange during the Vietnam War— have recently expressed health concerns associated with their exposure to residual amounts of the herbicide on the plane surfaces (United States Department of Veterans Affairs 2012). These veterans were not sprayed by Agent Orange themselves, but believe that close proximity to the toxin was enough to have caused them harm. The continued danger of Agent Orange is reflected in a number of ways, including the realization that research on the health effects of Agent Orange has been extensive and it continues. The Department of Veterans Affairs encourages anyone with health problems that were exposed to Agent Orange visit their local VA Environmental Health Coordinator (United States Department of Veterans Affairs 2014).

One of the deadliest weapons developed in the twentieth century was napalm, which was created by American chemist Louis Fieser during World War II. The U.S. military first used napalm bombs in France when the Allies attempted to liberate the country from Nazi rule. U.S. pilots dropped napalm bombs over Dresden, Germany, toward the end of the war. Napalm was used by Serbian forces in the 1990s during the Yugoslav Wars and the United States used a form of napalm following the Iraq invasion in 2003 ("Operation Iraqi Freedom"). It was during the Vietnam War, however, that napalm was most widely used as a weapon and garnered its reputation as a dirty weapon.

Napalm is gelled gasoline used as filling for incendiary bombs and in flamethrowers; it is derived from a combination of acids of the types exemplified by lauric acid and naphtenic or oleic acid (Fieser et al. 1946). The use of napalm is harmful to human and plant life alike. The jelly-like substance of the chemical adheres to its target's surface (including the human body) while it continues to burn. As a result, a person hit with napalm does not suffer first or second degree burns, but almost always third (burns that go all the way through the skin), fourth (through the skin to the underlying muscles, tendon, and ligaments, generally resulting in death), or fifth or sixth degree burns (determined during autopsy, as the burns go through bones).

The most poignant and relevant scene of *Apocalypse Now* involves napalm strikes along the Nung River. The attack helicopters arrive and while they are blasting the countryside with napalm the chopper loudspeakers blare the song "Ride of the Valkyrie," from Richard Wagner's opera *Die Walküre* (an interesting use of a high culture reference in a popular culture film). It is during this scene when one of the most classic popular culture quotes is uttered. Lieutenant Colonel Kilgore, taking pride in his military's ability to torch the forests of Cambodia, states, "I love the smell of napalm in the morning . . . it smells like victory." While this military man finds glory in the destruction brought about as a result of napalm bombings, the local ecosystems—including countless human lives—are being destroyed nearly instantly. War *is* Hell.

Lesson Learned: When victories include napalm, no one really wins.

Undead and Loving It:
What's So Bad about Being a Zombie?

Zombies have been prominent for some time now in the world of popular culture, including many films that depict the "living dead" phenomenon. Maybe this is partly because of movies like *Apocalypse Now* that inspire nightmare scenarios that involve either mass extinction or mutant creatures like zombies. Among the earliest films on zombies were *Invasion of the Body Snatchers* (1956), *Night of the Living Dead* (1968), and *Dawn of the Dead* (1978).

One of the main characters in George Romero's 1978 film *Dawn of the Dead* solemnly intones that "when there's no room in Hell the dead will walk the earth." While this theological issue may or may not be the cause of their popularity, there is no questioning the fact that in modern popular culture, it's the time of the season for Zombies. Why exactly are the Walking (and Eating) Dead so ubiquitous today, with such high-grossing movies as *Twenty Eight Days Later* (2004), *Shaun of the Dead* (2004), *Zombieland* (20009), and *World War Z* (2013) doing record business, and the comic book *The Walking Dead* (2003–) becoming the basis for a popular AMC Television series of the same name (2010–)?

First of all, the topic itself is something philosophy has been grappling with for centuries in a purely theoretical way. The so-called Zombie Problem (otherwise known as the Problem of Other Minds) has been a conundrum for centuries (How do we really know other people have thoughts like ours and aren't just mindless beings that look like they are thinking beings?), and modern-day cognitive scientists are asking ever more complex questions about the nature of consciousness. The topic of personal identity is also a perennial topic of discussion, and Zombies have been a theoretical test case for this. If you should actually lose your mind, would you still be the same individual? Moral status, too, is a longstanding issue in ethics—Is rationality the determining factor in whether or not one is a moral being and, if so, are there degrees of rationality that should be taken into consideration? Philosopher Rene Descartes's famous statement "I Think, Therefore I Am" at least conceptually leaves open the difficulty of proving that there are thinking beings other than us.

But, for all the ancient arguments associated with Zombies, it was George Romero's classic 1968 film *Night of the Living Dead* that reanimated and reconfigured the ways in which Zombies are addressed and—if you'll pardon the expression—gave new life to the undead. In many ways, the countless recent movies, graphic novels, television series, and other media depictions are all variations on the brain-eating, uncomprehending, relentless beings that Romero unleashed upon us almost fifty years ago.

One can ask a basic existential question: Would it really be a bad thing to become a Zombie? As the 1956 science fiction film *Invasion of the Body Snatchers* demonstrated, being a pod person has its advantages—at least, you won't need to set an alarm clock again if you never have to sleep. All thoughts would be gone, so presumably all worries would disappear, too. The only real concern you would have would be finding something to eat—and even if you cannot find anything, that too should have no really bad effect, since you're already dead. Why worry, be a Zombie!

What disturbs us about Zombies is exactly their lack of concern with anything except the most basic survival needs. Zombie-ness has become a metaphor for humans unconcerned about their environment and oblivious to everything but their own blinkered existence. In *Shaun of the Dead*, for instance, it takes some time for the lead character to realize his world has been infested by Zombies since they so resemble the Walkman-wearing, shuffling, self-absorbed human beings he's seen every day on his way to work.

Perhaps another important reason why Zombies have become so fashionable in the early twenty-first century is because many of us, due to the fact that humans are living much longer than ever before, have come to see quite a few of our loved ones severely afflicted with mental deterioration or in a persistent vegetative state. We increasingly wonder just what sorts of experiences these people are having, and whether or not we would wish to exist in such a state ourselves. It is a deeply disturbing existential phenomenon, and might well be mirrored in the popular culture depictions of Zombies today.

Many of the popular representations of Zombies, such as *World War Z* and *The Walking Dead*, speculate that the rise of Zombie-ness is due to a plague of some sort, and unless human beings find a cure for this, it will lead to the ultimate destruction of humanity itself. This, too, can be read as a metaphor for environmental degradation and the likely ill effects if humans do not confront the challenges of such a danger until it is too late. After that, we too would be brought back to our most basic selves, struggling not for meaningful projects but rather just to survive in an increasingly inhospitable world.

Thus, whether brought about by human actions or some other means, the rise of the Zombies in popular culture can be directly connected with environmental concerns, and the need to thrive or die. At the least, it's given new meaning to the old expression "mindless entertainment." It is a thought-provoking phenomenon—and perhaps, by showing that we still have thoughts to be provoked, it can help us prove to our own satisfaction that we are not a Zombies ourselves—at least as of yet.

Lesson Learned: Zombies have no worries, and that's what worries us humans.

Pinocchio: "Give a Little Whistle"

Ethicists such as Thomas Aquinas, Joseph Butler, and Immanuel Kant grappled mightily with the question of the nature of our conscience—that inner voice that tells us when we are acting rightly or wrongly. But for all their learned writings, none of these wise gentlemen have had as major an impact on the popular understanding of the conscience as Walt Disney, who gave us its best-known representative—Jiminy Cricket, the dapper, devil-may-care bug with a song in his heart who is always willing to give advice to his pal Pinocchio on proper behavior. Voiced by the beloved Cliff Edwards (popularly known as "Ukulele Ike"), Jiminy is the kind of friend anyone would long to have. The year 2015 marked the seventy-fifth anniversary of the film, which is truly one of the most beloved popular culture classics of all time.

Like many Disney films, this one is based on a work from another source, Carlo Collodi's 1883 *Le Avventure di Pinocchio*, itself a famous piece of popular literature. But there are many important differences between the original source and its film adaptation, which was par for the course with Disney. The 2013 movie *Saving Mr. Banks* entertainingly shows how Walt Disney himself was responsible for making many changes from the original book *Mary Poppins* to its screen incarnation, much to the displeasure of its author, P. L. Travers. Luckily for Walt, *Pinocchio*'s author was long dead by the time he decided to make it into his second feature length cartoon (after the success of his first such cartoon, 1937's smash hit *Snow White and the Seven Dwarfs*, based on a German fairy story first published in 1812 by the Brothers Grimm).

One of the people who immediately recognized the difference between the original story and the Disney version was the famous Italian author and public intellectual Umberto Eco, who writes that "I remember the discomfort we Italian kids felt on first seeing Walt Disney's *Pinocchio* on the big screen. I should say at once that, watching it again now, I find it to be a delightful film. But at the time, we were struck by the stark

difference between the American Pinocchio and the Pinocchio we had
come to know both through Collodi's original text and through the book's
early illustrators. . . . And though I admit that Disney's Jiminy Cricket is
an extraordinary invention, he has nothing to do with Collodi's Talking
Cricket, who was an actual insect: no top hat, no tailcoat (or was it a
frock coat?), no umbrella" (Eco, in Collodi 2008:ix).

Indeed, not only is the Talking Cricket—a rather minor figure in
the picaresque tale—undressed and unnamed ("Jiminy Cricket" being
a popular American way of nicely saying "Jesus Christ" when upset),
he isn't even Pinocchio's friend. The cricket first appears in chapter IV,
where it is stated that he has lived in Geppetto's home for over a century
(unlike the vagabond Jiminy, who scuttles in to get out of the cold at
the moment of Pinocchio's "birth"). He scolds the marionette boy for
his misbehaving, which includes kicking people in the shin, lying, and
causing Geppetto to get arrested by pretending to be physically abused
by him: "Woe to any little boy who rebels against his parents and turns
his back on his father's house! He will come to no good in this world,
and sooner or later he'll be filled with bitter regret," the cricket solemnly
intones (Collodi 2008:14). Wise words, but not very friendly. He further
chastises Pinocchio for shirking his household responsibilities, and for
not desiring a proper education. If you won't go to school, he warns,
you'll have to get a job to support yourself. "Of all the trades in the
world," Pinocchio replies, "there's only one that really suits me. . . . That
of eating, drinking, sleeping, playing, and wandering wherever I like from
sunup to sundown" (15). The cricket laments that this attitude will only
lead to the poor house or to prison. When the puppet warns him that
his gloom-and-doom prognostications are starting to get on his nerves,
the cricket calls him a blockhead, which is literally true, but not nice to
say. Much to the surprise of anyone only familiar with the 1940 film classic, Pinocchio reacts to such rebukes in a manner different than in the
Disney version, where he is always contrite after being upbraided. In the
Collodi original, he grabs a wooden mallet and flings it at the criticizing
cricket. "Perhaps he didn't mean to hit him at all, but unfortunately he
hit him square on the head. With his last breath the poor Cricket cried
cree-cree-cree and then died on the spot, stuck to the wall" (15).

As Eco points out, Collodi's original puppet is much more mischie-
vous and genuinely naughty than the rather goody-goody Pinocchio in
the film version. However, he is never deliberately malicious. Like Mark
Twain's Huck Finn (whose own sense of right and wrong is beautifully
delineated in philosopher Jonathan Bennett's classic 1974 article "The
Conscience of Huckleberry Finn") he is in *need* of a conscience. It's just

too bad that the one he finds is such a prig. Walt Disney astutely realized that *his* puppet needed a pal, not a know-it-all. Yet Collodi's Pinocchio seems to do fine without the bug, which later reappears as a ghost, and at the end of the tale is charitable toward the puppet, when he sees how compassionate he has become toward Geppetto. When Pinocchio asks for the Cricket's forgiveness, he replies, "I'll have mercy on the father and also on the son. But I wanted to remind you of the cruel treatment I received, to show you that in this world, whenever possible, we should treat others kindly, if we wish to be treated with similar kindness in our hour of need" (Collodi 2008:154–55). As the Golden Rule tells us, don't hurl mallets at others' heads if you don't want mallets hurled at your own.

Collodi's book is filled with many bizarre characters and situations not found in the film. This is not surprising, since it was written originally as an ongoing serial, loosely structured. Collodi, a Florentine journalist and freethinker whose real name was Carlo Lorenzini, became bored with his own creation, and tried to kill him off. He did this by having the Fox and the Cat (called Honest John and Gideon in the film) hang Pinocchio from a tree—thereby getting his own comeuppance for killing the cricket, appropriately enough by means of another wooden contrivance. But, just as Arthur Conan Doyle found out when he tried to do away with *his* creation Sherlock Holmes by having him plunge to his death from the top of the Reichenbach Falls, the public wouldn't stand for such an ending, and Collodi was compelled to bring him back to life.

The Disney movie version of 1940 stands on its own as a true cinematic masterpiece. In many ways, it's even more disturbing than the original. For instance, in Collodi's work, the Fox and the Cat pay the price for their evildoing by becoming blind and paralyzed. Not so in the Disney story, where we never learn what becomes of them. And who can ever forget the chilling scene where the wayward boys turn into donkeys, and cry out for their mothers. Truly the stuff of nightmares.

Walt Disney was wise to spruce up the Talking Cricket, putting on a top hat, tying up his white tie, and brushing up his tails. Jiminy Cricket earns his Eighteen Carat Gold Official Conscience Badge from the Blue Fairy by giving good advice through personal example and sincere friendship. As Walt Disney so astutely understood, nobody likes to be scolded. We want a conscience with a touch of class. As Shakespeare—a high culture figure much referenced in popular culture—might say: "Thus conscience doth make crickets of us all."

Lesson Learned: We often prefer the "Disney Version" of reality because it makes everything happier than it really is.

The Truman Show: "It's all real—it's just controlled"

The two previous sections, on Zombies and Pinocchio, provided us with an opportunity to examine culture from an ethical standpoint. In this section, we will take a look at *The Truman Show* from the standpoint of the Ancient Greek philosopher Plato (428–347 BCE). One of the most famous parables in all high culture is the so-called Parable of the Cave, found in Book Seven of Plato's classic work *The Republic*. In it, a group of people are chained to their seats at the bottom of a deep, dark cave. Rather than being upset about this, however, they are perfectly happy, since they are constantly entertained by watching shadows being cast on the wall in front of them, which they take to be actual events. Behind them, mysterious figures cast the shadows, using wooden instruments backlit by a fire behind the prisoners. Plato is asking us all to reflect upon the question: Would you like to be one of the happy, if ignorant, prisoners, or would you rather break the chains and leave the cave, even if in doing so you might have to face an unpleasant, unpredictable real world? And are the shadowcasters kindhearted individuals who only want to make the prisoners happy, or malevolent jailers who wish to keep the prisoners befuddled by imagery and unaware of their true situation?

Plato's Cave has often been used as a metaphor for such modern forms of entertainment as motion pictures, television, and now computer games and other forms of "virtual reality." Can such entertainment, by keeping us "in the dark" and unaware of reality, ever be harmful? Perhaps ironically, one of the best explorations of this question can be found in a popular movie. Nineteen ninety-eight's *The Truman Show*, directed by Peter Weir, is the story of a young man (played by Jim Carrey) who doesn't realize that his entire life has been filmed from birth, and that all of the people he thinks are his friends and family are really paid actors. His life is the number one television show throughout the world, whose viewers live vicariously through the scripted adventures of the cast members and Truman's spontaneous, genuine reactions to them. Truman, it turns out, is the only authentic individual in a created world.

The entire situation, we eventually learn, is manipulated and controlled by a mysterious figure known only as "Cristof." Ironically, we also learn that Cristof himself doesn't like to be filmed or interviewed and values his privacy, even though he has been filming every waking moment of Truman's life. And Truman, we learn in a disturbing aside, was the first baby ever adopted by a television network. His entire life has been filmed and observed for almost thirty years. When asked why Truman doesn't seem to suspect that his environment is an artificial rather than actual one, Cristof responds: "We accept the reality of the world with which we are presented."

That may be so, but Truman is not quite so easily manipulated. For many years he has had dreams of escaping his island community, but is discouraged from doing so by his "friends." Whenever he expresses the wish to travel, he is told that the world outside is scary and dangerous, and he should be grateful for living in such a pleasant, stress-free environment. And, in an act of classical conditioning, Cristof has caused Truman to have a fear of water. As a child he witnesses what he thinks is his father drowning, though it is really just an actor pretending to be his father, and pretending to die.

Various events—including a movie studio light that accidentally falls from the sky, and the unexpected reappearance of his "dead" father (the actor wants to be back on the show, and sneaks onto the set)—as well as the continuing love Truman has for a young woman he had only fleetingly known (and who was removed from the show by Cristof because this didn't accord with his script) cause him to begin to doubt whether his world really is so wonderful. He starts to suspect in fact that the people around him are just "role playing" rather than talking with him honestly. Even his own "wife" and "mother," he begins to suspect, are not who they seem to be. And when he finally does try to make a break for it from his island paradise, he realizes that escape doesn't seem to be an option. When he tells his supposed "best friend" that he suspects that the world around him isn't what it seems to be, the response he gets is the chilling words: "It's all real—it's just controlled."

There are many fascinating themes in this film: the desire to be authentic; the growing overlap between entertainment and reality; the performative aspects of everyday life; the search for truth in a world of illusions; and the important role of celebrities in modern society. The names of the characters are also significant: "True Man" versus "Cristof," a rather malevolent or un-Christlike all-seeing "creator." The film also anticipates the actual popularity of later so-called "reality shows" such as Survivor and Big Brother, as well as the increasing use of unseen video cameras to capture people's movements without their knowledge.

Interestingly enough, The Truman Show's set seems unrealistic, yet it was filmed in an actual location: Seaside, Florida, a planned community in the "New Urbanism" style. Many of the actual residents of the town have bit parts in the film, which is a sly criticism of such utopian planned communities.

One criticism of the film was that Jim Carrey's own screen personality is too exaggerated to reflect Truman's ordinariness. And it seems rather implausible that the many fans of the show—numbering perhaps in the billions—start to root for Truman as he seeks to escape his own version of Plato's Cave and enter the same mundane world they all live in. Still, *The Truman Show* is a fascinating exploration of our deep-seated desire to be authentic, and our horror at being manipulated. It's important to note that at least one of the prisoners in Plato's parable does break free of his chains and leaves the Cave, no longer satisfied by the shadows, in search of the real things outside of his controlled environment.

Lesson Learned: No matter how exciting the shadows on the wall might be, it's unethical to deceive people about reality.

3

Television and Popular Culture

Television has been a staple source of popular culture for generations now. Throughout its existence, and especially before the advent of personal computers, TV helped to shape people's views and understandings of the world and events that took place locally, nationally, and globally.

The desire to transmit moving images goes back to the 1890s, the time in which motion picture technology was being developed. Just as radio could allow people to hear human voices projected over the airwaves, so it was hoped that pictures could be transmitted, ideally combined with sound. Pioneers such as Philo Farnsworth, Lee de Forest, Vladimir Zworykin, and John Baird worked diligently (and often in competition with each other) to be the first to master this new art form. By 1927, around the same time that talking motion pictures were invented, the process of projecting images through the airwaves became possible. The word *television* is itself a combination of the Greek word *tele*, meaning "far" and the Latin word *visio*, or "sight," so from its origin television was a hybrid.

While television came into existence in the late 1920s, the Great Depression, followed by World War II, prevented its further development and commercialization. It wasn't until after the war's end that television sets began to be ubiquitous in households, taverns, and places of business.

Advancements in technology, beginning with such simplistic creations (from today's standards) as the remote control and extending to cable television and then satellite TV, and now high definition and recording devices (e.g., DVRs) that allow us to record multiple shows at the same time, are among the features that make television viewing so popular for so many people. Television is so popular that it was found in 114.7 million households in 2011 (Stelter 2012). Although this figure represents the vast majority of American homes, it also represents the first time in the previous twenty years that the number of such households had *dropped* when compared to the previous year (115.9 million in 2010) (Stelter 2012). This slight decline in television viewership is attributed to the aging of television viewers, especially the Baby Boomers who helped to make TV so popular. "The median age of broadcast television viewer is now the highest ever at 54. Twenty years ago, it was 41. The most-watched scripted series in the 1993–94 season was *Home Improvement*, with a median viewer age of 34. Today, it's *NCIS*, with a median viewer who is 61" (Blake 2014).

Despite the many other entertainment options available to people, there is no denying that television is still a major component of popular culture. In this chapter, we have four short stories about TV shows that were popular at different times in the past fifty years and that still remain a part of popular culture today. We will conclude with two stories on commercials. Commercials go hand in hand with television. Commercials help to offset the cost of TV programming. Commercials are also an important feature of popular culture in general, as American society is dependent upon the consumption of mass-produced items. We learn about these goods designed for consumption, among other ways, via popular culture. Furthermore, popular culture contributes to the accumulation of capital, and capital accumulation is a fundamental driving force of capitalist economies (Glyn 2006). In short, popular culture in general, and television specifically, are driving forces that help fuel consumerism and capitalism. Perhaps it's not surprising that one of the most popular TV shows of the early twenty-first century, *Mad Men*, is all about the advertising business and how it operates behind the scenes.

Americans are, more or less, used to commercials and it is something we put up with when viewing television. Interestingly, while many people find commercials to be disruptive to television viewing, there are a number of commercials that we actually find to be entertaining (e.g., Super Bowl commercials, beer commercials) and/or informative (e.g., infomercials). These too can be become iconic forms of popular culture.

To Boldly Go: Star Trek as a Guide to the Future

The first two examples to be discussed in this chapter, *Star Trek* and *Columbo*, were popular decades ago; in other words, with the typical median age television broadcast viewer. *Star Trek*, in particular, is still relevant today because of the many variations of the TV show and the many movies made over the years. We are going to discuss the original *Star Trek* series, the one that first made a significant cultural impact on society.

In its original version, *Star Trek* was on the air from 1966 through 1969, just missing out on the growing Earth Day movement of the early 1970s. But, even though set in outer space, no series has ever done more to show an appreciation for the earth itself. While there have been many subsequent *Star Trek* series, including *Star Trek: The Next Generation* (1987–1994), a prequel series (*Star Trek: Enterprise*, 2001–05), and the new "re-booted" *Star Trek* films directed by J. J. Abrams, it is the classic original series, created by Gene Roddenberry (1921–1991), that continues to fascinate.

The original show gave us such iconic characters as the stalwart Captain James T. Kirk; his Vulcan lieutenant, the stoical Mr. Spock; and the ship's emotive doctor Leonard "Bones" McCoy. The mission of the crew of the U.S.S. *Enterprise* was to "explore strange new worlds, to seek out new life and new civilizations, to boldly go where no man has gone before" (later changed to "where no one has gone before" on *Star Trek: The Next Generation* to avoid sexist language).

While seemingly exploring "strange new worlds," the real world which *Star Trek* explored was that of Planet Earth. An explicitly humanistic enterprise, *Star Trek* set out not only to entertain but also to change people's thinking. Initiated in the heated 1960s, it explored such controversial topics of the time as racism, war, religious bigotry, and the growing youth movement. By setting such topics well into the future and giving them a science fiction veneer, the show allowed its viewers to confront these issues and think about them in new ways—to boldly go where they might otherwise have feared to tread.

In regard to environmental issues, perhaps the best episode from the original series was "The Mark of Gideon," originally broadcast in Season Three (the final season of the original series), in 1969. It addresses the topic of overpopulation, an issue that had only recently been brought to the forefront of people's attention by Paul Ehrlich's 1968 book *The Population Bomb*. Captain Kirk beams down onto a planet named Gideon to see if it is ready to join the Federation. At first, Gideon seems to be an actual paradise: it is germ-free, and death itself has been virtually overcome, with all of its inhabitants living to a great age. But, it turns out, that seeming advantage has become a trap. With the birth rates on the planet not declining, and with no one dying, it has become dangerously overpopulated. The love of life which has motivated all of its inhabitants is now causing tremendous hardships as everyone must fight for resources and space on a planet whose carrying capacity is becoming unsustainable.

The crew of the *Enterprise*, under the temporary command of Lieutenant Spock, slowly learns the truth from Gideon's ambassador Hodin—Captain Kirk has been kidnapped, and his blood used to create a virus which Hodin plans to use to infect his own people. He has inoculated his own daughter with the virus, so that she will be the cause of a lethal plague that will now be unleashed upon the inhabitants of Gideon. In the nick of time—usually the case in *Star Trek* episodes—Kirk is saved, and McCoy manages to cure Hodin's daughter so that she will not infect her fellow citizens. An angry Kirk chastises Hodin for his mad scheme, and argues that the best approach would be a rational use of birth control methods rather than a planned destruction of life. Remember, this episode was broadcast in 1969, just a year after Pope Paul VI's encyclical *Humanae Vitae* ("Of Human Life"), which denounced artificial means of birth control as immoral and as against nature. This episode, like so many others of the series, most definitely boldly went were most other series had never gone before.

For fans of the show, its cancellation in 1969 was a tragedy, but like the mythical Phoenix that rose from the fire and sprung back to life, in 1979 the first of a series of movies starring the original cast was produced. Perhaps the most beloved of these, and also one of the highest grossing, was 1986's *Star Trek IV: The Voyage Home*—often called the "Save the Whales" film. Made during the Reagan era, when the United States seemed to be turning away from the Earth Day movement of the 1970s to a more consumer-based society unconcerned with sustainability issues, the film is a plea for preservation and sensible environmental policies. It deals with the timely topic of species extinction. To save Earth from an alien probe, Kirk (now promoted to admiral) and his crew violate Starfleet directives to go back in time to twentieth-century America to retrieve the only sentient beings who can prevent the Earth's destruction—humpback whales. The probe, Kirk has learned, is trying to communicate with the now long-dead whales (an intelligent species that earthlings had allowed to become extinct), who ironically are now the only hope for preserving the species—namely humanity—which had caused their destruction. While Kirk is demoted back to captain for his disobedience, his actions save the day, and also saves the whales as well as humanity.

Much of the film was shot on location in 1980s San Francisco, and, for all the importance of its overall theme, it has a lighthearted tone and a sense of fun that perfectly captures the original series' ethos. As Roger

Ebert put it in his knowing review of the movie, the scriptwriters (as well as the film's director, none other than Mr. Spock himself, Leonard Nimoy) no doubt had a lot of fun creating the scenario: "When they finished writing the script for *Star Trek IV*, they must have had a lot of silly grins on their faces. This is easily the most absurd of the *Star Trek* stories—and yet, oddly enough, it is also the best, the funniest and the most enjoyable in simple human terms. I'm relieved that nothing like restraint or common sense stood in their way" (Ebert 1986). As Ebert and others perceptively point out, while in most *Star Trek* episodes the villains are Klingons, Romulans, or other alien species, in this case the villains are humans— namely, hunters who have ruthlessly massacred whales over the centuries without any concern for their intelligence or role in the ecosystem. In the telling words of Mr. Spock: "To hunt a race to extinction is not logical." The imperturbable Vulcan, as he emerges back in 1980s America, adds: "Judging by the pollution content of the atmosphere, I believe we have arrived at the late twentieth century." A classic line—amusing but also thought-provoking, like *Star Trek* itself. The message of the film is that by saving the whales we save ourselves, thereby showing the interconnectedness of all species.

Star Trek IV: The Voyage Home* was, fittingly enough, chosen as one of the best environmental films of all time by the United Kingdom's Environmental Graffiti website, itself one of the top environmental sites worldwide.

To quote from Mr. Spock yet again—"live long and prosper." What better slogan can there be for those concerned about environmental sustainability?

Lesson Learned: If we want to live long and prosper, as individuals or as a species, we need to take care of our environment.

Columbo: "Just one more thing"

Some shows, such as *Seinfeld* and *Star Trek*, pass the test of time. They are still avidly watched and referred to years after being no longer on the air, and their catch phrases like "yada, yada, yada" and "set your phasers to stun" have entered the popular vernacular. Only time will tell if more current shows such as *The Big Bang Theory* (discussed later in this chapter) will also live on in this way, or instead join the countless other TV shows that once were number one in the ratings and now are mainly forgotten.

Surely, one show that, at least for now, seems to have met this test of time is the detective series *Columbo*, which first appeared on television in 1971 and continued to appear in various forms until 2003. Even those who professed never to watch the show knew about its main character, so ably performed by actor Peter Falk. His filthy raincoat, his disheveled hair, his nagging wife, and his forgetful nature were all part and parcel of a beloved iconic figure.

The *Columbo* episodes, as fans will recall, were not typical "whodunits." Instead, we the viewers knew from the beginning the identity of the murderer (often played by character actors such as Jack Cassidy, Ray Milland, Patrick Macnee, and even *Star Trek*'s Leonard Nimoy and William Shatner). The fun was anticipating how detective Columbo would find out "who dunit" and trap the murderer into confessing. In most cases, the arrogant killers underestimated Columbo's investigative prowess. By "playing dumb" he lulled them into a false sense of security. They would give him vital clues without realizing it. Columbo's most irritating technique was to leave a room and then return, with a befuddled look on his face. Scratching his head, he'd say "Just one more thing . . ." and ask a seemingly innocuous question. The killer, by then eager to see the last of this annoying fellow, would quickly answer, but would later find out that the question was not so innocent after all, when Columbo returned to say "You're under arrest."

In many ways, Columbo was a modern version of the Ancient Greek philosopher Socrates. Socrates too was known for his unkempt appearance, his nagging wife Xanthippe, and his distracted way of acting. But more important, as Shakespeare would say, there was method to the madness of Socrates, and by implication Columbo. For their outward appearances did not correspond to their inner natures. More to the point, there are many similarities between Columbo's detective techniques and Socrates's method of discovering truth. Both were polite but persistent, and while people with nothing to hide usually enjoyed their company, those who did not wish to have their alibis or ignorance probed would react in exasperation or with violent threats to both men. Suddenly, Socrates would no longer seem such a befuddled character. It's a shame that Peter Falk never performed as Socrates, as he would have been perfect for the part. Of course, like all analogies, one shouldn't take such comparisons too far. Columbo, after all, solved all his crimes, whereas it's debatable whether Socrates ever solved anything at all. Still, it is nice to see that one can make real connections between a high culture figure such as Socrates and a popular figure like Columbo.

Of course, as seen throughout this book, popular culture itself is a dynamic field. Once-beloved cultural icons can become tomorrow's forgotten figures. Indeed, while most young people today may still know *Seinfeld* or *Star Trek* even though they've long been off the air, it seems as though *Columbo* is beginning to fade as a popular figure. Perhaps, if one wants to find a more contemporary version of Socrates, the television character *Monk* or even *The Big Bang*'s Sheldon might be more recognizable. Still, we suspect that for a sizeable number of people, Columbo will always remain an iconic figure, for what better expresses the pursuit of truth than his wonderful expression "Just one more thing . . ."?

Lesson Learned: Just one more thing, never underestimate anyone, especially when they can put you in jail.

Seinfeld: "I think I can sum up the show for you with one word: Nothing!"

Some TV shows become so popular that they not only reflect a society's norms and values, they help to shape popular discourse. Such is the case with *Seinfeld*. *Seinfeld*, co-created by Jerry Seinfeld and Larry David, aired its first episode on July 5, 1989; it returned as a short-run late-spring replacement show in 1990 (May 31–June 21). *Seinfeld* began its run of brilliance in earnest on January 23, 1991, and aired its last episode on May 14, 1998, after a total of 180 episodes. The series finale was watched by 76 million people, a figure that still ranks third highest all-time (behind only *M*A*S*H** with 105.4 million viewers in 1983 and *Cheers*, which attracted 80.4 million viewers in 1993). In 2004, *TV Guide* ranked *Seinfeld* number one on its list of the fifty greatest TV shows of all time.

Despite the fact that *Seinfeld* has been off the air for nearly two decades now, a new generation of viewers are watching it for the first time in syndication. As *TV Guide* (2004) explains, "Even following its 1998 finale, *Seinfeld*'s life was far from over. The reruns still draw huge audiences in syndication, and they show no signs of slowing down" (36). More than ten years after this *TV Guide* article was published, *Seinfeld*, a comedy based on observational humor, remains extremely popular within the world of popular culture. In November 2004, the show was immortalized by the Smithsonian Institution when it entered the *Seinfeld* "Puffy Shirt" into the National Museum of American History. In the 1993 "Puffy Shirt" episode (#66), Jerry is tricked into wearing a puffy shirt created by Kramer's girlfriend, Leslie. Jerry wears the shirt at an appearance on the *Today* show to promote a charity event. Jerry is mocked by Bryant Gumbel. Leslie, the infamous "low-talker," mumbles quietly through most of her conversations and Jerry and Elaine, like most people, simply nod in agreement to whatever she says because they cannot hear her. Just prior to his appearance on the *Today* show, Jerry sees the puffy shirt for the first time and tells Kramer that he refuses to wear it. But, Leslie has worked out a deal with retailers to stock the shirt on the condition that Jerry wear it and promote it on *Today*. Jerry thinks the shirts looks ridiculous. Kramer tells Jerry that he can look like a pirate, to which Jerry replies, "But, I don't want to be a pirate!"

The sports world often pays homage to *Seinfeld* episodes, especially the pirate-themed puffy shirt episode. On July 5, 2014, the Brooklyn Cyclones, of the New York-Pennsylvania League (NY-P) paid tribute to the twenty-fifth anniversary of *Seinfeld* by having its players take batting practice in puffy shirts; a fan reeled in a slice of marble rye bread with a fishing rod from the suite level; a man named George Costanza announced the third inning; the first three thousand spectators to the temporarily renamed Vandelay Industries Park received a Keith Hernandez "Magic Loogie" bobblehead; there was an Elaine Benes dancing contest; the foul poles were renamed Festivus poles; and an information kiosk was repurposed for an "airing of grievances" (Atkins 2014).

On November 16, 2014, the Bakersfield Condors, a professional hockey club affiliated with the Edmonton Oilers in the ECHL (a premier AA hockey league), had its players wear puffy shirts in honor of the twenty-fifth anniversary of *Seinfeld*. The players' names on the backs of the puffy shirt–styled hockey shirts were replaced with *Seinfeld* characters' names, such as Kramer, Puddy, Uncle Leo, Joe Davola, and Bubble Boy (*CBC Sports* 2014).

Sports announcers on ESPN often repeat the pirate line from *Seinfeld* when covering highlights of the Pittsburgh Pirates. And this is only the beginning, as news, weather, and sports reporters often reference classic *Seinfeld* one-liners. Many of these one-liners are used by regular people in a variety of contexts. Here are a few examples of popular culture *Seinfeld* phrases: "Not that there is anything wrong with it"; "You double-dipped the chip"; "Low talker"; "Close talker"; "Anti-dentite"; "Regifter"; "Are you the master of your own domain?"; "It's in the vault"; "man hands"; "serenity now"; "No soup for you"; "Happy Festivus"; and "Yada, yada, yada."

Seinfeld was once criticized as a show about "nothing." To which Seinfeld and David responded in their typically clever way by creating a couple of *Seinfeld* episodes in which the character Jerry Seinfeld attempts to sell the pilot episode for his TV show idea "Jerry" to NBC. In "The Pitch" (#43) episode, Jerry and George discuss their idea with NBC executives. During their meeting, Russell Dalrymple, the head of the network, asks Jerry and George what the show would be about.

GEORGE: I think I can sum up the show for you with one word: Nothing!

RUSSELL: Nothing?

GEORGE (smiling): Nothing.

RUSSELL (unimpressed): What does that mean?

GEORGE: The show is about nothing.

JERRY (a little worried about the pitch, turns to George): Well, it's not about nothing.

GEORGE (to Jerry): No, it's about nothing.

JERRY: Well, maybe in philosophy. But, even nothing is something.

In his 2006 book *Seinology: The Sociology of Seinfeld*, author Tim Delaney argues that *Seinfeld* was not a show about nothing; instead, it was really a show about *everything*. The show discusses a wide variety of everyday topics and social situations that confront people on a regular basis. *Seinfeld* has particular relevancy to sociology, as the show centers on relationships, group dynamics, everyday norms and social expectations, marriage and family, gender issues, religion, and so on. The very design of *Seinfeld* makes it perfect for teaching life lessons. However, because one the authors of this book has already written a book on *Seinfeld*, we will limit our discussion here to one more specific topic area discussed by *Seinfeld* years ago that has only grown in popularity in contemporary society since the subject was first introduced on the TV show. This topic is Festivus.

The topic of Festivus represents one of the most significant contributions of *Seinfeld* to popular culture and was introduced to the public in "The Strike" (#166) episode. In this episode, we learn that Festivus is an alternative, secular holiday to the religious holidays that dominate American society in December. George's father Frank Costanza created Festivus because he grew tired of all the commercial and religious aspects of religious holidays, especially the idea of gift giving at Christmastime when many people forget the "true" meaning of the holiday. Frank tells the story of the birth of Festivus to George's friends. He mentions how he almost "came to blows" with another shopper while they both reached for the same gift at a department store. Frank thought that there must be a better way to celebrate a holiday and as a result, he created Festivus—a festival for the rest of us.

Festivus does not involve gift giving or a tree. Instead, it entails putting up an aluminum pole, and absolutely no tinsel, as Frank despises tinsel. Festivus also includes friends and family gathering together on Festivus—December 23—to share in a festive meal and such activities as "feats of strength" contests and the "airing of grievances." For George, the feats of strength contests were an annual nightmare as he had to try to pin his father with the aluminum pole. As Frank explained, Festivus continues until the host of the party is pinned by a guest. The airing of the grievances marks the official start of Festivus. All invited guests gather around the Festivus dinner table and take turns airing their grievances about those who have upset them during the past year. Frank begins by saying, "I got a lot of problems with you people!" After the airing of grievances, guests eat dinner and proceed to the feats of strength. It is the airing of grievances that might cause the biggest problem in most family and friends gatherings.

It is fascinating that the idea of Festivus, a made-up holiday that was introduced to the world of popular culture via a 1997 *Seinfeld* episode, has continued to grow each year. Nearly all news programs and newspapers discuss Festivus every December. In fact, there is now a Church of Festivus (Go to: www.ChurchofFestivus.com). As a matter of full disclosure, Tim Delaney (one of the authors of this book) created the Church of Festivus. He is also an ordained (online, of course) officiate who performs weddings, blessings, and a variety of other Festivus ceremonies. And while he has not worn a puffy shirt while officiating a wedding, he is willing to, if duped by a "low talker."

Lesson Learned: TV shows can entertain us, influence popular culture, establish new holidays such as Festivus, and lead to the creation of a new church, the Church of Festivus—A Church for the Rest of Us!

The Popularity of The Big Bang Theory: Giving Scientists and Nerds Some Love

Seinfeld was the top comedy, and one of the best overall TV shows, of the 1990s. The four main characters were close friends, a bit shallow, and were, more or less, regular folks trying to make a living and survive in the Manhattan urban environment. The idea of basing a comedy on a group of friends is a long-established formula in Hollywood. One popular hit show simply called itself *Friends* and had a significant impact on popular culture (e.g., the hairstyles of Jennifer Aniston's character "Rachel" were duplicated by millions of women in the real world). These six characters were also close friends, essentially regular folks who were also trying to survive and find their way in the Manhattan environment.

Most TV buddy shows are short-lived but a few, like *Seinfeld* and *Friends*, have gone on to become mega hits. But those shows are so twentieth century, what has your buddy-based format created for us lately, Hollywood? The best answer is, *The Big Bang Theory*. This show involves a group of close friends living in an urban environment, albeit the Pasadena area just north of downtown Los Angeles, and has properly blended a number of surefire aspects of the successful, buddy-show concept. Created by executive producers Chuck Lorre and Bill Prady, *The Big Bang Theory* premiered on CBS on September 24, 2007. The network renewed the show for its eighth season (2014–15) and has committed to extend it for a ten-year run. And why wouldn't CBS renew the show? With a viewing audience of 23.4 million in its seventh season, it is, by far, the most popular comedy on television. ABC's *Modern Family* was a distant second most popular comedy with a 2013–14 viewing audience of 14.5 million (Raymond 2014).

The Big Bang Theory has been popular since it premiered, but its ratings were much more modest at the beginning. During its first three seasons, the show averaged about thirteen million viewers, a high figure in this day in age of cable television, DVRs, Netflix, and other alternatives ("cord-cutting") to network television viewing. During its fourth season, *Big Bang* finally surpassed *Two and a Half Men* (then with Charlie Sheen) as the highest-rated comedy. By November 2012, the show reached a new high with 17.6 million viewers (Paul 2012). The number of viewers has only climbed since then. For example, more than eighteen million people tuned in for the September 2014 premiere of *The Big Bang Theory*'s eighth season (Ward 2014). It should be noted, that these are U.S.-only figures and that the show is popular in many other countries, especially in China where young, "nerdy" adults have come to embrace the scientific characters on *Big Bang*.

Interestingly, in May 2014, China banned the streaming of *The Big Bang Theory* in its country because it feared the show's popularity and influence on its young science-driven, geek culture–dwelling citizens (Toomer 2014). To their credit, geeky, scientific nerds in China have learned to bypass the Chinese censorship of the *Big Bang*. Such an act of defiance among these Chinese can be summed up in one appropriate *Big Bang* catchphrase—"Bazinga!" (For those of you not on top of your popular culture slang, "Bazinga" is a catchphrase uttered by the *Big Bang* character Sheldon who uses the word following a clever prank. It might also be helpful to look at the usage of "Bazinga" as an exclamation point to a witty remark or trick.)

An analysis of *The Big Bang Theory* reveals that the show, among other things, utilizes many key aspects of the buddy-show genre. Described below are a dozen ways *The Big Bang Theory* has utilized a tried and true formula for success:

1. Casting: Every successful show needs a strong cast, this is especially true with comedic sitcoms. Big Bang started with five main characters, four best friends and a "hot girl next door." These characters are: Leonard Hofstadter (Johnny Galecki), Sheldon Cooper (Jim Parsons), Howard Wolowitz (Simon Helberg), Raj Koothrappali (Kunal Nayyar), and the girl next door, Penny (Kaley Cuoco). Johnny Galecki and Kaley Cuoco were already sitcom veterans, but Jim Parsons has become the breakout star earning a great deal of respect (e.g., the Emmy Award for Outstanding Lead Actor in a Comedy Series) in the industry. The cast is devoid of a weak link, and this explains why the show has been nominated for so many awards, winning many, including the People's Choice Award for "Favorite Comedy."

2. Emphasizing the Breakout Character: The Sheldon Cooper character has become the breakout favorite character and as a result enjoys a great deal of focus on the show. Sheldon, although mostly lovable, is also a type of "anti-hero" because he is constantly insulting the people that he loves and we, the viewing audience, along with his friends on the show, accept it gleefully because he

really doesn't seem to understand when he is "hurting" the people he loves. Sheldon is like a modern-day Vulcan, because he has trouble with emotions and reading other people's emotions and is logic-driven (Raymond 2014).

3. Strategic Addition of New Characters: *The Big Bang Theory* has done a great job of adding two additional regular cast members, Bernadette Rostenkowski-Wolowitz (Melissa Rauch), the now-wife of Howard Wolowitz; and Amy Farrah Fowler (Mayim Bialik) the "girlfriend" of Sheldon Cooper. "Amy and Bernadette have brought a whole new element to the show. Both characters started in small roles and that allowed fans to slowly get used to them. Now they fit perfectly into the show, and they've allowed Penny's character to expand beyond just her storylines with the guys" (Paul 2012). The addition of Amy and Bernadette has led to interaction between seven close friends and has allowed for far more storylines.

4. Right Time, Right Place: As previously stated, *The Big Bang Theory* really hit its stride in the fourth season and it was not a coincidence that this also involved the move from Monday to Thursday nights. Thursday nights, since the time of NBC's "Must See TV" lineup that lumped powerhouse shows (beginning with *The Cosby Show* and including such shows as *Cheers*, *Seinfeld*, and *Friends*) together, has become the most important night of the week for advertisers, according to Lisa Vebber, NBC's former head of scheduling (Raymond 2014). Although NBC won the 2013–14 season-long demographic battle, unseating last year's champ, CBS, CBS was still the most-watched network (Mitovich 2014). Thus, *Big Bang* benefits from its Thursday time slot on CBS.

5. Syndication: It should come as no surprise that *The Big Bang Theory* does well in syndication as well. It currently airs on a variety of affiliates, but the biggest boost came from TBS (Paul 2012). A syndicated show provides an opportunity for people who did not watch the show originally to start all over while also viewing new episodes in the same week.

6. A Significant Catchphrase: Many successful shows have benefited from a highly identifiable catchphrase that catches the public's long-term attention span. *Happy Days* had Fonzie (Henry Winkler) saying, "Ayyyyye" and *Different Strokes* had "What you talkin' bout Willis," uttered by Arnold Jackson (Gary Coleman), and *The Big Bang* has Sheldon saying "Bazinga!" Give it time, folks, as soon everyone will be saying it. If we're wrong, well—Bazinga!

7. Real Locations: The four buddies on *Big Bang* often go to a nearby comic book store but this comic book store is really a generic setting and not universally applicable for viewers. The Cheesecake Factory, however, is a specific restaurant where the characters go to eat, and the long-time place of employment for Penny. Viewers of *Big Bang* will always think of the show's characters when they dine at, or hear about, the Cheesecake Factory.

8. Proper Pacing of Jokes: A comedy should, of course, include a number of jokes and humorous moments. However, in an attempt to build character storylines, there must be some balance between the drama and the comedy. The timing of jokes is also critical. Adam K. Raymond (2014) of *New York Magazine* suggests that *Big Bang* has perfect pacing when it comes to jokes—4.3 per minute. Raymond also points out what keen viewers have already noticed: that there is a balance between obscure and everyday references that are made into jokes. *The Simpsons* is the king of this balancing act.

9. Will They or Won't They?: It seems as though nearly every show, successful or not, attempts to build upon an age-old premise that the tension between two characters, with at least one of thing having a crush on the other, based on romantic desires will intrigue viewers. Such a premise exists because viewers do indeed enjoy the "will they or won't they (hook up)?" This premise worked well on *Cheers* between Sam and Diane and on *Friends* between Ross and Rachel (he's her lobster—fans of *Friends* get this reference). On *The Big Bang Theory*, we have Leonard and Penny. Leonard developed an immediate crush on Penny, the hot girl who just moved in next door. For years the tension existed, and finally, they did hook up (sorry if

that's a spoiler alert). But then they broke up. And then they got back together. You get the point here. Develop tension. Regular viewers are now left to wonder "will they or won't they" get married before the series ends?

An interesting addition to the "will they or won't they" is the relationship between Amy and Sheldon. Both characters have had little or no sex in their lives, Sheldon by choice, Amy because of lack of cooperation. Amy has been pursuing Sheldon for sex for quite a while and he refuses to act upon it; he is, essentially, an asexual human being. Fans of the show are interested in whether or not anything will ever come from this relationship. In the Season 9 episode of "The Opening Night Excitation," (December 17, 2015) Sheldon and Amy finally had sex— and both of them enjoyed it!

10. Bromance: Although the "will they or won't they" element is missing, bromances have become all the rage during the twenty-first century. A bromance involves a close nonromantic relationship between men. The friendship between Howard and Raj, especially before Howard started dating and eventually married Bernadette, qualified as a bromance. Raj is so inept when it comes to women, he literally cannot speak to them without consuming alcohol. Many of today's shows are utilizing a bromance factor to build tension.

11. References to Popular Culture: The authors of this book are especially happy that *The Big Bang Theory* constantly references various TV shows, comics, films, and personalities that these characters worship, often to the chagrin and confusion of their female counterparts (Eames 2014). And while the characters reference obvious examples of popular culture, such as *Star Trek, Batman, Superman, Game of Thrones,* and so on, they also reference more obscure characters in popular culture, such as *Red Dwarf, Doctor Who,* and *Hitchhiker's Guide to the Galaxy* (Eames 2014).

12. Celebrity Cameos: Once a show becomes popular, there is an increased likelihood that a celebrity will make an appearance, and such cameos can be beneficial to both the celebrity and the show. True to its geeky essence, the

celebrities that appear on *Big Bang* are heroes to geeks everywhere. Among the celebrities who have made cameos are Summer Glau, James Earl Jones, Carrie Fisher, George Takei, Stan Lee, and Bob Newhart. *Star Trek: The Next Generation*'s Wil Wheaton has appeared quite a few times as Sheldon's nemesis (Eames 2014). From the world of science, we have cameos from Stephen Hawking, Steve Wozniak, Brian Greene, and Buzz Aldrin (Eames 2014).

As we have demonstrated above, *The Big Bang Theory* is very popular and its fame, seemingly, can be directly tied to its commitment to using many elements of a proven formula for television success. However, we could also put forth the idea that *Big Bang* is popular because of its uniqueness—an attempt to attract geeks, nerds, and fans of science. The terms *geek* and *nerd* were once used by popular kids insulting socially inept and awkward kids, especially those who preferred time in the science lab rather than on the sports playing field. Today, the idea of being a nerd or geek has been openly and warmly embraced by science- and technology-driven upwardly mobile young adults. It is rare when a network sitcom attempts attract such an audience, but clearly a number of decision makers saw the geeky handwriting on the wall.

The core of the show, while based on the friendship of the four guys, is really about how these guys are men of science, especially physics. All four of the leading male characters are employed at Caltech and have science-related occupations, as do Bernadette and Amy; only Penny, an aspiring actress, has no scientific connection. That nerds and geeks are suddenly the "cool" people, combined with the traditional elements of a successful sitcom, explains why there is little wonder *The Big Bang Theory* is so popular.

Lesson Learned: The nerds and geeks of the world are taking over—Bazinga!

Commercials That Entertain Us:
"Quick, get back, the commercials are about to begin"

Throughout most of the history of television people tuned in to be entertained or to receive information on sports, news, and the weather. We took for granted that commercials were part of the deal. After all, it takes advertising dollars to pay for free television programming. Still, commercials were generally deemed an intrusion on our television viewing as they seemed to always pop up at the worst time, such as during a dramatic plot twist. Many viewers took this opportunity to go to the bathroom or get a snack. Paid movie channels like HBO and Cinemax allowed people to bypass commercials altogether, but programming is limited with these types of channels. The creation of TV programming recording devices such as the VCR and then the DVR allowed viewers the opportunity to fast-forward through the commercials to the program. There are occasions, however, when TV commercials actually entertain us as much as, if not more than many of the programs we watched. The popularity of Super Bowl commercials helps to illustrate this point.

While events such as the Olympics or the FIFA World Cup draw the largest worldwide television audiences, it is the annual Super Bowl, which crowns the National Football League's champion, that is consistently the number one rated program in the United States. According to Nielsen (2014), the FOX network drew an average audience of 111.5 million viewers for the 2014 Super Bowl, making it the highest rated title game of all time. But not all of these viewers watch the Super Bowl because of football; instead, many are watching the big-budgeted commercials. For these viewers, they take restroom and snack breaks during the game and rush back in front of the TV screen to watch the commercials.

Super Bowl ads are so popular that numerous websites are dedicated to rebroadcasting them. Critics offer up reviews that include "The Five Best" and "The Five Worst" commercials. The general public often voice their own opinions about the best and worst of the commercials. Viewers tend to really like commercials that involve cute babies and pet animals. Beer and snack-based commercials are staples among the Super Bowl ads.

Because of the large viewing audience and lasting popularity of Super Bowl ads, companies that air commercials during this sporting event pay a steep price. According to *Advertising Age* (2014), FOX, the network that aired Super Bowl XLVIII on February 2, 2014, averaged around $4 million for thirty seconds' worth of ad time during the game. This price tag set a new TV record; that is, until the following year, when 2015 Super Bowl ads cost $4.5 million per thirty seconds (Busbee 2014). CBS will air the 2016 Super Bowl (the fiftieth installment of the NFL title game) and as early as February 2015, the network's chairman Les Moonves announced that thirty-second ads would cost at least $5 million (Crupi 2015).

The popularity of Super Bowl commercials, along with other cult-like following of televised advertisements, reflects the value our society's members place on a desire to be entertained while consuming products. We all have to make certain purchases (e.g., food, clothing, office and home supplies) and we enjoy conspicuous purchases (by, e.g., attending the theatre, movies, or sporting events), but if we can be entertained while spending money, that seems to make us happier. Marketers and advertisers know this too. Consequently, they try to create clever ads that not only entice us to purchase their product, but present it in such a manner (using, e.g., a logo, a jingle, a clever catchphrase, or babies doing cute adultlike things such as trading stocks) as will keep the product alive in our minds. Thus, even though we have to buy toilet paper, making one wonder why is it even necessary to air commercials for toilet paper, there exists competition, and a variety of product features, even with toilet paper (such as softness, variety of colors, single packs to family size packs, and so on).

Beer, like toilet paper, is another one of those products that seems as though it has a built-in consumer base. After all, if you are a beer drinker do you really need a commercial to remind you that beer exists and that it's ready for purchase (for those of legal drinking age)? Beer drinker or not, beer commercials are often among the funnier and more entertaining of all commercials. Among our favorites are the Miller Lite "Man Laws" commercials that aired during the later years of the first decade of the 2000s. The "Man Laws" are a series of commercials that attempt to instill the unwritten code of manly men laws by which to live. In these TV commercials, the manly men of the "Square Table" (a takeoff on King Arthur's round table) analyze a number of social situations and provide words of masculine authority known as "Man Laws." Male viewers are expected to abide by these rules because, well, they are men. The members of the Square Table are chaired by Burt Reynolds and include actors, athletes, an astronaut, and a regular "Joe" (Delaney 2012a).

The first "Man Law" commercial involves the men of the Round Table discussing whether or not it is okay to date a woman who has dumped your friend. And, if it is okay, how long must you wait before asking her out? This is a scenario that most men have come across some time in their life, and that's the point of these rules, to establish guidelines, or codes of conduct in typical life situations. Astronaut Brian Binnie suggests, "You've got to wait at least a month." Moderator Burt Reynolds disagrees, "No, not a month." Comedian Eddie Griffin offers an alternative view, "I was always taught you've got to wait two Saturdays or a new hairdo, whichever comes first." Again, Reynolds strongly disagrees. He reminds the group of the informal male expectation that due to honor among male friends it is ethically wrong to hook up with a woman who has wronged a pal. Nearing a group decision, comedian Jackie Flynn, asks,

"But what if she's drop-dead gorgeous?" At this prospect, even Reynolds realizes a compromise must be reached. Eventually the group agrees that a six-month waiting period must be enforced. The ruling becomes a "Man Law" and is recorded as such by an elderly scribe.

In another commercial, the group contemplates whether or not it is okay to put fruit in their beer. One member suggests that it helps to prevent scurvy, to which the elderly scribe replies, "I had scurvy once." Mr. Reynolds is dead set against putting fruit in beer. (Note: This commercial would seem to be a direct attack against Corona drinkers who put a slice of lime in their beer and to a lesser extent Blue Moon drinkers who garnish it with an orange slice.) Reynolds suggests that we might as well put a little umbrella in it and call it a "beera colada." The Man Law solution: "Don't Fruit the Beer." The implication of this rule is that putting fruit in one's beer is unmasculine.

The Men of the Square Table answer other important questions posed by manly men, such as: "If you bring Miller Lite to a party and not all of it is consumed, can you take the remainder with you as you leave the party?" Many of us know people who bring food or drink to a communal party and then take any leftovers home with them. This is generally viewed negatively. The Men evoke the "Tuck Rule": one beer max, but only if the beer will fit in your pocket. If a friend buys a round of beer from the bar, is it acceptable for the friend to stick his finger in the opening to bring back several beers to the table at once? Man Rules dictate: No, "you poke it, you own it." How about when toasting with beer, should you clink the top or the bottom of the bottle? Man Rules dictate: The bottom, because clinking the top is like swapping saliva and thus qualifies as kissing. Among the many other issues addressed by the Men of the Square Table, "Is the high five officially played out?" Man Rules say "yes," but have granted a continuance until a replacement can be found. It seems we are still trying to phase out the "high five," but clearly no viable alternative has arisen.

The Miller Lite "Man Laws" commercials were clever and offered an important public service to men searching for a code of conduct in this ever-changing world of gender expectations. Unfortunately, these commercials did not improve sales. And while it's nice to entertain the public, advertisements are about making money for companies. We offer this final "Man Law": It's great to entertain, but when it comes to TV commercials, one must make it rain (heaps of profits).

Lesson Learned: The "Men of the Round Table" would be alarmed at the growing number of people fruiting their beers.

Infomercials: "But wait, there's more!"

Some commercials are not meant to be entertaining in the same manner as most Super Bowl commercials or Miller Lite's "Man Laws" commercial. Instead, they rely on being informative, long in length, and heavily dependent on sales gimmicks and spokespersons, often famous for some reason other than the product's design or use. These commercials are so long that they themselves become a TV program. We refer to such commercials as "Infomercials."

Resulting from the words *information* and *commercial,* an infomercial is a program-length commercial designed to look like regular television programming that enlightens or instructs and may often include a discussion or demonstration of specific products, or a product line, to an audience. Infomercials are designed to encourage people to consume specific products and represent a money-making mechanism for many companies. It is estimated that infomercials bring in $91 billion in sales each year (Watson 2014).

Infomercials often involve testimonials from celebrities, or from ordinary folks, who claim to have used the product and enjoyed highly positive results. Infomercials are characteristically accompanied by marketing sales pitches, such as: "But wait . . . There's more!" and "If you call now we'll double your order at no extra cost!" Sales pitches may also try to add a sense of urgency by saying something like, "There are a limited number remaining," or, "Once they're gone, they're gone forever!"

In the earliest days of television, companies created their own shows so that they would have a medium to promote their goods and services. The Federal Communications Commission (FCC) eventually got involved and placed limits on how much advertising can take place on any given show. Among the earliest versions of an infomercial in the United States was the advertising of Ginsu steak knives, which were promoted as being capable of cutting through anything (Delaney 2015). The first full-length infomercial in the United States aired in the 1970s on XETV, based in the San Diego area, with a one-hour program on Sundays that advertised homes for sale locally (Melkonyan 2009). While the FCC limited commercial time to eighteen minutes per hour in the 1970s, XETV was located in Mexico and broadcast its programs in English to an American audience to avoid U.S. communications laws (Delaney 2015).

Teleshopping, a variation of infomercials became popular in the United Kingdom during the 1980s; it remains popular throughout many parts of the world today. In the United States, infomercials arose following the passage of the Cable Communications Policy Act of 1984 that, among other things, deregulated television commercial airing policies (FCC 1984). Initially, infomercials were aired late at night or the early hours of the morning. Over time, their popularity and the saturation of cable television outlets led to a proliferation of infomercials. Some cable stations show just infomercials while others rely on infomercials for the majority of their programming hours (Delaney 2015).

Tim Hawthorne, the man behind "As Seen on TV," suggests that the history of infomercials is entrepreneurial. "Entrepreneurs from all kinds of fields, such as franchising, computer hardware and print advertising were getting into the television marketing field selling new and unique products not available at retail. In 1984, infomercials could be produced for $15,000 to $25,000 per production and generate as much as $50 million in sales, and one out of three could be a hit" (Hawthorne 1993). There are retail stores today that still carry "As Seen on TV" products.

The popularity of infomercials almost seems improbable, considering that many people look at commercials as unwanted intrusions on their viewing pleasure. The popularity of recording devices (e.g., DVRs) is partially explained by viewers' desires to bypass commercials completely (Delaney 2015). Despite this, millions of viewers tune into infomercial programming and, as a result, infomercials represent a moneymaking machine for many companies. *Consumer Reports* (2010) indicates that infomercials reduce marketing costs to as little as one-tenth the size of a traditional advertising campaign. Infomercials generate billions of dollars worldwide in annual sales and cover a diversity of products ranging from fitness workouts and juicers, to psychic hotlines, blankets that serve as bathrobes, and spray-on hair.

The early 1990s skit television show *In Living Color* brought us many memorable moments including an ongoing parody of the infomercial genre. The classic line, "But, wait, there's more" was a trademark of the skit. The classic infomercial line is used in Keenen Ivory Wayman's 2000 hit film *Scary Movie* as well.

Lesson Learned: We are often irritated by thirty and sixty second commercials during regular programming, but enjoy thirty or sixty minute commercials.

4

Social Media and Popular Culture

Progressive, creative, and liberal thinking allow for the invention of new technologies in the many spheres of social life, including forms of communications. Once upon a time, if we wanted to communicate with persons not in our immediate vicinity we would have to send messages via long-distance runners, or in some cases carrier pigeons or smoke signals. Over time, humans found other ways to communicate long distances, including the introduction of the Pony Express, telegraph wires, telephones, radio and television, and then computers. The creation of computers led to the formation of the Internet, which now allows for immediate long-distance social interactions through a series of networking sites.

The Internet is a relatively new, but influential and prevalent aspect of popular culture in contemporary society. The Internet was created in an effort to sped communication between people separated by long distances. While there might be some debate as to who exactly created the Internet (remember, Al Gore told CNN's Wolf Blitzer on March 9, 1999, that *he* created the Internet), many people have contributed to its creation and growth. Al Gore, for example *did* help pass legislation that advanced the information technology, but he was not the person who "created" it. According to Leiner and associates (2014), "[T]he first recorded description of the social interactions that could be enabled through networking was a series of memos written by J. C. R. Licklider of MIT in August 1962 discussing his 'Galactic Network' concept. He envisioned a globally interconnected set of computers through which everyone could quickly access data and programs from any site." Thus, the Internet was intended to be a widespread information infrastructure designed to help speed communication, especially among intellectuals conducting scientific research. And while the Internet still helps intellectuals conduct research, its everyday usage is far removed from such lofty endeavors.

The Internet has led to the creation of a virtual world (cyberspace) that in turn has led to the reduction of face-to-face interactions in favor of electronic communications. Electronic forms of communication help to shape the world of social media. Social media, then, refers to cyber communication and the nearly countless array of "internet based tools and platforms that increase and enhance the sharing of information. This new form of media makes the transfer of text, photos, audio, video and information in general increasingly fluid among internet users" (*Social Media Defined* 2014). People use social media for business, pleasure, and other reasons via such platforms as Facebook, Twitter, Instagram, Linkedin, Pinterest, and so on, all with the inevitable conclusion of forming virtual worlds of reality. Social media is capable of spreading information (ranging from the mundane, such as a Facebook friend's birthday, to the more serious news events of the day) so quickly that the concept of "trending" has become fashionable. Trending occurs when something significant happens in the world and people immediately use social media to talk about it and then others follow suit. A quick and huge spike in electronic talking about a topic causes it to be labeled as "trending." For example, the top two trending items on Facebook in 2014 were: the 2014 World Cup, which indicates that social media is a global cyber community (consider, 80 percent of Facebook users live outside the United States); and the Ebola outbreak (*Associated Press* 2014). Facebook has a "Trending Now" page so that its users can easily find the latest trends in social network news.

In this chapter, we will look at two social media sites, Facebook and Twitter; the Information Highway; the increasing role of passwords; a social media star; and, how street gangs communicate in the cyber world.

Facebook: Tracking Our Every Move

Chances are that you or someone you know has a Facebook, or some other social network, account. As of the first quarter of 2015, there were more than 1.44 billion monthly active Facebook (FB) users (Statista 2015) and, collectively, these folks spend a total of 640 million minutes on FB each month (Statistic Brain 2014a). Nearly half of all FB users log on every day and spend an average of eighteen minutes per visit. FB has followers in many nations across the globe. The international appeal of Facebook is attributed to the seventy languages in which Facebook is available (*The Post-Standard* 2012a).

Facebook offers many things to many people. Some users view FB as a means to keep in touch with friends and family; some use FB to track down (stalk, in rare cases) old friends and flames or to make new friends, while others use it as a political or religious forum to inform or attempt to force their views onto others. Potentially, there is so much information on one's FB news feed that this social network site has become a source of valuable information to people, similar to the function that newspapers once held for the masses. One of the most intriguing aspects of the posts made by users on FB is our ability to "like" a post. There used to be a "dislike" feature, but FB got rid of it, even though many users wish that the option still existed.

The "like" button first appeared on Facebook in 2009, and despite the seemingly cynical view of the world that many people possess, FB users like a lot of things. As of early 2012, FB averaged 2.7 billion daily "likes." FB users "like" many things, but especially specific posts made by other users, and photos (250 million photos are posted per day) (*The Post-Standard* 2012a).

Facebook was founded in 2004 by Mark Zuckerberg and his college roommates Eduardo Saverin, Dustin Moskovitz, and Chris Hughes, while he attended Harvard University. FB has become such a social phenomenon that *Time* magazine named Mark Zuckerberg the 2010 Person of the Year because of his influence on culture (Grossman 2010). FB, a free online social mixer site originally designed for college students only, but now open to anyone (over thirteen years old), allows users the opportunity to maintain a large number of friendships. However, the name *Facebook* is a little misleading, as there are no face-to-face associations on FB; rather, they are "virtual" relationships (Delaney 2012b).

Contemporary Western society is characterized by people who spend a great deal of time communicating with one another in the virtual world (cyberspace) rather than face-to-face interactions. This phenomenon is an aspect of *virtual socialization* and its influence on our lives is ever-increasing (see chapter 12 for a further discussion on Facebook and friendship). The amount of time Americans spend online has increased each year for at least the past decade (Delaney 2012b). Time spent online generally comes at the expense of spending less time with personal face-to-face relationships. Twenty-four percent of social network site users surveyed responded that they have missed important moments in person because they were busy trying to share those moments on their social network

(Laird 2012). In a 2008 study, 65 percent of Americans were found to spend more time with their computers than with their significant others (Kelton Research and Support 2008).

Not surprisingly, research has found that narcissistic users spend the most time on FB (Smith 2011). Such FB users spend a great deal of time self-promoting. Self-promotion on FB is described as "any descriptive or visual information that appeared to attempt to persuade others about one's own positive qualities" (e.g., posting celebrity look-alikes; attempts to garner as many friends as possible; and constant posting of new photos in an attempt to show how much fun one is having). A number of FB users take advantage of the social network site by embellishing on their lives. Research indicates that 24 percent of Americans and 28 percent of Brits admit to exaggerating or lying on a social network site about who they've met or what they've done (Laird 2012).

FB affords its members an opportunity to set up personal profiles (it also encourages users to fill out all demographic fields); upload photos; post their achievements, likes, and dislikes; create specialized buddy lists; and keep in contact with friends. The concept of "friend" is important with FB, as members are able—and encouraged—to ask other members to be their "friends." (It seems as though FB will not be happy until everyone is on the social network site.) If accepted as a friend, or "friended," the friends can view each other's personal pages and share information. Friends can sign each other's "walls" as well. Many FB members, especially younger ones, attempt to secure as many friends as possible. Having more than one thousand FB friends is not unusual for younger people. However, roughly half of all FB users have fewer than one hundred friends (Laird 2012), while the average teenage user has about three hundred (Smith 2014).

While much can be said about FB and its users, we limit our focus here to the FB profile aspect wherein users are asked to provide a great deal of personal information. FB users are happy to provide some bits of information because they are curious about the same things with regard to their friends. For example, as depicted in the 2010 Academy Award winning film *The Social Network*, it was the relationship status of persons that intrigued Zuckerberg's schoolmates at Harvard and inspired them to check the sites of friends and fellow students. Currently, FB users are still interested in this feature. We also like the reminders of upcoming FB friends' birthdays—it seems like FB remembers things that we don't.

But, Facebook has far more information on us than our relationship statuses and birth dates. They know where you live, your hometown, your high school and college, what degrees you possess, the names of your friends and family members, your location (through a GPS monitoring system), your phone number, whom you are dating, and so on. The amount of data FB possesses about its users is almost frightening, especially when one takes the time to ponder, Who else has access to this information? FB makes a great deal of its data readily available to the public. Here is a sampling of demographic data on FB users:

- Daily active users in the U.S.: 128 million

- Daily active users in the UK: 24 million

- Number of FB users in China (even though it is blocked): 87 million

- Percentage of Chinese FB users that are male: 24.9%

- Number of FB users in India: 100 million

- The country with the most active FB users: Canada

- Percentage of teens that are friends with their parents on FB: 70%

- Percentage of FB users that are male: 42%

- Percentage of FB users that have earned a bachelor's degree: 30%

- Top city (among the top 50 population centers) by percentage of single people on FB: Detroit (Smith 2014)

The data above are a mere sampling of the demographic information that FB has on its users. Among the concerns of the authors of this book are not just the demographic data at Facebook's disposal, but all the other information, such as the geographic location of its users, their purchasing habits, their personal habits, their background information, and so on. Furthermore, one has to, or one should, be concerned about what FB does with all this information. We know, for example, that every time a user "likes" a product or an advertisement, they have made a "connection" to that company, and they will be tracked and courted by that company. But what other data are being shared? And whom is FB sharing this information with? And to what end are they sharing this information? And what's with "Throwback Thursday," wherein FB users are encouraged to post photos from their past; is this for a chronological age profile on users? We live in a society where people are concerned about the National Security Agency (NSA) and its alleged spying on U.S. citizens, and yet many of these same people are on social network sites such as Facebook where they volunteer a great deal of private information. Some of these same people also have a GPS in their car, or own a smartphone with a built-in GPS. And they worry about being spied on? We have no idea how many private and governmental agencies have access to our would-be confidential and personal bits of demographic and general information. We do know, however, that Facebook has a great deal of information on us. Does that make Facebook "Big Brother?"

We have learned something else interesting about Facebook and the idea of Big Brother and unknowingly sharing information with undocumented others. *The Wall Street Journal* reported in May 2014 that Iran-based cyber spies are targeting U.S. officials via social network sites like Facebook. These cyber spies develop connections to their targets through FB and try to trick them into giving up information (Gorman 2014). Cyber spies such as these may also hack into FB files on all its users. Considering this, we would suggest that perhaps "Bigger Brother" is watching "Big Brother." It's quite disconcerting to think of a world with a Big and Bigger Brother watching and reporting our every move. And, somewhere out there right now, someone is reading this and looking for a "like" button. Someone else, however, may read this and add the authors' names to "a list."

Lesson Learned: Facebook, like "Big Brother," is watching you.

The Popularity of Twitter:
60 Million Tweets a Day . . . and Counting

Twitter is another social media site, and while it is not nearly as popular as Facebook, the number of people on Twitter is impressive. As of July 2014, there were nearly 650 million people on Twitter with an estimated 135,000 new Twitter users signing up every day (*Statistic Brain* 2014b). Twitter subscribers set up an account and become an "author" of their posts. These posts are sent to "followers" (an accepted circle of subscribers) to read, or they may go to all Twitter accounts (the default setting of Twitter).

Twitter was founded by Jack Dorsey, Biz Stone, and Evan Williams in March 2006; it is essentially a real-time short messaging service that works over multiple networks and devices. In countries around the world, people follow the sources most relevant to them and access information via a Twitter account as it happens—from breaking world news to updates from friends and celebrities (Delaney 2012a). Twitter and simplicity go hand in hand. Twitter used to ask, "What are you doing?" Now it asks, "What's happening?" Answers, called tweets, must be fewer than 140 characters in length. Like Facebook, which asks, "What's on your mind?" when you want to post a status update, most people pay little attention to the question prompt and proceed to tweet about a topic of interest. And people do like to post tweets, an average of 58 million per day as of July 2014 (*Statistic Brain* 2014b). A tweet may contain text, photos, and videos. Authors generally use a hashtag to identify the subject of their tweet. A hashtag is a word or phrase preceded by the symbol # (originally known as the "number" or "pound" sign), which clarifies or categorizes the accompanying tweet. For example, if people were at a protest rally in Times Square they could post their tweet and conclude it with: #protest-TimesSquare. This way, other Twitter users who might be looking for information on the protest at Times Square could conduct a Twitter search using a hashtag and such topics as #protesttoday or #TimesSquareprotest.

It is also common for Twitter users to retweet. A retweet works much in the same manner as "sharing" a post on Facebook, as it involves re-posting someone else's original tweet. Sometimes people type "RT" at the beginning of a tweet to indicate that they are re-posting someone else's original comment (*Twitter.com* 2014). Retweets may appear on one's home timeline or profile timeline.

Twitter is popular with entertainers and athletes who want to attempt to control the flow of media information about themselves. By making their own tweets, they do not have to rely on hoping that the traditional media writes/says something favorable. Many followers of famous celebrity Twitter authors wait impatiently for updates about their daily activities, most of which are actually quite mundane bits of information. According to *Twitter Counter* (2014), the following celebrities led the way with the largest number of followers: Katy Perry, 62.3 million; Justin Bieber, 58.5m; Barack Obama, 52.1m; Taylor Swift, 49.4m; YouTube, 47.5m; Lady Gaga, 43.2; Britney Spears, 40.1m; Justin Timberlake, 39.5m; Rihanna, 38.6m; and Ellen DeGeneres with 36.8 million followers rounded out the Top Ten. It is interesting that the President of the United States only ranks third in this list, with Taylor Swift swiftly closing in on him.

In some cases, celebrities may follow other celebrities and direct tweets toward them. This is also true with athletes, as often an athlete in one sport might tweet about an athlete in another sport in appreciation of something they just did during a game. For example, a baseball player such as Clayton Kershaw might tweet about a LeBron James slam dunk while he was watching the play on television. ESPN's *SportsCenter* often shows the tweets that one athlete posts about another. As one would suspect, athletes are popular on Twitter and have legions of fans. Like Facebook, when looking at the list of "Top Ten" athletes on Twitter, we are reminded that Twitter is a part of a global social media market. As a result, we are not surprised to learn that international soccer players dominate Twitter's "Top Ten Athletes" list: Cristiano Ronaldo, 32.2 million followers; Kaka, 21.6m; LeBron James; 17.4m; Neymar Junior, 15.9m; Ronaldinho Gaucho, 11.2m; Wayne Rooney, 10.3m; Andres Iniesta, 10.0m; Gerard Pique, 9.6m; Shaquille O'Neal, 9.1m; and Kevin Durant, 8.8 million (*Twitter Athletes* 2014).

There are people on Twitter who utilize the social media site for reasons other than keeping up with the latest celebrity and sports news. Twitter serves as an outlet for breaking news about the world of politics, emergencies (e.g., earthquakes, tornadoes, and snowstorms), traffic updates, criminal proceedings, medical updates on such topics as Ebola, and so on. The power of Twitter to address important issues was demonstrated early in its history, as it became all the rage during the 2008 U.S. presidential campaign, primarily because Barack Obama used Twitter to provide real-time coverage of news events as they occurred. The June 2009 presidential election in Iran propelled the credibility of Twitter in the world of politics.

> Protestors took to the streets of Tehran after accusing that hard-line president Mahmoud Ahmadinejad had stolen his reelection. The Iranian government was able to control traditional news outlets, but it was no match for people who sent tweets of the events in Iran. Twitter was considered such an important source of news during the Iranian post-election demonstrations that a State Department official e-mailed Twitter co-founder Jack Dorsey to delay scheduled maintenance of its global network while Iranians were using it to sway information and inform the outside world about the mushrooming protests around Tehran. (Delaney 2012a:423)

Naturally, Twitter complied with the request because of the great exposure it received. Twitter has continued to play a significant role in politically charged events. During the 2014 American protests against police shootings of unarmed black men, Twitter became the at-the-moment way for protestors to keep in touch with one another. Independent news outlets rely on Twitter so that they can get to the scene of trending events; in turn, they post their raw footage on Twitter (as well as other social media sites). The traditional news agencies also follow Twitter looking for news tips about breaking news. Everyday Twitter users also use the social media site to keep up with breaking news events as they trend.

While instantaneous information may be a good thing, it should be pointed out that tweets are unconfirmed sources of information and are often ripe with biased opinions about events, especially political events. One thing is for sure: Twitter is being used as a source of information, as the number of Twitter search engine queries per day equals 2.1 billion (*Statistic Brain* 2014b).

Lesson Learned: If you want to know what is trending in the political world, or if you want to know what your favorite celebrity had for lunch, you can find it all on Twitter.

The Information Highway:
Some of the Most Unpleasant People Travel on this Highway

While it is common for people on Twitter to tweet, which sounds sweet, and for people on Facebook to "like" things on a regular basis, a large number of people surf the cyber world and find news items and then make hateful or hurtful comments. We refer to such people as "haters." The *Urban Dictionary* (2014) defines a "hater" as: (1) a person that simply cannot be happy for another person's success. So rather than be happy they make a point of exposing a flaw in that person; (2) a person who doesn't have to actually hate the other, but rather wishes to knock the other down a notch.

As it pertains to the cyber world, we would define haters as people who post, generally, angry and/or uninformed comments about a topic, usually with the intent, or leading to the ultimate effect, of harming someone (e.g., the subject of the post, or another person who has posted a comment). Haters can be found on Facebook but they are different from anonymous folks who show up on other sites. For one thing, you know who they are because FB identifies everyone who makes a comment; and second, if you are offended enough by a post, you can either "hide" them from your newsfeed, or "unfriend" them. If the person who made the offensive comment is not a direct friend but made a post on the thread, you can limit your newsfeed to specific people only.

Interestingly, the *Urban Dictionary*'s definition of "hater" is followed by a thread of comments, many of which offer up their own ideas as to the definition of a hater. Among the comments:

- A term used by suburban people.

- The most non-insulting "insult" in existence

- To be a hater is to discriminate [the post was misspelled] or hate something, someone, or a certain type of something.

- People that make up reasons to hate certain people just because they aren't as wealthy or successful as them.to be a hater is to discriminate or hate something, someone, or a certain type of something [*sic*].

Just by looking at the *Urban Dictionary* site you get an idea of who a hater is. One person left a comment: "a hater is y'all people here; y'all haters."

Another interesting aspect of haters and their posts is the relationship between the intensity of hate and the usage of proper grammar. There is generally an inverse relationship; that is, as the level of hate goes up, the level of proper grammar goes down. Either that, or most online haters are either poorly educated or simply do not care about using proper English. Educated people, of course, can be haters too. And, their usage of proper grammar will also decrease as they post rants on a social network site.

"Haters" can be found on nearly all online sites that provide news or entertainment stories and allow for comments from the public, especially comments from anonymous sources. Bloggers often feel the brunt of haters. In some cases haters really care about the subject topic at hand and want to get their point across, while in other cases there are people who post hateful comments for kicks and grins. The ability to remain anonymous fuels the bravery of many haters. An example of haters that express hate primarily for kicks might show up following a story about a celebrity and some minor detail of his or her life, such as whom he or she is dating, or how and where he or she spent vacation. There is usually an overly sensationalized headline to accompany the story, designed to catch the attention of online users. The authors found countless instances wherein people posted comments such as: "Who cares?" and "Who is this person and why should I care?" Such laughable comments. The answer to the question, "Who cares?" is: Obviously, *you* care about the story or you would not have taken the time to read it and then make a post. In response to the question, "Who is this person and why should I care?": Take the ten seconds you used to write the post and do a Google search and find out. A little extra knowledge is a good thing.

While nearly any mundane topic, such as the latest happenings of the Kardashian sisters, can stir the emotions of haters, it is generally the more controversial subject topics that raise the ire of folks. One such topic that is guaranteed to stimulate conversation and hateful comments is gun control. Gun control in relation to a school killing is especially guaranteed to generate haters on both sides of the issue. Sadly, there seem to be an increasing number of shootings at schools that lead to multiple deaths. The murderous rampage near the University of California, Santa Barbara, had occurred at the time of this writing. Elliot Rodger, described as a "mentally disturbed" person, had promised a "day of retribution" in a YouTube video of himself explaining why he was about to do what he was about to do (Ellis and Sidner 2014). And what he did was fatally stab three men in his residence, shot two women to death in front of a sorority house, shot a man to death inside a deli, exchanged gunfire twice with police and injured thirteen people before he fatally shot himself in the head while sitting behind the wheel of his wrecked BMW (Ellis and Sidner 2014). Inside the car, police found three handguns—all legally purchased—and more than four hundred rounds of unused ammunition (Ellis and Sidner 2014).

Elliot's father Peter Rodger works in the film industry, and among his credits was assistant director on the first *The Hunger Games*. Elliot Rodger was not popular and lived anything but a dreamy fun-filled life. He was mentally anguished for a number of reasons, but in his 140-page account of his life, he ranted against women who had ignored him or rejected him over the previous eight years (Ellis and Sidner 2014).

The most important details of this story often get lost in the land of cyber hate. We should be trying to find out why Rodger did not receive the help he needed and use this as a lead to a discussion on mental illness. There are many other related topics as well. But the one that generates the biggest buzz online is gun control. Predictably, there are those who strongly believe that if there were stricter gun control laws this tragedy might have been avoided; there are also those who adamantly believe that guns cannot be blamed for this killing spree and use the occasion to remind people of their constitutional right to bear arms. An intellectual discussion on topics such as gun control can be, or should be, quite enlightening as in reality both sides have good points to make. In online forums, however, people are not generally patient enough to consider one person's point while offering their own. The conversation quickly deteriorates. Below is a sampling of comments shortly after the mass killings occurred:

> P. Walters—Why would anyone be care what a friggin sorority skank things of them? they were doing him a favor by rejecting him lol, no one should date a sorority chick.

> QuoVadisAnima—This is a horrible tragedy, however, the anti-gun assertion makes little sense given that half of those killed were stabbed, and half of those he wounded were hit by his car—the suggestion that this wouldn't have happened if he hadn't been armed is irrational.

> Willy G—This is what I believe to be true. If our great nation was to take our guns, the only civilians who would possess them would be thugs!!! So until we get rid of these non job having pieces of garbage I say leave well enough alone! Remember how well prohibition went?

> Thinkitover—There is evidence that he was in therapy and had been for some time. Apparently the screening process is, the form if filled out (with whatever information true or false the applicant wishes) and the form is read and a gun is issued. Checking into this young man's application would have turned up the fact that he was mentally unstable—although I will admit that may not have been enough to keep him from qualifying for a gun permit.

> LoreneFaircheld—This was tragic but it wasn't the fault of the NRA. Prohibiting law abiding citizens from owning guns will not stop the nut-jobs from obtaining guns illegally.

> Ingvild LoreneFairchild—Actually, yes, it will, and pretty much the rest of the world stands as proof.

> Big2Tex—The NRA supports the notion that the mentally ill should not have guns. Being in "therapy" does not mean one is

mentally ill. If that were the case, the gun grabbers would get their wish, virtually no one could legally own a gun therefore all the criminals would be free to commit mayhem. It appears Rodger gave plenty of warning that he was off the mental reservation but no one was paying attention. Maybe because he was a California liberal. Hey, he could look like Obama's son just like Trayvon.

The online quotes above are a mere sampling of the posts that were available at the time of this writing. Many topics such as school shootings will generate multiple online forums that will generate millions of comments. While some people try to stay close to the subject at hand, others will try to push an agenda, which will further trigger an extreme counterposition. Books could be written about online haters, but who needs them because all we have to do is go online at any given time and there is sure to be a forum with people posting hateful or misinformed comments.

Lesson Learned: There are a lot of haters in the cyber world.

The Password Is: "Frustration"

One of the most popular TV game shows of all time was *Password*, hosted by Allen Ludden, which appeared in various formats from 1961 until 1975. Two contestants were paired with two celebrity guests; each team was asked to guess a specific word (the password), with one member of the team giving the other words that were similar to the password as clues. Whichever team guessed the correct word with the fewest clues would win.

In a classic 1972 episode of the beloved sitcom *The Odd Couple*, Ludden's real-life wife Betty White (then starring in the equally classic sitcom *The Mary Tyler Moore Show*) and her partner are paired on *Password* against sportswriter Oscar Madison (played by Jack Klugman) and his partner and roommate Felix Unger (Tony Randall). Madison becomes increasingly frustrated as the overeducated Unger gives clues that are esoteric and obscure. For instance, for the password "Bird," Felix gives the clue "Aristophanes." A befuddled Oscar can only hopelessly answer, "Greek?" During the commercial break, after Felix tells him that "everyone knows" that the Ancient Greek playwright Aristophanes wrote a play called "The Birds," Oscar berates his friend and tells him the clues have to be clearer and less complex. "'Aristophanes' is *ridiculous!*" he yells. After the break, it's Oscar's turn to give the clue and, to his amazement, the password is "Ridiculous." Looking intently at Felix, and with great anger in his voice, Oscar intones: "*Aristophanes.*" After a moment's pause, Felix hesitantly answers: "Ridiculous?" The buzzer sounds announcing they've won the round, and they are both suitably jubilant, although predictably Felix goes back to his old ways and loses the match for them when he later gives another obscure clue. *TV Guide* in 1997 would declare this particular episode to be the fifth-greatest TV episode of all time.

Oscar's frustration with passwords is one that most of us can relate to on a daily basis. As technology continues to intrude upon our every waking moment, we begin to realize that we need a password for nearly everything. Some of us have so many accounts that require a password we could fill an entire sheet of paper with them. As Thomas Way, a computer science professor at Villanova University explains, "We are in the midst of an era I call the 'tyranny of the password'" (*The Citizen* 6/27/14:A6).

In an earlier era, many of us would choose a simple password, such as the name of a favorite sports team, our birthdate, or our dog's name. But with the proliferation of accounts we all need to constantly access, and with the ever-increasing danger of such accounts being hacked, it is foolhardy to use such easily cracked codes. Indeed, many accounts now require more sophisticated passwords—even more sophisticated than the erudite Felix Unger could have come up with—consisting of combinations of letters, numbers, and symbols, some capitalized, some not. It is hoped that these complex passwords will be more difficult for miscreants to access or guess. That may well be true (although most hackers would say they haven't met a code they couldn't break and welcome the challenge), but the upshot is, we all have to now try to remember codes that are by their very structure literally unmemorable, or at least unmemorizable. We have probably all had the unnerving situation of typing our password into an account we need to access immediately, such as a bank account, only to be told we've gotten it wrong. Quite a few of these only allow a limited number of attempts, after which they freeze and lock us out.

In frustration, we often do the things we're warned against. We write down the passwords and put them in our wallets, purses, or cell phones, thereby making it simple for anyone who steals such items to access all of our most intimate information. Or we still try to use simple, easily decoded phrases or series of numbers, just because we can remember them. While realizing that this increases our vulnerability, the other option—trying to somehow recall a myriad of meaningless symbols—seems to lead to the danger of driving us batty.

Must secure passwords be so frustrating? Keith Palmgren, an instructor at the SANS Institute, a cyber security research and education organization based in Texas, holds that it isn't necessary for passwords to be so mind boggling. "Whoever coined the phrase 'complex password' did us a disservice," he states, suggesting that in fact it would be more effective to use entire sentences, including spacing and punctuation, as a password. These would be much easier to remember. "This sentence is an example" of such a password (*The Citizen,* 6/27/14:A6).

Other options that seem to be increasing are the use not of words and symbols as access to our data, but biometrics, such as thumbprints, iris patterns, and face recognition. Given that these are unique to each person, it's felt that they are much more secure, and save us from the problem of remembering passwords. While these may indeed be more effective means of protection, it's important to note that they are not foolproof. Popular Culture has many examples of ways in which even these methods can be breached, as for instance in the 2002 Tom Cruise futurist film *Minority Report,* where the lead character, in order to deceive personal recognition devices, has his irises replaced.

Like it or not, passwords are here to stay. Balancing ease of access with legitimate fears for security will remain a constant problem. Passwords are a real, if annoying, part of modern life. As Oscar Madison would no doubt put it, they are both necessary and *ridiculous.*

Lesson Learned: If you want the freedom of the Internet, you need the security of a good password.

Michael Stevens, Social Media Personality.
Answering Your Questions on a Vast Array of Subjects

The different genres of popular culture all have their stars. There are movie and TV stars; star musicians and singers; radio DJ stars; star comedians; star writers; sports stars; and celebrities who are stars just because they are popular personalities. It should come as no surprise, then, that social media has its own stars as well. In fact, there is even an annual conference called VidCon, where thousands of attendees hope to meet their favorite YouTube celebrities. Among the more fascinating social media personalities is Michael Stevens.

Michael Stevens answers people's questions, some of which are quite odd and others of which are scientifically driven, and posts his responses online via his Vsauce channels on YouTube. According to the YouTube site, Vsauce was created by Stevens in the summer of 2010. Stevens encourages people to send him questions and ideas via his Twitter site: twitter.com/tweetsauce. Visitors to the YouTube site are invited to subscribe to Vsauce for "Mind-Blowing Facts & The Best of the Internet." As of mid-August 2014, there were more than 7.5 million subscribers. At this same time, Vsauce included four channels: Vsauce, Vsauce2, Vsauce3, and WeSauce. Each of the channels produces videos to answer questions or to provide a variety of facts, some beneficial, some useless. The number of combined subscriptions to Stevens's Vsauce network of channels exceeds twelve million, and his videos have been viewed nearly 1.2 billion times.

Stevens admits that he is not an expert on all the questions that he answers (in fact, he is hardly an expert on any subjects), and even acknowledges that some of his research comes from Wikipedia (a highly questionable nonacademic site) and YouTube videos, but he also searches academic papers in seeking accuracy in his responses.

From his Vsauce channel, we can see that some of the most popular questions he has answered include: "What if everyone jumped at once?" (13.7m views), "Why do people kiss?" (11.2m views), "What color is a mirror?" (10.2m views), and the intriguing question, "Why don't we all have cancer?" (2.7m views). Stevens provides a lengthy and usually interesting answer to every question he receives. He concludes his answers with a signature signoff: "And as always, thanks for watching."

To answer the first question, "What if everyone jumped at the same time?" Stevens begins by describing the rotation of the earth on its axis and around the sun. He mentions how our combined jumping would have little, if any, measurable impact because, among other factors, the total weight of humans around the world is insignificant compared to the total weight of everything else on the planet.

Why do people kiss? Many of us could offer up answers to this question, including because we love someone and want to share intimate and/or passionate moments with others. Stevens calculates that each of us will spend about 20,160 minutes of our lives kissing. The longest recorded kiss exceeded fifty-eight hours, so if you want to break the continuous kissing record you have your work cut out for you. Stevens says that although kissing seems kind of weird and gross it's quite enjoyable, especially with a loving significant other. Kissing burns two or three calories per minute. But, perhaps the real reason we enjoy kissing is because the act itself releases epinephrine, a hormone important to the body's metabolism. Epinephrine provides a type of "rush" that gives people a natural "high." Thus, kissing makes us high. Stevens also connects "good" kissing to signs of a good lover and further concludes that a good kisser is important to evolutionary growth of the human species.

To answer "What color is a mirror?" Stevens describes the importance of a prism and the role of the spectrum of light. Thus, one might conclude that a mirror is the color of anything it reflects. However, Stevens explains, there is always a speck of green in a mirror. In a "mirror tunnel" (series of mirrors arranged to reflect back upon themselves), a little bit of light is lost in each mirror, but the color green is the least likely color to disappear; therefore, the color green is more evident.

While there are many more frequently cited questions than "Why don't we all have cancer?" we believe this to be one of the most important. Stevens begins his answer by describing how each of us has millions of dead cells covering our body; we are literally covered by dead stuff. When we are in a room with a sunbeam shining through and see millions of tiny objects dancing around, 80 percent of that material is dead human skin. For the most part, we are made of living things, millions of living cells, each designed to keep us alive. Our bodies are not perfect, however. Some cellular mistakes may cause bodily harm while continuing to reproduce, with cancer as a result. According to Stevens, cancer is caused by cellular mistakes. Because there are more than two hundred types of cancer, it is unlikely that all cancer will be eliminated, but science is finding a way to combat cancer in a growing number of people.

If you want a fuller explanation to these and the countless other questions answered by Stevens you can go to the Vsauce channel.

In December 2010, the Vsauce2 and Vsauce3 channels were opened. The WeSauce channel opened in 2012. Each of these channels also provides information in an entertaining format. To date, with nearly 2.5 million views, the most popular video on Vsauce2 is "7 Banned Foods from around the World," as follows: chewing gum is banned in Singapore; ketchup is banned in cafeterias in France; a town in Indiana has banned eating watermelon in the park; New York City banned large soft drinks (the law was repealed) when Michael Bloomberg was mayor, and in response the state of Mississippi banned attempts to try to ban large soft drinks (Mississippi, by the way has the highest rate of obesity in the USA); many nations have banned horsemeat; buying salmon from an unlicensed dealer in the United Kingdom; sassafras is banned in root beer (because it might cause cancer); the UK government is trying to get the

United States to lift its ban on Scottish haggis. (Interestingly enough, the article's headline says seven banned foods, but the article describes eight.)

Vsauce3 has different hosts and is dedicated to fictional worlds and video games. Like WeSauce, Vsauce is still working on increasing its total subscription memberships. WeSauce features the videos, primarily musical playlists, of fans of Vsauce channels.

Lesson Learned: People will take advice from non-experts if the answers provided are entertaining.

Street Gangs and the Cyber World: Claiming Digital Turf

The Internet is utilized by billions of people around the world. Chances are, if people have electricity, or some power source, they have access to the World Wide Web (www). As we learned in the introduction in our discussion of social media, the Internet was created as a mechanism for scientists to share research and data. The vast majority of people online are not engaged in such lofty goals. In fact, the cyber world is often used for illegal purposes.

Among those using the cyber world for illegal purposes are street gangs. Tim Delaney has conducted a great deal of research on street gangs. He has observed gang activity up close and personal, but you, or anyone else, can conduct research from the safety of your own home, or anywhere you have access to the net. A quick Google search of "Gangs and the Internet," which yields more than eleven million links, will illustrate the point that street gangs use the Internet. A research study conducted at Sam Houston State University indicates that gang members spend time online for many of the same reasons as conventional folks; that is, they watch YouTube videos and use social network sites like Facebook (*Science Daily* 2013). The study also indicates that street gangs use the net to search out information on other gangs and more than half watch gang-related videos online.

Other research paints a more ominous picture of street gangs online. "As social media has increasingly become part of daily lives, both gangs and law enforcement are trying to capitalize on the reach of this new digital world" (PoliceOne.com 2014). There are indeed gang videos online that show gang members, or reputed gang members, pointing their guns at the camera, acting tough and demonstrating bravado. The gangs are shown fighting rival gangs, throwing parties, and hanging out with girls. Images such as these are designed to lure socially alienated youth, especially from the lower socioeconomic classes, to go through the initiation process and become a gang member. Terms such as *cyberbanging* and *Internet banging* might be used to describe the activity of gang members online.

Nation gangs may have their own websites. Gangs such as the Crips and Bloods have undisguised online sites: www.crips.com and www.bloods. com. The Crips site includes general information about the gang, YouTube videos provide links to news stories, interviews with prison gang members, information about shootings with rival gangs, and so on. Specific gangs may showcase their illegal exploits, make threats, and honor their deceased and incarcerated members on a "digital turf." As Glazer (2006) explains, "Crips, Bloods, MS-13, 18th Street and others have staked claims on various corners of cyberspace. 'Web bangers' are posting potentially incriminating photos of members holding guns, messages taunting other gangs and boasts of illegal exploits on personal Web sites and social networking sites" (p. 1). The National Gang Crime Research Center, has trained hundreds of police officials in acquiring intelligence about gang memberships, rivalries, territory, and lingo from gangs' web pages (Glazer 2006).

In its 2011 National Gang Threat Assessment, the FBI addressed the emerging trend of street gangs on the Internet, and the Bureau has begun training its personnel in tactics to combat street gangs that use the Internet (National Gang Intelligence Center 2011; Delaney 2014). Street gangs have become increasingly savvy and are embracing new and advanced technology to facilitate criminal activity not only on the streets but in cyberspace as well. "Gang members use prepaid cell phones, social networking and microblogging websites, voice over Internet Protocol systems (e.g., making phone calls from one's computer), virtual worlds, and gaming systems that enable them to communicate globally and discreetly. Street gangs are also increasingly employing advanced countermeasures to monitor and target law enforcement while engaging in a host of criminal activity" (Delaney 2014:132).

It is safe to say that street gangs are using the Internet for both recreational and gangbanging activity. There is no evidence to suggest that they are doing academic research, however.

Lesson Learned: Thanks to street gangs, we have to worry about becoming victims of a "drive-by shooting" on the information highway.

5

Music and Popular Culture

We recently saw the following message posted on Facebook: "Music, a mind-altering noise with the potential to induce joy, happiness, memories, bliss, merriment, and mirth." That pretty much sums it up. There is an old saying that music can soothe the savage breast. How many of us, no matter how bent out of shape we might be, nonetheless find solace by listening to our favorite tunes? It can be a classical recording of a Beethoven symphony, a hip hop hit, a patriotic tune, or even a commercial jingle. For some reason (which we'll explore in detail below), music has a power that in many ways is greater than that of any other popular art. In fact, the philosopher Arthur Schopenhauer (1788–1860) went so far as to say that music was the highest of all the arts, since it best captured the nature of reality and it alone was truly immortal.

While that may be going a bit too far, it does seem that music can lift individual and community spirits: a national anthem performed at an event can give rise to patriotic sentiments throughout the audience, and music can give voice to our personal feelings and life circumstances. Regardless of one's taste in music, there is a genre for everyone. People enjoy music from a variety of genres, and since the advent of recordings in the 1870s it has been possible to share such experiences over and over. Before that time, if you wanted to hear music, you either had to perform it yourself or attend a musical performance. In fact, people often amused themselves by singing songs and playing instruments in the comfort of their own homes, which is how so many of the popular songs we now know were passed on for posterity.

In the following stories, we will take a look at the Beatles invasion, which helped establish rock and roll as the number one genre for decades;

we will take a look at a living legend assumed to be dead (no, not Elvis!); and we will examine some recent controversies in the realms of popular culture and music, such as the fact that today, for the first time ever, it is possible to own all sorts of recordings without paying for them, to the consternation of the music's creators. The ways in which music can represent differences between men and women will also be explored, as will the fact that success in the recording and performing industries can often "give voice" to individuals who are otherwise marginalized. The love we have for attending performances can itself be a bonding factor for communities and can help to keep alive the careers of performers decades after their original works were published—a kind of pop culture resurrection, as it were.

As an old folk song (one that Schopenhauer would have loved) once put it, "All things shall perish from under the sky/Music alone shall live/ . . . never to die."

It Was Fifty Years Ago Today: The Beatles Live On

For fans of the Beatles, the year 2014 was a time for great celebration. It was on February 9, 1964, that the Beatles made their first appearance on the popular CBS television program *The Ed Sullivan Show*. While the group had already had several hit songs in their native England, this live television appearance marked the beginning of what came to be called "Beatlemania," and indeed sparked an entire movement called "The British Invasion," in which countless other pop music acts from the United Kingdom came to the United States, many appearing on *The Ed Sullivan Show* as well as on other programs. The Beatles themselves returned twice more that February, and the fervor and pandemonium they inspired only increased (a nice depiction of this time can be found in the amusing 1978 movie *I Wanna Hold Your Hand*, directed and co-written by Bob Zemeckis, in which four young women, loosely analogous to the four Beatles, are transformed by their experiences in breaking into the Sullivan show set and, in one case, the hotel room where the Beatles are staying New York City).

That was just the beginning of the Beatles' "invasion" of America that year, as their manager Brian Epstein booked them on a series of tours across the country. After that, the exhausted Fab Four headed back home, not to rest, but rather to star in their first motion picture, named after one of their hit songs, *A Hard Day's Night* (a title said to be taken from one of Ringo Starr's laconic Liverpool expressions). Other rock and roll stars such as Elvis Presley had already headlined motion pictures and Epstein thought this would be a good way to keep up the enthusiasm generated by the group by allowing fans to see them who otherwise would not get the live experience. The director of the movie was Richard Lester, who had in earlier films already pioneered the use of rapid editing cuts connected with music. The match between his innovative technique and the Liverpool lads' whimsical humor and fresh appearances was a great success, and the film did record business at the box office, and was followed the next year by their second film (also directed by Lester), *Help!*

What almost no one at the time (least of all the Beatles themselves) could have predicted is that a half-century later the Beatles would be as prominent in popular culture as they were when they first "invaded" the U.S.A. Countless websites, articles, and television programs commemorating the original *Ed Sullivan* experience were promulgated in 2014, and the two surviving Beatle members, Paul McCartney and Ringo Starr, reunited at that year's Primetime Emmys Award show, as well as on a special CBS commemoration of the original *Ed Sullivan Show* appearance that was filmed on the same set (at that time the set of *Late Night With David Letterman*) and featured homages from such contemporary recording artists as Alicia Keys, Katy Perry, Keith Urban, and Pharrell Williams. Still, it was the appearance of McCartney and Starr, then aged seventy-two and seventy-four respectively, that brought down the house with versions of the songs they had played on the same stage fifty years before. Paul was quoted as saying, "When I was asked to do this show, I was wondering if it was the right thing to do. Was it seemly to tribute yourself? Then I saw a couple of American guys and they said, 'You don't understand the enormous impact that show had on America.' So then I understood and I decided to show up" (*The Beatles: 50ᵗʰ Anniversary Collector's Edition*).

After the performance, the two surviving Beatles led their respective bands on world tours, keeping the drive alive for those who wanted to recapture in some way the magic that the Fab Four had first brought about. And Paul was there to induct his bandmate Ringo into the Rock and Roll Hall of Fame in 2015 (having himself been inducted as a solo artist in 1999).

The Beatles stopped playing live performances just a few years after their original American tour, when they realized that the screaming throughout the songs by their countless fans drowned out the music and made for an increasingly unsettling experience. By then, they had begun devoting more and more of their time to creating new works in the recording studio, which would eventually lead to their masterpiece *Sgt. Pepper's Lonely Hearts Club Band* (1967), a work whose musical complexities were accentuated and often created in the studio, and which would have been impossible to duplicate live.

The Beatles' last live performance (other than their iconic brief gig in 1969 on their Apple Headquarters roof, which ended with John Lennon's dry remark, "I'd like to say thank you on behalf of the group and ourselves and I hope we've passed the audition"), was at Candlestick Park in San Francisco, California, on August 29, 1966. The park at that time was the home field for Major League Baseball's San Francisco Giants. Due to structural and other problems, Candlestick Park—which later had become the home field of the National Football League's San Francisco 49ers and the site of countless other rock concerts and related events—was abandoned after the end of the 49ers' 2013 season and its demolition scheduled to occur. How fitting, therefore, that the last event held there was a concert by none other than a person whose own last formal concert as a Beatle had taken place at the same location. "Sir Paul McCartney last played Candlestick Park on August 29, 1966, with some guys named John, George and Ringo. The Beatles' last concert was at the Stick that afternoon, a tidy 11-song, 35-minute performance largely drowned out by the din of screaming teenagers and their admiring parents. On Thursday night, it was Candlestick's swan song with Sir Paul at the mike" (Swartz 2014).

In many ways, the Beatles are the archetypes of a modern pop culture phenomenon. As we defined it in chapter 1, a *popular culture phenomenon* involves any instance when an aspect of one form of pop culture crosses over to at least six other genres of popular culture. Even though the group disbanded in 1970 and, due to the untimely and tragic deaths of John Lennon in 1980 and George Harrison in 2001, can never reunite, their legacy lives on and indeed continues to dominate many areas of popular culture: movies; television; social media; music; radio; cartoons and comics; books; fads; fashion; technology; and trends. The Beatles remain the foremost ambassadors of popular culture, and given the fact that they are taken seriously, written about frequently, studied assiduously, and continue to influence new generations of musicians, it is safe to say that they have crossed the frontier into high culture as well.

On Saturday, July 6, 1957, "the 15 year old Paul McCartney, wearing his flash white sport coat and black drainpipe trousers, circled from his home in Allerton to St. Peter's [Church]. He'd come at the suggestion of Ivan Vaughan, a class-mate, to see the Quarry Men, a skiffle group for which Ivan sometimes played tea chest bass. And, there might also be the chance of chatting up some girls" (Jones 1991:70). Paul was impressed by the versatility and quick wit shown by the group's leader, sixteen-year-old John Lennon, and after the show Vaughan introduced the two of them when they gathered in the Church Hall. "Paul remembered thinking 'I wouldn't mind being in a group with him.' Years later, John was to say: 'That was the day, the day I met Paul that it started moving'" (Jones 1991:70). A plaque commemorating this event, with John's statement emblazoned upon it, was unveiled forty years later, in 1997. Truer words were never spoken—after that historic meeting, popular music, and popular culture, would never be the same.

Lesson Learned: Some popular culture phenomena stand the test of time.

Searching for Sugar Man

In 2012, an amazing documentary film appeared, with little fanfare, at the annual Sundance Film Festival. Written and directed by Malik Bendjelloul—a former actor and reporter from Sweden who, while he had done extensive work in television, had never before produced a film—the movie detailed the career of an American singer/songwriter known only as "Rodriguez" who had put out two rock albums in the early 1970s (including one with a song called "Sugar Man"). His bluesy rock-folk songs, with their incisive social commentary, were similar in tone to other successful performers of the time, such as Bob Dylan, the Grateful Dead, or Crosby, Stills, Nash, and Young. Unlike them, however, Sixto Rodriguez, alas, was not a success, and shortly afterward disappeared completely from the music scene.

While editing and directing documentaries for Swedish television about recording artists, Bendjelloul had heard stories about Rodriguez, particularly the astonishing fact that his albums had become wildly popular in, of all places, apartheid-era South Africa. "A largely inexperienced filmmaker when he started the project," writes Bruce Weber, "Mr. Bendjelloul edited *Searching for Sugar Man* in his Stockholm apartment and paid for most of it himself" (Weber 2014). It took him more than three years, with little encouragement from others, to complete the film, and he had no way of knowing whether it would be received any better than Rodriguez's own initial work had been.

Searching for Sugar Man records the efforts of two dedicated South African fans, Stephen Segerman (who laughingly remarks that his own nickname of "Sugar" comes from his interest in "Sugar Man"), a Cape Town record store owner, and reporter Craig Bartholomew Strydom, both of whom attempted to find out what had happened to their favorite recording artist. Rumors abounded that "Sugar Man" had killed himself, either due to despair over his lack of success, or perhaps due to a drug overdose (as, sadly, had been the case with so many of his contemporaries). Because of his obscurity, as well as the difficulty South Africans had in gaining information from the world outside during the apartheid times, when the country was isolated by international sanctions, it was almost impossible for Segerman and Strydom to get even basic facts. All they had to go on were Rodriguez's record albums themselves and the cryptic lyrics therein. Only after the fall of apartheid in the early 1990s, and the concurrent rise of the Internet, were they able to get any details. Amazingly enough, they learned that Rodriguez was in fact alive and well and living in Detroit, where he had been working as a handyman since his career as a musician had ended.

Thanks to their efforts, Rodriguez was invited to give a series of concerts in South Africa. At first, he thought the invitation was a put-on, but upon arrival he and his daughters came to realize the love that the people of South Africa still had for him. Several of the best-known South African bands were able to back him, since the musicians all knew his albums by heart.

Why were Rodriguez's songs so popular in South Africa? In part, it was because his lyrics confronted the same sort of social problems that were occurring in South Africa at the time: racial inequality, oppression, and ignorance. As a Hispanic American, neither black nor white, his persona was one that crossed boundaries in that segregated country. And basically, his fans in South Africa recognized what American audiences hadn't—that Rodriguez wrote and performed some damn good songs. It wasn't because of lack of talent but rather due to bad breaks that he hadn't gotten the recognition he deserved.

Searching for Sugar Man records this remarkable story in detail. The love and respect that Rodriguez finally received, after more than thirty years of seemingly being forgotten; his humility and lack of anger for the years of obscurity; and most of all his sheer talent all shine through in this heartwarming documentary.

The film itself won numerous awards, beginning at its first showing at the Sundance Film Festival, where it was given the Special Jury Prize and the Audience Award for best international documentary. A flurry of other awards soon followed, including the British Academy Film Award, the Directors Guild of America Award, and perhaps best of all, the Academy Award for Best Documentary at the Eighty-Fifth Academy Awards ceremony in February 2013. Humble as ever, Rodriguez chose not to attend the ceremony, so that he wouldn't take attention away from filmmaker Bendjelloul.

Malik Bendjelloul's perseverance had paid off. The noted film reviewer Roger Ebert gave it one of his highest endorsements: "Do some stories exist only because we need them to? . . . *Searching for Sugar Man* is a documentary that enlists us in the process of its search. Using archival footage, it shows both Segerman and Bendjelloul pressing ahead in a quest that became increasingly frustrating. The information they eventually dislodge about Rodriguez suggests a secular saint, a deeply good man, whose music is the expression of a blessed inner being. I hope you're able to see this film. You deserve to. And yes, it exists only because we need for it to" (Ebert 2012).

Thanks to the renewed interest the film brought to him, Rodriguez's career belatedly took off. He was soon performing gigs across the world, and started to get the recognition he should have received earlier in his own country. His two initial albums were reissued, and, unlike the first time, not only did they sell well, he received the financial benefits from them as well.

However, as often happens with popular culture sensational stories, complexities arose. While Rodriguez definitely did seem to be a goodhearted, humble individual, no one could have lived up to being called "a secular saint." Reporters and other interested parties began to ask difficult questions about what had happened to the money received from the sales of his albums in South Africa, especially since none of the royalties came to Rodriguez himself. Various lawsuits were launched to try to determine where the money went.

In addition, older stories on the Internet made it clear that there were other things left out of the documentary, including the fact that Sugar Man also had been popular in Australia, and had in fact toured there in the late 1970s and early 1980s. As Ryan Lenora Brown put it, in an article entitled "Sugar Man: Did the Oscar-Winning Documentary Mislead Viewers?": "It's a story ready-made for Hollywood, and watching the film, it all seems almost too good to be true. That's probably because it is" (Brown 2013).

Saddest of all, shortly after receiving the most prestigious awards any filmmaker could ask for, and without ever completing a second movie,

Searching for Sugar Man's director committed suicide. As with so many such tragedies, it was not clear why Malik Bendjelloul chose to end his life, but this depressing event most certainly put a damper on the overall "feel good" story of the documentary.

Still, *Searching for Sugar Man* must be judged for its effectiveness as a popular culture phenomenon. The film did very well at the box office, and continues to be a favorite on the Internet through Netflix viewings. It is often shown at film festivals. And best of all, Rodriguez continues to perform, both live and in television and radio appearances. His albums are selling, and a new generation can appreciate his talent. And, for his many fans in South Africa, the search for Sugar Man came to a wonderful conclusion. Rather than dying horribly in pain and obscurity, their hero returned again to them to continue to spread joy with his words and music. As Malik Bendielloul understood, this is indeed a great story, and perhaps the closest any of us will get to a modern-day resurrection.

Lesson Learned: If your biggest fans think you are dead and then they learn you are alive, that's a popular culture resurrection.

Hip Hop and Rap Music:
Giving "Voice" to Those Who Have None in
Major Decision-Making Arenas

Music provides most of us with an opportunity to express ourselves, and this is true whether we are consumers or producers of music. The majority of us are consumers of music; that is to say, we enjoy the music that others have produced. While listening to music we allow ourselves to be transfixed for moments in time, as certain songs remind us of specific places and past times with significant others. Some of us are musicians who produce new tunes for others to enjoy.

Music has many social functions, including the expression of happiness, sadness, and disgust over social injustice. For example, patriotic songs contain lyrics designed to show support for the country's decision to go to war and for the brave men and women who fight. Other songs may demonstrate disapproval of decisions made by politicians, including the choice to wage war. One genre of music, however, has been created for the sole purpose of expressing a community's dissatisfaction with the racism that characterizes American society, principally by articulating its effects. This genre is rap and hip hop.

Rap and hip hop came about because African Americans were tired of structural racism in the United States, which disproportionately has relegated them to the lowest socioeconomic strata. Rap music afforded them a chance to voice their displeasure at a social system that has led to their being treated as second-class citizens. Rap rose out of the Afrocentrism movement that followed the civil rights movement of the 1960s. Poetry and rhymes were especially important in this movement, and were generally accompanied by African music or drumming (Delaney 2012). Among the more popular performers were the Last Poets of Harlem. By the early 1970s, soul and funk artists such as Barry White and Isaac Hayes had started using raps in their songs (Keyes 2002).

The relatively tame lyrics and themes of early rappers through the 1980s gave way in the 1990s to raps characterized by rage and profanity. Gangsta rap emerged during this period, and was centered on notions of street credibility and "keeping it real." In other words, these rappers were from lower socioeconomic status (SES) backgrounds and their raps centered on real-life events such as being victimized by law enforcement and the social system. Gangsta rappers such as Easy E and Tupac Shakur, and later Dr. Dre and Snoop Dogg, used their actual gang affiliations to legitimize their street credibility. Having street cred is of little importance to those who control the means of production, as they dominate the socioeconomic arenas of society; conversely, lower-SES people, such as gangbangers and rappers, find street cred to be important. Thus, it could be argued that those with power seek "Wall Street cred" because their power comes from their financial clout, while gangsta rappers and their fans seek credibility on the actual streets.

Having street cred is still an important element of gangsta rap today. The biggest stars boast about gang life and being shot and having survived. And while gangsta rap is primarily a "black thing" a number of Hispanic rappers (such as Pitbull) and a few white rappers (Eminem) have also emerged to the forefront because they too feel disenfranchised from mainstream society.

Not surprisingly, gangsta rap, with its roots among gang members turned rappers has influence among street gangs and would-be gang members. In Delaney's (2014) research on upstate New York street gangs, he found that one of the most notorious street gangs in Syracuse was named after a hip hop group, and the same is true of an infamous Rochester street gang. Both Syracuse and Rochester have relatively serious gang problems, with homicide rates consistently three to five times the national average, most of which is attributable to gang members. As with any large city, street gangs in Syracuse and Rochester have taken control of a great deal of the illegal drug trade. The high unemployment and poverty rates contribute to the sense of hopelessness that many African American youth feel in these two cities.

The Syracuse street gang Boot Camp was notorious for being the first gang in Syracuse, and one of the earliest in the nation, to be taken down by federal authorities via the Racketeer Influenced and Corrupt Organizations (RICO) Act. RICO was originally designed so that law enforcement could put on trial all the members of an organized crime syndicate and not just those arrested. In other words, if the people at the top of the hierarchy were not directly tied to criminal activities they could still be prosecuted because of their membership in the criminal organization. The idea of applying RICO to street gangs was unique and unheard of until the early 2000s. RICO statutes were used to imprison Boot Camp members in 2003. Among their criminal activities were murder, conspiracy, racketeering, and a host of other violent offenses.

As for their connection to rap and hip hop, the members of Boot Camp took their name from hip hop supergroup "Boot Camp Clik." Boot Camp Clik originated in Brooklyn, New York, in 1993. The members of Boot Camp Clik include renowned artists from Brooklyn: Buckshot (from the group Black Moon), a famous underground rapper and leader of Book Camp Clik; Smif-N-Wessum, also known as Cocoa Brovaz (from Tek and Steele); Heltah Skeltah (a hip hop duo with members Rock and Sean Price); and OGC (Originoo Gunn Cappaz consisting of rappers Starang Wondah, Louieville Sluggah, and Top Dog) (U.S. Military 2012; Delaney 2014). Boot Camp Clik was a huge success in the underground world of rap. They added personal experiences to their raps and they are considered the first rap group to infuse reggae elements into their music. Boot Camp Clik's rise to stardom in the rap world during the 1990s inspired many hip hop artists and influenced many black youth, including a soon-to-be notorious street gang in Syracuse.

In Rochester, another upstate New York city with a serious gang problem, the notorious street gang Dipset was named in honor of a hip hop band. The name "Dipset" comes from the "Dipset Anthem," a rap song by The Diplomats" (Flanigan 2003). The lyrics to this song are filled with references to gangsters, drugs, drive-by shootings, homicide, and treating women as "hos." The word *dipset* is believed to be a code for "run," as in "run away, the cops are coming." In the gang world, Dipset became associated with The Diplomats because of their anthem song. The Diplomats were founded by Cam'ron and Jim Jones in 1997. Over the course of the following six years, many artists joined the Jones brothers' band. In 2003, The Diplomats released the album *Diplomatic Immunity*, which featured a remix of "Hey Ma" (a platinum single from Cam'ron's third solo album in 2002) as well as the lead single, "Dipset Anthem." The Dipset anthem, besides being a favorite hip hop song among rap fans, would also influence a group of gangsters in Rochester who would embrace both the message and the name offered by this anthem (Delaney 2012).

Hip hop and rap represents more than a genre of music. For many of its fans, it represents a way of life, a life consumed by violence and hopelessness. Rap artists become heroes to many lower SES youth, especially African Americans, because they "keep it real" and rap about social happenings that they can relate to.

Lesson Learned: Rappers and hip hop artists give voice to disenfranchised youth who feel that their needs and concerns are going unheard.

Why Should I Pay for Music
When I Can Download It for Free?

It would be great if everything in life was free, wouldn't it? Imagine going to the grocery store and everything was free, or going to an auto dealership and driving away with a new car without paying for it, wouldn't that be great? Logic and a little bit of common sense remind us that if everything were free no one would earn a salary to provide that good or service, and if no one got paid to work, why would they work? How many among us would be willing to work all day for free? And, even if we did work for free for free products, how would the production costs be covered? Karl Marx dreamed of a utopian society wherein everyone takes just what they need and they all provide their working skills and labor for free. Such societies are known as communistic, and none exist. Even Marx came to realize there were some flaws in his proposed socioeconomic system. The system most of us are a part of includes some sort of variation wherein we work, get paid for our labor, and then receive a wage to pay for goods and services.

While nearly everyone clearly understands the principle that people should be paid for their labor, there exist a number of people who think it is okay to steal the products of musicians and the music industry. This seems quite odd: we don't walk into a clothing store and think it's okay to walk out with clothes without paying for them, do we? And even those who do think it's okay to steal specific items such as clothing or jewelry generally acknowledge the reality that if caught, they might go to jail. People who illegally download music generally seem to think that it's okay to do so and that, if caught, there will be no negative repercussions. After all, "All I did was download a few songs, what's the big deal?"

The idea that downloading music for free is an odd one. Most of the same people who download music illegally would not think it was okay to steal from their friends, family, or department stores, so again we ask, Why do some people think it's okay to steal music from musicians? We know people do download music illegally. Chances are, readers of this story know someone who has done this, or perhaps they have done so themselves. People have been making copies of sound recordings without paying for them for decades now. In the 1960s, people would use such crude techniques as placing a tape recorder near a radio or turntable to record the music being played. Over the years, and with the advent of technology, people, most of them high school or college aged, have downloaded and shared music taken from the Internet.

Many people who download music illegally may not be aware of the fact that the Recording Industry Association of America (RIAA) considers this theft of intellectual property (copyrighted material); in other words, criminal activity. Just who is the RIAA? They are the trade organization that supports and promotes the creative and financial vitality of the major music companies. "Its members are the music labels that comprise the most vibrant record industry in the world. RIAA members create, manufacture and/or distribute approximately 85% of all legitimate recorded music produced and sold in the United States" (RIAA 2014).

The theft of intellectual property from the music industry is indeed illegal; it is piracy. As the RIAA (2014) explains, although downloading one song may not seem that serious a crime, "the accumulative impact of millions of songs downloaded illegally—and without any compensation to all the people who helped to create that song and bring it to fans—is devastating." The people who help create a song include songwriters, recording artists, audio engineers, computer technicians, talent scouts, marketing specialists, producers, publishers, and many others. The RIAA (2014) believes that global music piracy causes $12.5 billion in economic losses each year and is responsible for more than 71,000 jobs lost, a loss of $2.7 billion in workers' earnings, and a loss of $422 million in tax revenues.

The RIAA would like to emphasize a couple of key points. First, there are more than thirteen million licensed tracks available on the Internet that are available for legal purchase. Second, music theft is a real offense and subject to criminal prosecution, generally leading to expensive fines. College students in particular receive the brunt of the wrath of the RIAA because they are responsible for the largest amount of the music pirated. To combat this thievery, the RIAA obtains the Internet addresses of individuals who use file sharing programs (from the file sharing companies themselves), send the offenders warning letters and/or bills for the estimated dollar value of the material stolen, and then threaten to sue if the perpetrator refuses to pay (Delaney 2012a). Most recently, the RIAA has attempted to work with colleges and universities in an attempt to curtail this criminal behavior by resorting to the extreme method of cutting off college aid to students who illegally download music off the Internet. Many college students justify their behavior by claiming that they want to sample music before deciding whether to purchase an entire CD. But, how many college students really buy an entire CD anymore? A number of people believe that music should be shared with others freely. Most students, however, do admit that downloading music without paying for it is wrong.

Under federal copyright law (Title 17 of the United States Code), recording companies are entitled to between $759 and $30,000 per illegal download infringement. The law also requires as much as $150,000 per track if the jury finds the infringements were willful (*The Citizen* 8/1/09). There have been some highly publicized cases of people who illegally downloaded music being fined huge sums of money. For example, on July 31, 2009, a federal jury ordered a student to pay $675,000 to four record labels. The student admitted in court that he had downloaded and distributed thirty songs online, but he also said that he would not pay the fine and if the decision stood, he would simply file for bankruptcy (Lavole 2009). A housewife and mother of four, Jammie Thomas-Rasset, from Brainerd, Minnesota, violated music copyrights and was ordered to pay recording companies $1.92 million—$80,000 per song for the twenty-four songs she copied. She told the court she did not have that kind of money because she had limited financial means and shrugged off the decision, saying she wasn't about to worry about it (*Post-Standard* 6/19/09). She did, however, also say she would appeal the decision.

The authors asked a number of their students and searched online chatroom discussions to see whether or not anyone has actually paid a fine of any sort, and most stories we heard involved a student saying that he or she received a warning from the RIAA and they either stopped their activity or continued. In either case, we could not find anyone who paid a large fine. So, what does this tell us about the power of the RIAA or the willingness of people to stop illegally downloading music (and movies)? The answer is revealed in our lesson learned.

Lesson Learned: Wait, I have to pay for music that I download illegally from the Internet?

Beyoncé and Jay-Z:
Representing the Differences between Women and Men through Song Lyrics

Musicians, singers, and everyone else involved in the creation, production, distribution, and sale of music are surely opposed those who illegally download their work. After all, like the rest of us, they want to be paid for their time and labor. It is true, however, that some artists are better paid and more successful than others. While many musicians struggle financially to make ends meet, some artists can afford to turn their backs if their fans download a few songs illegally. Among the more successful performers in the music industry are singers Beyoncé and Jay-Z, who happen to be married to one another.

Beyoncé Giselle Knowles-Carter was born September 4, 1981 in Houston, Texas. She is a multi–Grammy Award winning American rhythm and blues, soul, and pop singer and an actress. She performed in a variety of singing and dancing competitions in her youth and rose to stardom in the late 1990s as the lead singer of the successful R&B girl group Destiny's Child. The band was managed by Beyoncé's father, and they became one of the most financially successful girl groups in history. The group disbanded in 2005, and Beyoncé went to become an even more popular singer with her solo career. She created an alter ego named "Sasha Fierce" for her third album, "I Am . . . Sasha Fierce" (2008). Beyoncé married Jay-Z in 2008. She is a self-described modern-day feminist and is as popular today as at any time in her career.

Shawn Corey Carter, born December 4, 1969, is known by his stage name Jay-Z, he is an American rapper, record producer, and successful businessperson. Like his wife Beyoncé, Jay-Z has enjoyed a successful financial career, in his case as a hip hop artist. He has sold multimillion copies of his albums and has been nominated for, and won, more than a dozen Grammy Awards. Together, Beyoncé and Jay-Z represent one of the truly elite musical couples in the world.

Beyoncé and Jay-Z have collaborated in ways beyond matrimony; they also share the stage together. In 2014, the power couple embarked on their On the Run Tour. It's interesting to note, however, that the lyrics of some of the more famous songs each has produced reflect differences in perspectives on some key social issues. The explanation for these differences may reside with the differences in their individual musical backgrounds, with Beyoncé's songs characterized by ideals of love, commitment, monogamy, and female sexuality and empowerment and Jay-Z's with a hip hop perspective. Then again, perhaps Beyoncé represents a stereotypical female perspective on certain issues and Jay-Z represents the male perspective. It might also be that the genres of music that Beyoncé and Jay-Z come from reflect certain gender perspectives. Let's take a look at some specific song lyrics from the two singers.

It was an *Entertainment Weekly* article written by Kyle Anderson (2014) that drew our attention to the song lyrics of Beyoncé and Jay-Z. On the topic of "the romantic significance of jewelry," Beyoncé, in her song "Countdown," says, "Still love the way he talk, still love the way I sing/Still love the way he rock them black diamonds in that chain." Jay-Z, in the song "Money Ain't a Thang," says, "Said she loved my necklace, started relaxing/Now that's what the fuck I call a chain reaction." On the topic of "wardrobe consulting," Beyoncé says in "Upgrade U," "Partner, let me upgrade you/Audemars Piguet you/Switch your neckties to Purple Label." Jay-Z counters in hip hop fashion in his song "Change Clothes," "No bra with that blouse, that's so necessary/No panties and jeans, that's so necessary."

On the topic of "the supernatural," Beyoncé, in "Haunted," sings, "My haunted lungs, ghost in the sheets/I know if I'm haunting you, you must be haunting me/My wicked tongue, where will it be?" Jay-Z offers his view on the supernatural in "Heaven," and raps, "Getting ghost in the Ghost, can you see me? Can you see me?/Have mercy on a Judas, angel wings on a 'ghini.'" On the topic of "choosing love over possessions," in "Single Ladies (Put a Ring on It)," Beyoncé sings, "Don't treat me to the things of the world/I'm not that kind of girl/Your love is what I prefer, what I deserve." Jay-Z offers a different perspective on this matter in the song "Can I Get A . . ." when he raps, "If I was broke would you want me/ if I couldn't get you finer things/Like all of them diamond rings bitches kill for/Would you still roll?"

The final area of comparison between the lyrics of Beyoncé and Jay-Z resonates with most of us: the idea of "delayed gratification." In "Check On It," Beyoncé sings, "I can tell you wanna taste it, but I'm gone make you chase it/You got to be patient, I like my men patient/More patience you take might get you in more places." Jay-Z, in "Big Pimpin'"—and this song title alone should tell you he is looking at delayed gratification differently than Beyoncé—raps, "I'll be forever macking/Heart cold as assassins, I got no passion/I got no patience and I hate waiting/Ho, get your ass in and let's ride."

As we can see from this sampling of song lyrics, Beyoncé and Jay-Z possess different perspectives on fundamental issues, and yet, it works for them, to date, anyway.

Lesson Learned: Beyoncé and Jay-Z teach us that women want to make men "work for it" and that men "want it now."

Straight Outta Compton: Dr. Dre and Beats

In 1988, N.W.A. (Niggaz Wit Attitude) released its debut album *Straight Outta Compton*. Produced by Dr. Dre and DJ Yella, the release of this album signaled the beginning of West Coast and gangsta rap and the subgenre hip hop. The album title refers to the group's hometown of Compton, California, a city known for its notorious street gangs. Dr. Dre is also from Compton, and since the release of this album this southern Los Angeles city has been forever associated with gangsta rap.

NWA was active from 1986 to 1991 and included such famous people as Ice Cube, Easy-E, and MC Ren, in addition to Dr. Dre and DJ Yella. Ice Cube left the group in 1989 because of a royalty dispute. He has since gone on to become a famous solo rap artist, movie and TV star, producer, screenwriter, and director. Along with Snoop Dogg, Ice Cube (birth name O'Shea Jackson) is one of the most famous rappers of all time.

Ice Cube's fame and fortune pales in comparison to Dr. Dre's, however-er. Dr. Dre (birth name Andre Romelle Young), like Ice Cube, is a rapper and record producer, but he is also an entrepreneur. And it's his entrepreneurship that we wish to describe in this short story. While most younger folks are certainly aware of his primary product, other readers may not be aware of how this rap artist became hip hop's first billionaire. Louis Stewart, an economics teacher at Centennial High School (Compton) teaches his students that this Compton native did not become wealthy because of sports but instead because of his business savvy. Stewart explains that "Dr. Dre's rise from the streets of Compton to rapper to music producer" led to his becoming the "co-founder of Beats Electronics, the high-end, bass-heavy headphone and speaker company" (Jennings 2014:A1). In case you missed this high end transaction, Apple Inc. recently purchased Beats for $3.2 billion, making Dr. Dre Compton's and rap's first billionaire.

Originally, Beats was a product line consisting primarily of headphones and speakers under the brand "Beats by Dr. Dre" co-founded and owned by Dr. Dre and Jimmy Iovine, chairman of Interscope-Geffen-A&M Records. The headphones are bulky and oversized, which, ironically, is more of a throwback to days of yore (1960s and 1970s) when everyone who listened to music with headphones had such large earphones. During the years in between the early consumer headphones and Beats, people were subjected to a market dominated by small earplug type headphones that were bothersome and uncomfortable to the ear. Interestingly, this same trend is mirrored in the cellular phone industry. The first cell phones were bulky and people worried about getting cancer from their radiation, then cell phones kept getting smaller, so small they could easy fit in your pocket. And that was the selling point of cell phones for some time: smaller is better. As cell phone technology improved and people started streaming videos on their phones, there was a perceived need for larger cell phones so that we could enjoy our videos on larger screens. Cell phones are getting so large now they are beginning to resemble iPads and risk no longer fitting in one's pocket—one of the drawing points of cell phones just a few years ago.

That Beats are so big seemed to be a drawing point for younger people who, apparently, wanted a nostalgic type of headphone. The attached image of Dr. Dre made them "cool" for urbanites and nonurbanites alike. Iovine's connections in the music industry made it easier to market Beats via product placement and branding deals. Beats are also desired by people who find them more comfortable to wear than the tiny earplugs. Suddenly, Beats was a product ready to take off in the world of popular culture, and that's just what it did. To be hip and current was to wear Beats. But Beats are popular for another reason: people love the sound of music through these headphones. There is a heavy bass emphasis to Beats which is popular with many listeners, especially the originally targeted consumers, fans of hip hop and pop music. Dr. Dre describes Beats as a product that allows people to hear what the artists hear and to listen to music the way he does (as an artist and producer). In 2011, Beats made a deal with Chrysler LLC to feature their brand of audio systems in its vehicles, and suddenly the speaker brand grew in popularity.

The Beats brand became so popular and profitable that in May 2014 Apple Inc. made Dre and Iovine an offer they could not refuse, a reported

$3.2 billion in cash and stocks to purchase the product line. And with that, Dre and Iovine became billionaires. A visit to Apple's website in August 2014 included this announcement: "There's a new instrument in the Apple family." The news blurb described how Apple's products are the leaders in "music in your pocket" and praised the company for its acquisition of Beats.

Dre's milestone has prompted some Compton community leaders who blamed him and his N.W.A. bandmates for casting the city in a negative light with their *Straight Outta Compton* album to reassess their feelings about this rapper (Jennings 2014). For years, Compton has tried to shed its national image as a gangsta town and now, instead of distancing itself from Dre, it has embraced him. During the summer of 2014, Compton mayor Aja Brown, no fan of gangsta rap, offered Dre a key to the city. She had ignored Dre when he was famous for being a rapper, but now that Dre is known primarily by kids as Beats by Dre, Mayor Brown promotes Dre's business achievements (Jennings 2014). A grassroots group in Compton that works to reduce gang violence in the community declared June 19 (2014) as "Dre Day." At the event, a number of youth indicated that they want to be just like Dre, a successful businessperson, and expressed their desire to attend college while citing Dre as their inspiration (Jennings 2014).

There is hope in Compton now. And interestingly, it has a lot to do with a now-favored son who was once straight outta there.

Lesson Learned: Once a badass rapper, not always a badass rapper.

6

Radio and Popular Culture

Radio (a wireless form of communication via the transmission of electro-magnetic signals sent through the atmosphere, or "free air," into a specially designed receiver) was once among the key representatives of popular culture. If you didn't own a record and a record player, you never heard the song played unless it was on the radio. Before television, radio was the primary source of news, weather, sports, and general bits of information. President Franklin D. Roosevelt connected with the public via a series of thirty evening "fireside chats" between 1933 and 1944 on the radio. With the advent of the auto industry and the shift away from mass transit to a car culture came our appreciation for the car radio. Adults and children alike loved to listen to the radio, and it was common for family members to prefer certain stations, as limited as they were. Radio was mostly limited to an AM band during its early years, then advanced to FM (a much clearer broadcast), and then evolved to satellite radio. Despite the many ways people can listen to music, learn about the news, weather, sports, and entertainment, radio remains a vital aspect of popular culture.

Disk jockeys have long been an important force in promulgating both music and points of view over the airwaves (as Tom Petty and the Heartbreaker's hit song from 2002, "The Last DJ," makes amply clear: "There goes your freedom of choice/There goes the last human voice/ And there goes the last DJ").

In this chapter, we will look at how the role of the DJ is changing in the age of free radio; how listening to the radio in the early twenty-first century is a radically different experience than it was in the previous century; the ways in which media experts can get their perspectives presented on radio interview shows; the famous "War of the Worlds" broadcast of

Orson Welles in the early days of radio, and what it had to say about the nature of radio's own "War of Popular Culture" with newspapers; the connection between radio and romance; and the political power of the human voice directed at individuals over the airwaves. In the words of Elvis Costello and the Attractions' "Radio, Radio" (a song that got them banned from *Saturday Night Live* after they played it unannounced in 1977): "Radio is a sound salvation/Radio is cleaning up the nation."

Disc Jockeys and Free Radio: Radio Beams are Transmitting in the Air at All Times

Like most industries and inventions, radio began from humble roots, including the discovery of electromagnetic waves and their potential. "Hans Christian Oersted was the first to proclaim, in 1820, that a magnetic field is created around a wire that has a current running through it" (American Experience 2014). It was not until the late 1880s that German physicist Heinrich Hertz produced electromagnetic waves and substantiated James Clerk Maxwell's (an experimental physics professor) 1864 theory that electromagnetic currents could be picked up from a distant location. Shortly afterward, Italian inventor Guglielmo Marconi brought electromagnetic waves out of the laboratory and into the world, beginning with short-distance broadcasts from his own backyard. In September 1899, he captivated the world's attention by telegraphing the results of the America's Cup yacht races from a ship at sea to a land-based station in New York (American Experience 2014). The idea that information could be transmitted from sea to land inspired the pursuit of spreading information over even greater distances.

A steady stream of inventions (e.g., amplification of sound waves and dial locations for stations broadcasting on designated frequencies) followed until radio became a rudimentary form of its current self. While AM (Amplitude Modulation) was the first band used by radio, FM (Frequency Modulation) was created as far back as 1933, but RCA's top executive, David Sarnoff, was pushing for the development of television and FM was kept from the public for more than a decade (American Experience 2014), and even then, many people could not pick up FM radio waves. The late 1920s through the early 1950s represents the "Golden Era" of radio because of its high quality broadcasts in comedy, drama, variety shows, game shows, and popular music shows. Television took over as king by the late 1950s, but radio remained popular as a pop culture force.

During the height of radio's reign as the primary disseminator of music, both in terms of those who wanted to hear their favorite songs on the radio and the artists who wanted a venue for their tunes, the radio disc jockey (DJ) came to acquire a revered status in the industry. This was especially true in the big markets and radio stations with a strong signal. Listeners would call their favorite station and ask the DJ to play a particular song (although this is still true today, it is not to the extent that it was in the 1950s and 1960s). Musicians or their managers would plead with DJs to play their records. Chuck Berry, a famous rock and roll star dating back to the early 1950s, went so far as to put a stanza of his lyrics to "Roll Over Beethoven" (a hit song for the Beatles, too) to attract airtime from DJs: "I'm a write a little letter/ Gonna mail it to my local DJ/ It's a jumpin' little record/ I want my jockey to play/ Roll over Beethoven/ I gotta hear it again today."

Representatives of record companies would offer gifts, or "payola," as it was known then, to DJs in order to get their signed stars on the air. It was routine for big-name DJs, such as Alan Freed to be offered and accept payola in trade for air time for that record company's artist. Record companies that would not participate in payola schemes would not get air play. The payola scheme would eventually become so blatant that a number of radio stations and DJs were brought to court.

Alan Freed, known as "Moondog," was a top DJ in the mid-1950s. He worked in Cleveland (WJW-850AM) in the early 1950s and then began work in New York City in 1954 at WINS-1010AM, a station that played Top 40 songs around the clock. He lost his job at WINS in 1958 as a result of his connection with the congressional payola hearings. But Freed had played a huge role in popularizing rock 'n' roll, not just in the northeast but across the country. He is a member of the Rock and Roll Hall of Fame in Cleveland. When listeners of WINS did not like a particular song they would move their AM dial to WMGM-1050AM and listen to DJ Peter Tripp's playlist. While WINS was more popular, Peter Tripp was another influential DJ during this era.

Another popular DJ was Robert "Wolfman Jack" Weston Smith. Wolfman Jack was a cult hero among rock and roll fans. He was immortalized following his appearance as himself in the highly popular film *American Graffiti* (1973). In the early 1960s, Wolfman Jack was hired to work in a studio and transmitter site owned by XERF-AM at Ciudad Acuna, Mexico. At well over 250,000 watts—five times the U.S. limit—the signal at XERF was the strongest in North America (Herszenhorn 1995). Anyone from New York City to Los Angeles could listen to Wolfman

Jack. And because he was stationed in Mexico he did not have to abide by U.S. laws, making him a hero to rock and roll fans who were embracing the "bad boy" image of rock. At night it was possible for Wolfman Jack's voice to be picked up in Europe or the Soviet Union. Now that is a powerful and prestigious DJ. Mexico would eventually curtail the signal strength of XERF and other stations with super high transmission power and Wolfman Jack, who would howl like a wolf on the radio and during personal appearances, would move on.

One other major DJ worth mentioning here because of his influence on popular culture is Casey Kasem. Kasem was the long-time host of the "American Top 40" (and its variations) from 1970 to 2009. His show was known for counting backward the top 40 songs of the week and allowed for a forum of "long distance" dedications wherein, supposedly, fans from across the country wrote letters to Kasem about some sort of sad or tragic occurrence that they endured and then requested a specific song be played in honor of someone.

There have been other famous DJs, including the likes of Shadoe Stevens and Ryan Seacrest, but for the most part, since the 1980s, most radio shows have relied on "morning teams" who bring humor and entertainment to the airwaves. The idea of more talk and less music was a hard one for older folks used to tuning their radio dials for music as they drove to work, but morning shows dominate nearly every AM and FM radio station today. Mark (Thompson) and Brian (Phelps), out of Los Angeles (KLOS-95.5FM), were syndicated to a huge, primarily West Coast market for more than a quarter of a century beginning in the mid-1980s until Mark Thompson retired. And of course we cannot forget Don Imus and especially Howard Stern. We will speak more of Stern in the next chapter.

The big-name DJ dominating a nightly radio show by him- or herself is mostly a thing of the past. Today, the coveted time slot for radio stations is during the "morning drive" when commuters are driving to work and parents are getting the kids ready for school. A quick tour up and down the AM and FM radio dial Monday through Friday mornings will yield an array of morning talk shows with DJ partners or teams of morning personalities. Some morning shows are outrageous and cutting edge and others are conservative and maintain a status quo viewpoint of the world. Some shows rely on sophomoric-level humor to entertain their listeners and news-based morning shows rely on a straightforward, "let's take this seriously" approach to broadcasting. Regardless of one's ideology and taste in morning radio shows, those who turn to the radio in the morning are looking for a show with DJs they can relate to. Morning talk show DJs talk about their personal lives (e.g., "I got in a fight with my wife and I'm in the doghouse," or, "My wife is about to give birth to our baby"), and we tune in each morning to hear the next segment of the drama that is their lives. Callers to morning shows are not asking for a particular song to be played, but instead want to comment about the subject at hand or offer a related story from their own lives.

Morning show DJs, then, have become the new radio stars. Regular listeners look forward to listening to their favorite show to keep up with the drama. One of the authors of this book fondly remembers his time living in Los Angeles and recalls the first day Mark and Brian went on the air for KLOS. For years, he listened to Mark and Brian loyally to keep up with the latest happenings in the world, but also the personal stories shared by this morning team. When he moved away from Los Angeles many years later he missed Mark and Brian as much as many of the people he met (not his closest friends, of course). He has moved quite a few times in his life, and like many people, when he moved to a new geographic location one of the things on the top of the "To Do" list was finding the "right" radio stations for the car and the morning commute to work. The right morning DJ show is an important factor in deciding what stations make the "preset."

Lesson Learned: Radio has come full circle; like nearly a century ago, when radio enjoyed the beginning of its "Golden Age," contemporary "Morning Shows" hosted by DJs bring us drama, comedy, personalities, interviews with stars, news, sports, and entertainment.

Why Listen to the Radio for Free When You Can Pay for It? Beaming to You from Outer Space

In the previous section, we examined the role of DJs in radio. We also mentioned Howard Stern. Stern became the most dominant of all radio "shock jocks" beginning in the mid-1980s. Born in 1954, Stern attended Boston University, where, among other things, he worked at the campus radio station, WTBU. After short gigs at various radio stations, Stern began working at WXRK (New York City) in 1986. For the next twenty years Stern would be the king morning radio jock. At his peak, Stern would have more than twenty million listeners and be broadcast in sixty different markets in the United States and Canada. His media influence did not end at radio, as he would make a film, host pay per view events and home video releases, become a best-selling author, and serve as a host on a TV talent show. Because of his forays outside of radio, Stern refers to himself the "king of all media." The jury is still out on that self-proclamation, but Stern is certainly among the top shock jocks as well a major figure in popular culture.

To claim the title of top shock jock on radio for two decades implies that *The Howard Stern Show* engaged in countless outrageous antics. Not surprisingly then, this top-rated DJ is also the most-fined radio host in the history of radio, with the Federal Communications Commission (FCC) having fined Stern and his bosses more than $2.5 million. The FCC regulates free/terrestrial radio stations, but it does not have jurisdiction over the content on satellite radio (it regulates the technical broadcast spectrum only). Stern regularly blasted the FCC on his radio program and often incurred the wrath of both the federal agency and the station ownership, as it was the station license that was most vulnerable to punishment. Having lost patience with the FCC, Stern announced in October 2004 that he was signing a five-year contract with Sirius Satellite Radio effective in January 2006. Stern was given two channels on Sirius, Howard 100 and Howard 101.

Terrestrial radio's loss would be satellite radio's victory. Sirius Radio had assumed, and rightfully so, that a significant number of Stern's audience would follow him to paid radio, and sure enough they did. Stern and his agent, in fact, received more than thirty-four million shares of stock (shares closed at $6.36 each at that time, making the stock worth over $218 million) on January 9, 2006, as part of a previous agreement to issue the stock if Sirius exceeded subscriber targets established in 2004 when they made the deal with Stern (*CNN Money* 2006). Sirius reported that it added nearly 2.2 million subscribers in 2005, a 190 percent increase from 2004, giving the station more than 3.3 million total subscribers (*CNN Money* 2006). Sirius had hoped to exceed six million subscribers by 2006. With Stern still at Sirius (as of early 2015), there were more than twenty-five million subscribers in 2013 (Sirius XM 2013).

So, what is satellite radio? Satellite radio is a paid broadcast service that beams a signal from a satellite in space down to Earth, most commonly to a car antenna. The same signal can extend to a coverage area of thousands of miles on Earth, compared to the typical forty, more or less, miles accessed by terrestrial radio stations. Thus, if you want to listen to Howard Stern, you pay to receive the Sirius XM signal, and turn your dial to Channel 100 or 101 anywhere in the United States and most of Canada.

The first satellite radio system in the United States was Sirius Satellite Radio, who petitioned the FCC to assign new frequencies for satellites to broadcast digital sounds both to cars and to homes. The FCC allocated a spectrum in the "S" band (2.3 GHz) for nationwide broadcasting of satellite-based Digital Audio Radio Service (DARS). The FCC gave licenses to two companies to use this band—Sirius Satellite Radio and XM Satellite Radio. Each of these companies paid more than $80 million for the right to use space in the S-band for digital satellite transmission (Bonsor 2014). The S-band signal travels more from farther than 22,000 miles in space to reach a car or home with complete clarity. The idea of never having to have to change a favorite radio station for an entire cross-country trip, static free, with few or no commercials is among the features that appeal to people willing to spend more than $13 a month.

Sirius and XM spent more than $3 billion combined for the development of receiver technology; satellite production and launching; state of the art broadcast studios; and building business relationships with radio producers and broadcast media (Space Foundation 2002). The two satellite radio companies realized that they would have to combine forces if they wished to survive financially. In 2007, they announced their plans to merge into one company, and in July 2008 the FCC approved the merger (Kharif 2008). As of 2013, there were just two space-based radio broadcasters: Sirius XM Radio and 1worldpace. Only Sirius XM is available in the United States at this time, but 1worldspace has a longer reach than Sirius XM (Bonsor 2014).

Satellite radio works much like satellite TV—one purchases a receiver and pays a monthly or six-month subscription fee to pick up a signal that can be seen/heard at home or in a car. Satellite radio offers mostly commercial-free stations, although Howard 100 and 101 are filled with commercials. There are talk, news, sports, traffic and weather, entertainment, comedy, religion, politics, family and health, and music stations available on Sirius. There are more rock stations than any other genre of music and some bands, such as Pearl Jam (22) and the Grateful Dead (23), have their own station. There are multiple stations under such categories as: pop, hip hop/R&B, dance/electronic, country, Christian, jazz/standards, and classical. There are more than ten Canadian and six Latin stations available as well.

Despite its large investment, Sirius XM has made profits. They reported a quarterly profit of $124 million the first quarter of 2013, an increase of $16 million compared to the same quarter a year earlier. At the end of the first quarter 2013, Sirius XM boasted 24.4 million subscribers (Szalai 2013). Howard Stern remains as a driving force behind the success of Sirius, attracting more than twelve million listeners per week. The other big boost in subscriptions to Sirius XM comes from the sale of new cars, as nearly 60 percent of new cars sold in the United States come equipped with the station, generally for a six-months' free trial period. Nearly half of the people who buy a new car with free Sirius XM renew their membership. Both of the authors of this text fall into this latter category, as neither really thought he would ever pay for radio, when it comes free, but following the purchase of their respective new cars equipped with Sirius XM, both have regularly renewed their subscriptions.

Lesson Learned: Like water, some people are willing to pay for radio, even when it is available for free.

Would-be Media Experts:
Here's a List of the Do's and Don'ts for
Conducting Radio Interviews

In the opening section of this chapter we discussed the role of radio disk jockeys and morning personalities. We should point out that they often interview "experts" in the specific topic being discussed in an attempt to add quality and integrity to their talk shows.

We might first want to consider why someone would want to go on the air to be interviewed by a morning show or radio personality. In other words, what's in it for the guest? First, let's consider guests from the fields of entertainment, news, or sports; it is understandable why they would subject themselves to questions, often unexpected and perhaps "ambush" types of questions, because that is part of their job description (to promote their product). For example, a local news show in Tucson, Arizona, might try to interview a celebrity meteorologist from the Weather Channel to explain some weather event affecting Tucson. The Weather Channel celebrity is expected by the Weather Channel, as well as by advertisers and fans to make a certain number of on-air appearances in order to help promote the brand. As another example, it is understandable that a star athlete would submit to a radio interview with announcers from outside his or her market, because it is part of the athlete's job to promote the team, the league, or some league-sponsored event. In both of these cases, the guest is already established in the field of entertainment, news, or sports and they are essentially engaged in an extension of their job by conducting interviews.

Secondly, an author who has just published a book, a musician that just released an album, or an actor who has a movie coming out will generally be happy to serve as a guest on a radio show because they want the opportunity to promote their latest product. There are also people who simply like to keep their names in the news and continue to be a part of popular culture, so they will gladly talk to media outlets, including radio. The Reverend Jesse Jackson and Rush Limbaugh types of people seem to fit this category of guest experts.

A third type of person who might be willing to serve as a guest on a radio show is the academic expert. Academics often serve as "experts" in their fields of study for radio (and television) shows. Radio (and TV) hosts like to be able to inform their audience that they have Dr. So-and-So from some university or college in their studio, because it seems to add an element of credibility to the discussion of a specific topic. For example, a professor who has been studying street gangs for decades might be asked to serve as a guest expert on a program addressing a recent gang-related incident in the news. Experts provide, or attempt to provide, insights and explanations to events that might seem to be beyond the understanding of the average person not familiar with a particular topic. If nothing else, it is nice to compare one's own opinion with that of an expert.

One of the authors of this book (Tim Delaney) has quite a bit experience being interviewed as an "expert" in a variety of topics. He can assure you that it seems a bit odd sometimes to be labeled an expert and that is why the word *expert* is often used here in quotations. (He's a humble "expert.") Like most academics, Delaney responded to a questionnaire in which his university's public relations department requested its faculty to list areas they feel comfortable being listed as an "expert." Nearly every college and university has a public relations (PR) department that sends a questionnaire to faculty members asking them what topic areas, if any, they are comfortable serving as a media expert on. Faculty members choose from a PR-generated list, and usually claim their teaching area(s) of expertise as the category(s) regarding which they are willing to respond to media requests. In this manner, once a news outlet sends out a general request (via social media) or contacts a school to find out if anyone on staff is qualified to be interviewed on a news event, the PR department will put them in touch with an appropriate faculty member.

The primary reason colleges promote their faculty as "experts" in any given area of specialty is the perceived prestige gained by having one of their faculty declared an "expert" by outside sources (e.g., news agencies). In addition, colleges recognize and appreciate the free publicity—from having faculty members' college affiliation mentioned (on-air).

Radio and television shows often designate a "go-to" person that they call on regularly because they have established a good working relationship with them. In some cases, it seems that an expert becomes a go-to person because he or she is always readily available. Below, Delaney shares his perspective on being asked to serve as an "expert" and also offers a list of "Do's" and "Don'ts" for those aspiring to become experts themselves:

During the early stages of my academic career, I appeared sporadically on local TV and radio programs and was interviewed in a few dozen newspapers. However, during a span roughly covering 2006–2011, I conducted numerous radio interviews nationwide and throughout Canada, appeared on TV a little more frequently, and had numerous book signings. What changed? I started writing popular culture books in addition to textbooks. The 2006 publication of my book *Seinology: The Sociology of Seinfeld* (about the TV show *Seinfeld*) is what steered the media's attention in my direction. I wrote a book on *The Simpsons* next. By this time, I had a number of radio stations that regularly interviewed me and looked forward to talking to me about future projects. A book titled *Shameful Behaviors* that promotes the premise that there is a growing culture of shamelessness in society and another book titled *Sports: Why People Love Them!* (co-authored with Tim Madigan) that promoted the positive side of sports followed and led to interviews on sports-based radio shows.

Prior to these publications, I had written a couple of social theory textbooks with a major publisher, and yet not a single radio or television station has ever asked to interview me on the concepts and contributions of such people as Auguste Comte, Emile Durkheim, Georg Simmel, or even George Herbert Mead. Imagine that: there was no interest by radio stations in interviewing an expert on social thinkers. However, if you write about Jerry Seinfeld, Homer Simpson, Miley Cyrus, or Lance Armstrong interest is piqued. While I still write textbooks, I have learned to incorporate popular culture features into them. Students and general readers seem to appreciate references to popular culture. It is this reality—that people like popular culture references—that inspired Delaney and Madigan's interest in writing this book. Presumably, you will hear one of us on a radio show near you in the near future.

The Do's and Don'ts of Radio Interviewing

- If you want an opportunity to promote your work with the media DO write popular books and DO NOT write dry, heavyhanded, and jargon-filled books.

- Do publish with a trade press if possible, as they will promote your book for you. DO NOT publish with the trade press if you need publications for promotion—as the academic world has a different value system than the general public.

- If your publisher DOES NOT promote its books to the trades or the media, DO consider paying some agency (such as RTIR) to advertise your book.

- The general public cares about things that are contemporary so DO keep your comments relevant and current and DO NOT reference something obscure for a mass media audience.

- DO NOT get into a heated battle with TV and radio hosts as they can keep slamming you on the air when you are off the air.

- Do be prepared for odd, maybe even idiotic questions. During one *Seinology* radio interview I was asked this question: "What is sociology?"

- Generally, DO NOT give short answers. Radio hosts want you to do their work for them. Elaborate. Thus, when I defined sociology as: "the scientific study of people interacting with one another, groups, organizations, and societies," the radio host reacted dumbfoundedly: "Oh, is that all?" I have entire books on explaining sociology, just how long should my answer be? The key is finding the balance.

- DO be prepared for TV and radio hosts mispronouncing your name and/or book title. Radio hosts have referred to my *Seinology: The Sociology of Seinfeld* book as: *Scientology; Seinology: The Scientology of Seinfeld; Seinfeldology;* and *Sociotology.*

- DO politely state the name of your book some time shortly after the radio host mispronounced it.

- DO talk energetically. DO NOT talk with a boring monotone voice that some professors unwisely utilize in the classroom.

- Be prepared for late calls. DO be patient. A 7:00 a.m. scheduled call may not arrive until 7:10 or 7:14 a.m. DO NOT blow them off because they called late. When scheduling interviews be sure to allow yourself the appropriate amount of time; that is to say, it may be a short five to ten minute interview or it may be a thirty to sixty minute interview, so make sure you allow that amount of time for the interviewer.

- DO be prepared for extended interviews. If things are going really well the host may decide to keep you on for an extra segment. As a rule, you should agree to this as the host is likely to promote you all the more. I once had a forty-five-minute interview extend to one hour and thirty minutes. But, the radio station was broadcast in a three-state area and my book (and school) was plugged numerous times.

- DO have your own website. Hosts will want to direct their audience to your website so that they can learn more about you and (ideally) buy your book.

- DO be prepared to have scheduled interviews cancelled or postponed. The host may call in sick that day or something unexpected may occur (e.g., a local disaster or emergency that changes the focus of that media outlet for the day).

- DO anticipate possible questions from the media. If you are doing a radio or TV interview from home, DO have some "cheat" notes nearby. If you are in the studio live, DO NOT bring notes.

- If you being interviewed by a "Morning Team" radio show, DO be prepared for numerous people speaking at the same time and for being confused as to when you are expected to respond. Be prepared for shallow conversations.

- If you are being interviewed by a single host DO be prepared for in-depth analysis and discussion of your book.

- No matter how early, or late, your scheduled interview is, DO be awake. Think of how annoying it is if your host is sleepy—DON'T be a sleepyhead.

- DO be prepared to for "poor" phone connections and not being able to hear some of the radio hosts (and their questions). DON'T yell into the phone to overcompensate for a poor phone connection.

- If you are being interviewed on terrestrial radio (free radio), DO watch your language, think of George Carlin's "seven dirty words" to avoid using; if you are on satellite radio DO NOT be surprised to hear DJs drop the "f-bomb." You should use your own judgment whether or not to join in using swear words.

- Do thank the host for having you as a guest. DON'T forget to plug your book and website or twitter page. And, be sure to send a followup thank-you message to whoever interviewed you.

- DO try to have fun. If it's not fun for you, DON'T keep doing interviews.

Not everyone is comfortable doing media interviews. Make sure you are up to the task. As professors have learned, teaching in class and casual conversations with others are quite different than being interviewed on a live radio show.

The authors recognize that most readers will not find themselves being interviewed on the radio but we also realize that it has become increasingly popular for many folks to self-publish, and self-published authors may find themselves—they hope—on the air promoting their work. For those of you hoping to be interviewed someday, we hope you learned a few lessons about being interviewed. And, for those of you not interested in being interviewed on the radio (or any other sort of mass media), we hope you learned a little something about what goes on behind the scenes as you listen to or watch others being interviewed.

Lesson Learned: Radio stations are far more likely to interview you if you talk about something interesting, like popular culture–themed topics, than they are if you want to talk about classical sociological or philosophical theory.

The Martians Are Coming: Orson Welles's War of the Worlds

One of the best-known popular culture stories in the history of radio, often referred to as the "Panic Broadcast of 1938" is that of Orson Welles's famous radio adaptation of H. G. Wells's 1898 novel *The War of the Worlds*. There have been many adaptations of this work. Younger people, for instance, are likely to think of the 2005 movie *War of the Worlds* starring Tom Cruise and Dakota Fanning, while older folks will recall the 1953 movie of the same name. But none of these had quite the impact on popular culture as did Orson Welles's original adaptation. It is said that thousands of people, upon hearing the broadcast, were convinced that Planet Earth was indeed under attack by creatures from outer space. They fled their homes and/or hid in fear, sure that the final days were at hand.

Orson Welles was a popular culture phenomenon who excelled in theater, motion pictures, television (especially commercials), recordings, and radio. Though he died in 1985, before the Internet became a prime means of communication, countless clips of him taken from his various movies and television appearances reside on YouTube, and a book consisting of edited transcripts of anecdotes he told at gatherings with friends—*My Lunches With Orson: Conversations Between Henry Jaglom and Orson Welles*—became an unexpected bestseller in 2013. A larger than life figure, in all meanings of that term, Welles was a trendsetter and ambassador of popular culture par excellence.

Born in 1915 in Kenosha, Wisconsin, Welles, even as a young child, was noted for his creativity, his love for disguises, his talent as a magician, and his ability to fool people. As Simon Callow details in his 1997 book *Orson Welles: The Road to Xanadu*, the sixteen-year-old Welles, whose only acting experience up to that time had been in school plays, appeared unannounced at the Gate Theatre in Dublin, Ireland, and told the managers that he was a famous American actor in his twenties, who would be willing to deign to appear in plays at their provincial establishment. As Callow notes, the managers probably weren't taken in by him, but they did admire his chutzpah and obvious acting abilities, and cast him in their next production. He was an immediate success, and shortly thereafter did in fact become a famous actor and the founder of the Mercury Theatre in New York City, which was noted for its experimental and provocative productions. Blessed with a mellifluous voice, Welles soon had an equally successful career in radio, recording lucrative voiceovers for commercials (something he would continue to do until the end of his career) and becoming the narrator of several radio serial programs. He was also the voice of "The Shadow," a crime-fighting superhero known by his famous tagline: "Who knows what evil lurks in the hearts of men? The Shadow knows!"

Not content to be an actor on radio, and merely reading other people's scripts, Welles—using the expertise of the writers and actors from his Mercury Theatre company—created his own series, *Mercury Theatre on the Air*. It was noted for its many adaptations of great works of literature, including such classics as *The Adventures of Huckleberry Finn*, *Les Miserables*, *Treasure Island*, and *Dracula*. But none of the adaptations created anything like the stir created by the broadcast on October 30, 1938, on Halloween Eve, a time when listeners might already have been rather jittery, of *The War of the Worlds*.

Trying to capture the essence rather than the literal text of his near-namesake Wells's book, Orson's version was set not in London in 1898 but in New Jersey in 1938. The broadcast begins innocuously with banal band music. But shortly thereafter, an announcer breaks into the regularly scheduled music to reveal strange happenings occurring in the New Jersey skies. Sounding very much like an actual radio news report of the time, "eyewitnesses" are interviewed, "reporters" give whatever sketchy information they can about the ongoing events, "government and military authorities" issue warnings, and details emerge about the evil intents of the alien invaders.

The show ends with a jocular announcement by Welles himself, reminding people that the next day is Halloween, and that the broadcast was his aural equivalent "of dressing up in a sheet, jumping out of a bush and saying, 'Boo!'" (Callow 1997:230).

But long before this avowal that the whole thing was a hoax, thousands of people, taking the reports as serious, had already fled to the hills or barricaded themselves in the basement. Or did they? In 2013, to mark the seventy-fifth anniversary of *The War of the Worlds* broadcast, *Slate* reporters Jefferson Pooley and Michael J. Socolow did their own investigation. They discovered that no such mass hysteria had actually occurred. Most listeners—especially those who were already familiar with Welles's cheeky persona—realized right away that it was a put-on, and an entertaining one at that. And yet, reports do persist that a general panic took place across America. What was the basis of such reports? According to Pooley and Socolow: "Blame America's newspapers. Radio had siphoned off advertising revenue from print during the Depression, badly damaging the newspaper industry. So the papers seized the opportunity presented by Welles' program to discredit radio as a source of news. The newspaper industry sensationalized the panic to prove to advertisers and regulators that radio management was irresponsible and not to be trusted" (Pooley and Socolow 2013). So one form of popular culture, newspapers, tried to use Welles's fanciful show to impede the growth of another form of popular culture, radio.

How can Pooley and Socolow be so sure that millions of people didn't panic? Simple—evidence shows that the original broadcast was not even listened to by all that many people. They write: "The night the program aired, the C.E. Hooper ratings service telephoned 5,000 households for its national ratings survey. 'To what program are you listening?' the service asked respondents. Only 2 percent answered a radio 'play' or 'the Orson Welles program,' or something similar indicating CBS. None said a 'news broadcast,' according to a summary published in *Broadcasting*. In other words, 98 percent of those surveyed were listening to something else, or nothing at all, on Oct. 30, 1938. This miniscule rating is not surprising. Welles' program was scheduled against one of the most popular national programs at the time—ventriloquist Edgar Bergen's *Chase and Sanborn Hour*, a comedy-variety show" (Pooley and Socolow 2013). As an aside, the fact that a *ventriloquist* was so popular in this medium is one of the stranger facts about the early days of radio. Think about it.

While America might not have panicked, the false reports did have positive results for Welles himself. It gained him notoriety and propelled him to the front pages of the nation's newspapers. He parlayed this newfound fame into an unheard-of contract from RKO Pictures to produce a movie he would co-write (with Herman Mankiewicz), direct, cast, and star in: 1940's *Citizen Kane*. Often called the greatest movie ever made, and a perennial on the list of all-time classic films, its plot, significantly enough, is about a newspaper publisher who deceives the public by manipulating the news. Welles was consistent in his themes.

Why does the story of "The Panic Broadcast" of 1938 continue to resonate? Perhaps in part it's because even if it wasn't true, it *should* have been. America in 1938 was filled with legitimate fears of communism, fascism, the eruption of another world war, and continuing economic uncertainties. An invasion of space aliens might well have seemed just another realistic fear to add to the list. Also, the methods used by Welles were quite ingenious. Think about whether a similar-type program, using the technological means we are familiar with today, would be able to fool many people. Interrupting broadcasts with serious-sounding but vague reports of ongoing disasters is something we've become all too familiar with in the age of international terrorism. If nothing else, Welles's broadcast is still cited as a cautionary tale about the ethical imperative not to fool the public by using such means, given the possibility—if not the reality—of actual panic.

As for Welles, it's also not coincidental that his last major movie, *F for Fake*, which came out in 1974, was all about hoaxers, including the art forger Emyr de Hory and the writer Clifford Irving, who fabricated the supposed autobiography of the reclusive billionaire Howard Hughes, only to get found out and end up imprisoned. Some took the film to be

Welles's own apology for fooling his audiences over the years, beginning with his magic tricks as a young child all the way to the tall tales he loved to tell in his old age on his many TV talk show appearances. But, as he tells his friend Henry Jaglom over lunch, *F for Fake* is "a fake confessional. I'm not really confessing. That fact that I confess to be a fraud is a fraud. It is just as deliberate and manipulative as that. No, I think I'm absolutely genuine—that's a lie. I *never* tell the truth" (Biskind 2013:107).

Did Orson Welles mean to panic Americans into believing their country was under attack by men from Mars? Only the Shadow knows for sure.

Lesson Learned: Popular myths are hard to kill when they seem so real.

"They're Playing Our Song:" Radio and Romance

The pop music group Roxy Music, fronted by soulful lead singer Bryan Ferry, had a hit song in 1980 called "Oh Yeah." Given its rather bland title, it's not surprising that the song is better known by its evocative refrain "There's a Band Playing on the Radio." In it, the narrator details his romantic experiences driving with his loved one. One particular song becomes their favorite, and every time they hear it on the radio it reinforces their mutual bond: "And so it came to be our song/And so on through all summer long/Day and night drifting into love."

However, as so often happens, the lovers eventually part ways. And now, whenever the narrator unexpectedly hears that particular song, rather than filling him with joy, the opposite effect occurs: "There's a band playing on the radio/And it's drowning the sound of my tears."

It's an interesting question whether "Oh Yeah" itself fulfilled the very role it depicts for those who might have fallen in love when first hearing it and then later broke up. Surely we have all experienced something similar. Why do some songs become identified with times of our lives, so that hearing them—even years later—can bring forth a rush of emotions? At times, these can be sweet and wonderful, as when we're driving with our soulmate and can look into each other's eyes and simultaneously emote: "They're playing our song." (But only momentarily—get your eyes back on the road, driver.). And at times, as Ferry's mournful voice so powerfully expresses, when driving alone the memories of a lost love we haven't thought of in years can suddenly fill our eyes with tears and make it hard to watch the road ahead.

No doubt, one of the most compelling reasons we listen to radio is not just to hear shock jocks or news reports or sports scores—it's to continually experience songs we've loved for years, sometimes since childhood. When it comes to favorite songs, we can listen to them over and over again, much like small children who can hear the same story ad nauseam yet still demand it be told again. And nothing's as likely as a love song to fill us with emotion.

But why is this the case? Music may have charms to soothe the savage breast, but it's still an open question why this is so. Tufts University professor Jamshed Bharucha writes: "All people have music, and only people have music. Despite similarities to vocalizations in animals, such as birdcalls and 'whale song,' music as we know it in its full richness cannot be found amongst other species. The nature of this mysterious phenomenon has baffled philosophers through the ages. Recently, however, the tools of cognitive science and neuroscience have started bringing to light some intriguing possibilities about the origins of music and its roles in society" (Bharucha 2007). Musical intelligence may in fact be "hardwired" into our brains. Even Plato, in his magnum opus *The Republic*, stressed the importance of music for education: a sense of rhythm can bring order to mundane reality and help us remember important details. In fact, it's probably true that each and every one of us can recall word for word the lyrics to dozens, if not hundreds, of our favorite songs. Bharacha continues: "A widely accepted theory of musical aesthetics is that a successful piece of music generates melodic, harmonic, and rhythmic expectations, based on familiar cultural patterns, and then violates these expectations to varying degrees. In their musical preferences, people seem to seek a balance between the fulfillment and violation of expectations" (Bharucha 2007).

Romantic love in particular seems also to comprise a balance between fulfillment and violation of expectations—we like our lovers to be both familiar but also mysterious. And music can help to evoke the strongest feelings in us, often in ways that cognitive scientists and neuroscientists still cannot fathom. In his fascinating 2006 book *This is Your Brain on Music: The Science of a Human Obsession*, rocker-turned-neuroscientist Daniel J. Levitin writes: "Musical preferences also have a large social component based on our knowledge of the singer or musician, on our knowledge of what our family and friends like, and knowledge of what the music stands for. Historically, and particularly evolutionarily, music has been involved with social activities. This may explain why the most common form of musical expression, from the Psalms of David to Tin Pan Alley to contemporary music, is the love song, and why for most of us, love songs seem to be among our favorite things" (Levitin 2006:246). Or, in the immortal words of Sir Paul McCartney of Wings fame (as well as another, lesser-known earlier band): "You'd think that people would have had enough of silly love songs/But I look around me and I see it isn't so."

The fancy word that describes what happens to us when we hear a specific piece of music and reexperience feelings associated with it is *redintegration*. The *Merriam-Webster Dictionary* defines this phenomenon as: "a. revival of the whole of a previous mental state when a phase of it recurs; b. arousal of any response by a part of the complex of stimuli that originally aroused that response." This is a complex term for something all of us have experienced at one time or another. In fact, a related word, *nostalgia*, has a similar meaning. Quoting again from *Merriam-Webster*, nostalgia is a state of "pleasure and sadness that is caused by remembering something from the past and wishing that you could experience it again."

Hearing a song identified with a particular emotion and/or time of one's life can actually allow one to experience that emotion and time again, if only for a fleeting moment. Radio is a means for allowing us to almost constantly relive our past. It's not surprising, then, that so many programs broadcast "golden oldies" or that so many songs themselves—like Roxy Music's "Oh Yeah"—address this phenomenon. Nor is it surprising that a popular musical play of 1979, written by Neil Simon, with lyrics by Carole Bayer Sager and music by Marvin Hamlisch, was entitled "They're Playing Our Song." That title alone would be enough to get one's attention.

Lesson Learned: We identify certain songs with periods in our lives, and that can either be a good thing or a bad thing, especially if romance was involved.

Radio and Politics:
From Father Coughlan to Rush Limbaugh

Understanding the nature of radio as an aspect of popular culture necessarily means coming to grips with so-called Talk Radio. In addition to disk jockeys playing recorded music and newscasters reporting on local, national, and world affairs, as well as sporting events and weather conditions, a large portion of the airwaves consists of individuals filling the time by talking. Sometimes the time is taken up with callers engaging in conversation with the host, but often hours go by during which a single voice is heard. What might be deadly boring if watched on television (where so-called talking heads are usually denigrated as being uninteresting to watch) can be strangely compelling when heard on the radio. Opinionated individuals thrive in this setting, none more so than Rush Hudson Limbaugh III, a political commentator and talk show host whose program, *The Rush Limbaugh Show*, has been on the air in one form or another since 1984. Opponents of Limbaugh's extreme right-of-center viewpoint often wonder how one man can say so much about so little for so long, while advocates marvel at his stamina and quick-wittedness. Other conservative radio talk show hosts, such as Morton Downey Jr., Bob Grant, G. Gordon Liddy, and Dr. Laura Schlesinger, have come and gone, but Rush seems indefatigable. Even deafness—an affliction that one might think would preclude a person from continuing on the radio—hasn't stopped him, in part because of successful cochlear implant surgery, and in part perhaps because he was never noted for listening much to other people to begin with.

While Rush may seem to be a modern phenomenon, notable figures with distinct political points of view have actually abounded throughout the history of radio. In the early days of the medium, one of the most famous of such individuals was a Catholic priest, who came to prominence in the 1930s, a time when Roman Catholics in general were not necessarily welcome figures in American popular culture. New York governor Alfred E. Smith, for instance, had been overwhelmingly defeated as the Democratic candidate in the 1928 presidential campaign at least in part because of fears that, if elected, he would take orders from the pope. A famous cartoon of the time showed Smith, shortly after his defeat, cabling the pope in Rome to "unpack!" Even as late as 1960, presidential candidate John F. Kennedy had to assure the nation that, if he were elected, the pope would not speak for him.

Father Charles J. Coughlin was, like Limbaugh in recent times, a firebrand and a force of nature, who dominated the airwaves with his popular radio program. Originally noted for his progressive views and support for newly elected President Franklin Delano Roosevelt, Coughlin soon became a strong critic of the New Deal. His broadcasts became increasingly vituperative. He began to praise the fascist regimes of Benito Mussolini and Adolf Hitler, and argued that America needed similar all-powerful leaders. In addition, his criticisms of international banking became more and more anti-Semitic in tone.

FDR, who was himself a master of the airwaves, famous for his "Fireside Chats" given over the radio, understood the power of Coughlin's voice. He appealed to Joseph Kennedy (father of future president John F. Kennedy), a well-known Irish Catholic supporter of the New Deal, to try to persuade Coughlin to tone down his attacks on the administration. When that failed to work, it was said that he convinced New York's Cardinal Francis Spellman to contact Pope Pius XI about Coughlin. For whatever reason, in 1942—shortly after the United States entered into World War II—Coughlin was ordered by his superior to stop broadcasting and return to his duties as a parish priest. He complied.

As often happens to popular cultures figures who seem to gain overnight success, Coughlin's fall was as rapid as his rise. After losing his listening audience he soon faded away from the public's conscience. Even though he lived until the ripe old age of eighty-eight, he never again had a radio program, and he died in obscurity. While one of the most famous figures of his time, today he is known primarily to students of the history of radio.

Nonetheless, in many ways Father Coughlan lives on through the voices of modern-day extremists of all sorts, who utilize the power of radio to promulgate their own views, and mesmerize their audiences with their rhetorical powers. Radio is a perfect medium for the human voice. Centuries ago, the Ancient Greek philosopher Aristotle warned against the danger of demagogues—people who claim to speak on behalf of "the people" (*demos* in Ancient Greek) while actually manipulating facts to fit their own preconceived views, and damaging the political process through distortion. Words are powerful tools, but wielded by masters of language with questionable intentions, the human voice can be a force for great destruction.

Lesson Learned: When it comes to ideology, nothing beats the human voice.

7

Newspapers, Comics and Cartoons and Popular Culture

As the journalist Neil Gabler memorably puts it, "The first portal through which entertainment slithered into life and then conquered it was journalism" (Gabler 1998:59). He goes on to point out that before the 1830s newspapers didn't really cover *news* at all. Instead, they were mostly broadsheets connected with specific political parties, were noted for their vituperative tone, and were targeted primarily at the rich and influential. Such papers were relatively expensive, and were often distributed to private clubs, which paid for a subscription and secured the newspaper on long wooden sticks for club members to share (a remnant of this can still be found in some public libraries today).

It was Benjamin Day of *The New York Sun* who hit upon the formula that made newspapers what we know today. He charged a penny (an affordable amount even in those distant days) for each issue, in order to attract a wider clientele. As Gabler (1998) notes, "Before the *Sun*, a typical daily newspaper in New York City could expect to sell roughly 1,200 copies, with the total circulation of all eleven daily papers in the city in 1833 reaching only 26,500. After the appearance of the penny press, readership skyrocketed. In June 1835, by one report, the combined circulation of the penny papers alone was 44,000" (pp. 59–60).

Since the time of the "penny press," newspapers have been the/a primary source of news for most members of society. Until the last decade, newspapers were an important source of popular culture news. Newspapers usually have multiple sections, typically including news, sports, weather, stock market and business information, obituaries, entertainment reviews, comics, and other areas connected with popular culture.

Many historians of newspapers point out that their growth was intimately connected with a facet of popular culture that traditionally receives little respect: the comic strip. As the stories below detail, the humble cartoon—whether in the form of a daily strip such as *Peanuts* or *Mary Worth*, or an editorial cartoon commenting upon issues of the day—helped to make newspapers a "must-read" for millions of people, who follow the adventures of their favorite characters. It has often been said that the comics are the first part of the paper that most people turn to.

Comic books developed from this original form, and have been published independently since their inception. Tales of such superheroes as Spider-Man, Batman, Captain America, and—the most famous of all—Superman were immediate best-sellers. Furthermore, the early-twenty-first-century popular culture world has been dominated by blockbuster movies based on these sources.

Yet the survival of both newspapers and comics are an open question in a time when people are no longer reading or subscribing to papers as they once did. The following stories will look at some of the issues facing newspapers, comics, and cartoons in the social media age.

USA Today: But What about Tomorrow?

While newspapers have played a tremendous role in promoting popular culture, as well as being referenced often in popular culture itself (think of such movies as *His Girl Friday*, *Citizen Kane*, *All the President's Men*, and *Spotlight*, as well as such television series as *Lou Grant*, *Kolchak: The Night Stalker*, and *The Newsroom*), it's not at all clear what the future of newspapers will be in a world of instant communication, rapidly changing technology, and a generation that seems to no longer get its information from traditional sources. Waiting for the paper to arrive in order to read the latest stock reports, sports scores, classified ads, or even obituaries is no longer necessary when we can call up such information at a moment's notice on our smartphones or personal computers.

The question of whether newspapers can survive the onslaught of new technology is not a new one. The same fears were expressed when radio came on the scene and people could listen to the news rather than read it, and yet papers continued to thrive. Likewise, the rapid development of television—with not only newscasts but documentaries, sports coverage, and other programming—cut into markets newspapers had previously monopolized. With competition from both radio and television, the availablility of advertising dollars became an issue, since advertising revenue is the life's blood of newspapers. But the papers boasted advantages over their competitors, especially in providing depth of coverage (most television reports would run a few minutes at most, whereas a newspaper could report a story for several pages, if necessary) and timeliness. If need be, papers could put out several editions a day. And, as will be discussed in the next two sections, papers had another advantage that radio and television did not—comic strips.

For all of that, by the 1970s newspapers started to look like a stale and pale reflection of what they had once been. Before television, most major cities had supported at least two, if not more, daily papers, often in morning and evening editions. Thanks to increasing production costs, the loss of advertising revenue, and continuing loss of readership, this soon became a rarity, with most cities reduced to a single newspaper, in some cases not even with daily delivery. The rise of the Internet as the primary means of accessing information dealt a further death blow to the industry.

But newspapers have always thrived by being innovative and rising to new challenges. Perhaps the best such example of this was the 1982 launch of *USA Today*. Founded by Al Neuharth of the Gannett Company, the newspaper's aim—as its name implied—was to be a bona fide national paper. Whereas a few newspapers, such as *The New York Times*, *The Washington Post*, *The Los Angeles Times*, *The Chicago Sun-Times*, and *The Wall Street Journal*, had a significant readership outside of their immediate geographical areas, each was still primarily identified with the city in its name. *USA Today* dared to be different: its base would be the entire United States. It would be distributed in all fifty states, as well as all U.S. territories.

And, unlike the other papers mentioned, which were noted for their in-depth articles and erudite approach to news reporting, *USA Today* would have a simple, reader-friendly layout, with short, punchy news items and easily accessible "bites" of information on sports, celebrities, business, and the weather. Oddly, however, the paper does not have comics. *USA Today* was geared for busy Americans, especially travelers, who were on the go and wanted a quick summary of what was happening across the country.

USA Today became wildly successful. One mark of this was the fact that, appropriately enough, it soon entered the vocabulary of popular culture. The phrase "*USA Today*" became synonymous with quick and easy information—or, as the saying goes from Western movies that quickened the pace of their storytelling by leaving out a lot of exposition, just "cut to the chase." No better proof of this can be found than the fact that *USA Today* became a *Seinfeld* reference. In the episode "The Yada, Yada" (#153), George discusses the virtues of his new girlfriend Marcy and her distinctive way of speaking. After beginning a story, she says "yada, yada, yada" as a way of leaving out the boring details, and just proceeds right to the end. Jerry meets up with them at Monk's coffee shop and they have the following exchange:

MARCY: You know, a friend of mine thought she got Legionnaire's disease in the hot tub.

GEORGE: Really? What happened?

MARCY: Oh, yada, yada, yada, just some bad egg salad. I'll be right back. (She gets up and heads toward the restroom.)

JERRY: I noticed she's big on the phrase "Yada, yada."

GEORGE: Is "yada, yada" bad?"

JERRY: "No, "yada yada" is good. She's very succinct.

GEORGE: She is succinct.

JERRY: Yeah, it's like you're dating the *USA Today*.

While Jerry and George appreciate this get-to-the-point approach to conversation, critics of *USA Today* find fault with its often too concise and sometimes very shallow summations of complex issues. And George himself was to find out later in the episode that the "yada, yada" approach could have its disadvantages, too, when Marcy tells him: "My old boyfriend came over late last night, and, yada, yada, yada. Anyway, I'm really tired today." Sometimes we really *do* want the details that "yada, yada" leaves out.

While *USA Today* marked a turning point in the history of newspapers, and although it remains the second highest-circulation paper (after *The Wall Street Journal*, which is itself attempting to become a more national newspaper), the things that initially made it distinctive are no longer quite as innovative. As mentioned above, almost no one today reads the paper for its sports scores, weather information, or stock market details when such information can be readily accessed on the Internet at any time. Celebrity "news"—including the latest escapades of popular culture ambassadors—now dominates its pages, but, again, such details can be found on countless webpages and blogs as well. Indeed, critics of *USA Today* fear that other mainstream newspapers, in order to survive, have emulated its "get to the point" approach and its reliance on celebrity gossip, to their detriment. The acclaimed HBO television series *The Wire*, in its final season, depicted the *Baltimore Sun* newsroom as a place where old-fashioned reporting is disparaged and sensationalized stories—even fabricated ones—are deemed more likely to win the paper acclaim, new readership and, hopefully, a Pulitzer Prize or two. It is not coincidental that the series creator, David Simon, is a former *Baltimore Sun* reporter.

To counter this growing trend, some papers have tried to go back to their original strengths in the hopes that that will sustain readership and help them continue into the twenty-first century. *The New York Times*, for instance, has been stressing its in-depth news reporting, as a way of differentiating itself from the "sound bite" era and also to reassertthe advantages newspapers still enjoy over other sources of information.

Can newspapers survive in the world of the Internet? *USA Today* has a strong online presence, and stresses that its mobile app on iPhones and iPads will once again allow busy Americans to access its information easily. Some of us who love comic strips would say that it should consider adding them to its revamped product as well. Whether or not *USA Today* can thrive in a world of rapid communication—a world it once was able to dominate—remains an open question. In fact, the overall challenge of whether newspapers can survive in the cyber age is a newsworthy topic in and of itself. It warrants more than just a "yada, yada."

Lesson Learned: How the news is covered is itself newsworthy, but please go beyond the yada, yada.

Newspaper Comic Strips:
Providing Humor and Drama in the
Funny Pages for More than a Century

Today there are comic books, underground comics, political cartoons, and webcomics; but the first comics appeared in newspapers, at the end of the nineteenth century. Newspaper comics came to known as "comic strips," because they appeared in sequences of drawings in interrelated panels, generally utilizing speech balloons or captions to fashion a narrative and allow the characters a "voice." As the term *comic* would imply, comics are generally meant to be funny (the comic strip section of the newspaper is known as the "funny pages") and provide readers with a joke and a laugh. Comics do, however, also take the form of dramas serialized as running storylines with regular, reccurring, and occasionally new characters.

The first comic strip, *The Yellow Kid*, first appeared in the *New York World* (owned by Joseph Pulitzer) in 1895 (Ross 2007; Pond 2011). Created by Richard Outcault, *The Yellow Kid* featured a bald, snaggle-toothed boy in a yellow nightshirt living in grungy alley ("Hogan's Alley") with other odd characters (Pond 2011). The "yellow boy" character became very popular in New York City, and, in 1897, William Hearst's *New York Journal* hired Outcault away from the *World*. Pulitzer responded by hiring George Luks to draw his own version of *The Yellow Kid*. Both strips ended in 1898 (Ross 2007). As an interesting piece of popular culture history, both of these newspapers—the *World* and the *Journal*—were known for sensationalism, each trying to outdo the other rather than sticking to reporting the truth. This practice became known as "yellow journalism" (Ross 2007).

The next comic strip to appear in a newspaper (in the *New York Journal*) was Rudolph Dirks's *The Katzenjammer Kids*, a story that starred a set of twin brothers, Hans and Fritz. Dirks was a German immigrant, and he is credited with being the first cartoonist to feature "sawing logs" to indicate that a character was snoring loudly, "swirling stars" to illustrate a character's pain, and word balloons for dialogue (Pond 2011). *The Katzenjammer Kids* is still running today as the oldest strip in syndication (Ross 2007).

In 1905, *Little Nemo in Slumberland*, by Winsor McCay, began running in the *New York Herald*. It was the first comic with a continuing storyline and is considered one of the most richly illustrated comic strips of all time (Ross 2007). In 1907, *Mutt and Jeff* became the first successful daily comic strip. The strip would run until 1962. In 1913, Krazy Kat appeared in the comics of the same name. In 1919, *Gasoline Alley* began. It was the first comic strip to have its characters age in real time rather than the standard comic strip device that suspends the aging process for its characters. *Gasoline Alley* is still running today. Throughout the 1920s and 1930s an increasing number of comic strips were introduced and syndicated in numerous newspapers across the nation. The 1930s would see comic strips that featured adventures and exploits—*Popeye, Tarzan, Buck Rogers*, and other action-oriented characters (Pond 2011). Dramas, or the soap opera variety of comic strips such as *Mary Worth* and *Judge Parker*, emerged in the 1940s.

One of the interesting and unique comic strips that emerged in the 1940s was *Brenda Starr* (1940). As one might assume, the lead character was named Brenda Starr, a redheaded reporter who often visited exotic places for a good story, adventure, good food, and a little romance. We would suggest that Brenda Starr was way ahead of Liz Gilbert (Julia Roberts) of *Eat, Pray, Love* (2010) movie fame. *Brenda Starr* first appeared in a *Chicago Tribune* comic book insert in June 1940, and then appeared in the *Tribune* newspaper and later in newspapers across the United States and beyond.

Throughout the 1950s and the rest of the twentieth century, the number of comic strips continued to grow. There were daily comic strips and Sunday edition comics, which often included comics not available during the week. Newspapers in different areas of the country would offer some of the same, nationally syndicated comics, as well as some that were more locally popular. While most comic strips (e.g., *Doonesbury, Mutts, Buckles, Adam, Classic Peanuts, Marvin, Get Fuzzy*, and *Pearls Before Swine*) are drawn as a series of panels (usually four, but sometimes from two to five), there are some comics (*Marmaduke, Close to Home*, and *Family Circus*) presented in a single panel format. Some single panel comics, such as *Family Circus*, are expanded to multiple panels on Sunday. Most of the multipanel comics are given additional panels in their Sunday editions as well.

Newspaper publishers are often faced with a tough decision when choosing which comic strips to carry, but sometimes they are not even given a choice. As Jeremy Boyer (2010), executive editor of *The Citizen* (Auburn, N.Y.) explained in an editorial: "The way the overwhelming majority of strips land in newspapers is through a syndication company, and those companies employ sales staff whose mission is to get their firm's strips on to as many pages as possible" (p.A4). Boyer announced that he was having a tough time deciding which comic strips to keep and which ones to eliminate, if any, and encouraged readers who make the comics page a daily must-read to share their thoughts with him. Delaney (2010) e-mailed Boyer and asked a number of questions. Boyer replied. When asked why *The Citizen* carried so few comic strips compared to Syracuse's *Post-Standard*, Boyer pointed out that comics are expensive and that *The Citizen* simply did not have a budget comparable to *The Post-Standard*'s. Boyer also mentioned that newspapers pay a weekly fee for each strip and some strips are more expensive than others. Additionally, Boyer pointed out that some comics that appear in a larger newspaper in an overlapping region have exclusive rights, meaning that the syndicate won't give them to nearby competing newspapers (such as *The Citizen*). He concluded by saying that the comic strip business is "quite an industry" (Delaney 2010).

Earlier, we mentioned the comic strip *Brenda Starr*. *Brenda Starr* ran until January 2, 2011, when *Tribune Media Services*, which owned the strip, put an end to its successful run (*The Post-Standard* 2010). In its final strip, a Sunday edition, Brenda has retired from *The Flash* newspaper and is leaving her farewell party. Her co-workers and friends are in the background. She is sad; a long successful chapter of her life is over. As she leaves the building she is handed a mysterious package by a deliveryman. She examines the contents and becomes very excited. Readers of the strip are led to believe another new adventure is about to begin. To make it clear, the cartoonist provides a thought balloon over Brenda Starr that reads, "Every ending is a beginning, and every beginning carries the seed of its own end. As a wise man once said, 'So it Goes . . .'" And with that, readers are left with the message that the cartoonist will miss us, the public, and acknowledges that we will miss Brenda; and yet, life will go on . . .

The overwhelming concern of cartoonists and fans of comic strips in the early twenty-first century relates to the fate of newspapers. As newspapers disappear, will comic strips also disappear? Will they appear on websites, or in underground newspapers? Or will they face the same fate suffered by Brenda Starr and so many other comic strip characters before and after her departure from the funny pages? Will the cartoonists be afforded an opportunity to say good-bye to readers and bring the storylines of their main characters to some sort of closure, like *Brenda Starr*?

Lesson Learned: It's not funny when your favorite comic strip ceases to exist.

You're a Good Man, Charles Schulz

One beloved comic strip that, in a sense, both ceased to exist and yet has continued to be published is *Peanuts*, created by Charles Schulz. Begun in 1950 with the original title *Li'l Folks*—Schulz hated the title *Peanuts*, which was imposed upon him by the syndicate that published the strip—it ran for an astonishing fifty years, ceasing publication in 2000, just a few days before Schulz's death. Unlike the creators of many of the comics mentioned above, Schulz was not only the sole writer of the strip, he actually drew each and every one himself, an almost unheard-of state of affairs in an industry where creators (such as Jerry Siegel and Joe Schuster of *Superman* fame, who are discussed below) usually lose control of their creations, and where the characters "live on" long after their originators depart, willingly or otherwise.

As David Michaelis points out in his 2007 book *Schulz and Peanuts: A Biography,* it's not too much to say that Charles Schulz and his creations—including Charlie and Sally Brown, Lucy and Linus Van Pelt, Schroeder, "Pig-Pen," Snoopy, and Woodstock—were impossible to separate from each other. The comic strip was Schulz's life, and he put many of his own whimsical attitudes into it. It's not surprising that he refused to relinquish control, and stipulated that, while the original strips could continue to appear after his death, no one else could take over *Peanuts*, as was done with other such strips as *Little Orphan Annie, Blondie,* or *Dick Tracy. Peanuts was* Charles Schulz.

Perhaps it's also not coincidental that Schulz—a man who was learned in the intellectual issues of his time—began to publish at almost the same time that Existentialism came into the American public's consciousness. Michaelis quotes Schulz as saying: "I'm not a philosopher . . . I'm not that well-educated" (Michaelis 2007:394). But, as Shakespeare might say, he doth protest too much. While it was primarily a humorous comic, *Peanuts* was labeled as "existential" from an early stage, as it dealt with such themes as loneliness, dread, contingency, and despair, all of which could be found in the works of such existential thinkers as Soren Kierkegaard, Friedrich Nietzsche, Martin Heidegger, and Albert Camus. In particular, one can find many similarities between Jean-Paul Sartre's 1944 play *No Exit* and the *Peanuts* world. Both seem to take place in a self-enclosed absurd setting, where characters (Estelle, Garcin, and Inez in Sartre's work, and Charlie Brown and the Little Red-haired Girl, Sally Brown and Linus, Lucy and Schroeder, among others, in Schulz's universe) never seem to connect, and engage in endless variations of unrequited love and abusive relationships. Yet, unlike in Sartre's hellish world, the *Peanuts* gang do form a genuine community, and by somehow surviving the daily travails of their environment through their constant philosophical questionings, they help us all to better understand the human condition. Like Sisyphus at the end of Camus's seminal essay, one must imagine Charlie Brown happy.

One example of the *Peanuts* community in action can be found in the strip appearing on Sunday, September 17, 1967 (the Sunday strips, by the way, took a full page in the newspaper and, unlike the daily strips, were titled *Peanuts featuring "Good Ol' Charlie Brown"*—one small way for Schulz to try to transcend the title he had been stuck with but never loved). In this particular strip, Charlie Brown stands, as is his wont, on the pitcher's mound during a typical losing game for his team. "Nine home runs in a row!! Good Grief!" he intones. His catcher, Schroeder, comes to the mound to ask him the cause of his outburst. "We're getting slaughtered again, Schroeder," he says. "I don't know what to do. Why do we have to suffer like this?" A perfectly reasonable question—indeed, regular readers of the strip might well ask that question about the *Peanuts* gang in general, as the team never wins a game, the love circles never close, and Charlie Brown never gets to kick the football Lucy holds so enticingly at the beginning of every football season. But Schroeder gives a rather perplexing response: "Man is born to trouble as the sparks fly upward." Not surprisingly, Charlie Brown can only reply by asking "What?"

At this point, Linus comes up to the mound to inform the befuddled pitcher/manager that Schroeder has quoted the Old Testament's Book of Job, seventh verse, fifth chapter. Linus—the resident intellectual, noted for his brilliance but also his insecurity and need to suck his thumb and hold onto his blanket to endure the world's travails—starts to explain why the problem of suffering is such a profound one. But his bossy sister Lucy interrupts him in midsentence, as she so often does in the strip, to assert, "If a person has bad luck, it's because he's done something wrong. That's what I always say." As Schroeder reminds her, that is exactly what Job's friends tell him when he is inflicted with boils and other unbearable sufferings, even though he knows he is a good and faithful servant to God. Unimpressed, Lucy tells him, "What about Job's wife? I don't think she gets enough credit!" Those who know the Book of Job will recall her advice to her husband when he asks why he is being made to suffer so: "Curse God and die." A very Lucy-like response.

The rest of the panels consist of other characters discussing various reasons why suffering may occur, with a thoughtful-looking Snoopy taking in the deep discussion. It is a master class on getting across rather profound observations in a ridiculous setting, not unlike a play by Samuel Beckett or indeed Archibald MacLeish's 1958 play *J.B.*, itself a variation of the Book of Job. To cap it all off, the final panel shows Charlie Brown, alone again on his sad pitcher's mound, with a forlorn expression on his face. "I don't have a ball team," he moans, "I have a theological seminary" (Schulz 1967–68:112). A pessimist might say this shows the futility of the *Peanuts* world; an optimist would say that, while the team never seems to win a game, it does have some great conversations. And most of all, they have learned to persevere.

One of the strengths of "Peanuts" was the way the Schulz was able to return time and again to the same themes and give them interesting—and often unexpected—variations. This is best demonstrated by the annual tradition, every autumn, of having Charlie Brown rush passionately down the field to kick the football Lucy is holding, only to have it snatched away at the last second. David Michaelis writes about this yearly event: "Schulz originally drew the football-kicking episode to show that Charlie Brown was incapable of combating Lucy's shrewdness. . . . From first (1952) to last (1999), each setup of the football encouraged Charlie Brown to one more act of determination and, ultimately, martyrdom" (Michaelis 2007:510).

But Schulz, in the very last such episode, threw a curveball to his readers. Lucy is suddenly called into the house by her mother. She asks her baby brother Rerun to hold the ball for her. When he enters the home she asks him anxiously, "What happened? Did you pull the ball away? Did he kick it? What happened?" To which Rerun slyly says in return, "You'll never know . . ." And neither will we. Perhaps good Ol' Charlie Brown finally did kick the ball after all.

In another complicated yet typical *Peanuts* scenario, Lucy—ashamed to be associated with a brother who clutches a security blanket—grabs the blanket from Linus and tells him she's hidden it and that he has to get used to being without it. Linus begins to hallucinate, faint, and fear for his sanity—rather extreme stuff for a "comic" strip—but Snoopy (usually lost in his own world of fantasy and often oblivious to the concerns of the humans around him, especially the "round-headed kid" who feeds him but whose name he can never remember) saves the day. Using his beagle sense of smell, he finds the blanket where Lucy has buried it, and digs it up and returns it to its happy owner. The overjoyed and fully recovered Linus thanks him profusely, and in the final panel, Snoopy, laying on top of his doghouse, muses: "Every now and then I feel that my existence is justified." It's hard to find a better example of existentialism in action.

As he drew the final *Peanuts* comic strip just days before his own death, one hopes that Charles Schulz appreciated all the joy that he had brought to the world by creating this timeless work. Like Snoopy, he had every right to feel that his existence was truly justified. And Charlie Brown and his crew remain a vital part of contemporary popular culture. The classic strip still appears in hundreds of newspapers (although as discussed above, their own existential reality is fraught with peril), and in 2015 a 3-D animated film introduced the gang to a whole new generation. Schulz, though, given his loathing for the syndicate title of his strip, might not have been thrilled to know it was called *The Peanuts Movie*. Good grief!

Lesson Learned: For a nobody, Charlie Brown was really somebody.

Underground Comics, Webcomics, and Political Cartoons: Cartoonists Expressing Themselves, but with an Edge

In the previous section on newspaper comics, it was mentioned that comics can be found in places other than the funny pages of a traditional newspaper. There are comics in underground newspapers, comics online, and political cartoons that generally reside in the news section of a newspaper (traditional or underground). Let's first take a look at underground comics.

Underground comics (sometimes referred to as comix) began appearing during the 1960s and '70s in reaction to the changing political climate and changing social mores. The Vietnam War, protests against the draft, sex, and drugs were among the subject areas covered in underground comics. Underground comics are often unrefined, edgy, crude in artistic style, and populated by a wide range of interesting and slightly bizarre characters. The authors of this book are familiar with, and fans of, a number of underground comic strips including *Fritz the Cat*, *The Fabulous Furry Freak Brothers*, *Zippy the Pinhead*, *Weird Fantasies*, *Bloom County*, *Doonesbury*, and *Life in Hell*.

It is difficult to chronicle underground comics for a number of reasons, but especially because of the nature of the newspapers they appear in. Consider, for example, that "underground" newspapers themselves often have a short life span, are limited to specific local markets, are not available on most newsstands, and are not delivered to one's home via a subscription like traditional newspapers. In addition, the cartoonists often lose interest in continuing the strips after a period of time, or if they do gain recognition they tame their cartoons for traditional newspapers or comic books.

As for the transition to comic books from underground comic strips, "Almost every cause created its own comic book: feminism, marijuana legalization, Black Power, anti-abortion and anti-war. Comics with explicit sexual content also flourished along with comix with gay and lesbian themes" (Moore Collection 2014). Most comic book companies are poorly financed and rely on revenues from sales in order to print the next issue. Many cartoonists print their own comix, and as a result, the print runs are low, especially compared to newspapers. As a result, many underground comics have disappeared in the face of insupportable costs and industry-wide financial instability.

Many underground cartoonists realized that if they wished to make a career drawing comics, they would have to turn to more stable sources of income. Some underground artists found success by drawing comic strips for such magazines as *Playboy* or *National Lampoon* (Estren 1993). Garry Trudeau took his comic strip *Doonesbury* to traditional newspapers after first drawing his characters in the Yale University student newspaper, the *Yale Daily News*. *Doonesbury* (the name is a slang term for a clueless person) first appeared as a continuation of a strip called *Bull Tales*, which had also appeared in the *Yale Daily News*. Although *Doonesbury* is often viewed as a liberal-leaning comic, the characters actually represent a wide array of professions and sociopolitical viewpoints. *Doonesbury* first appeared as a daily strip in 1970 and remains a mainstay in many newspapers today. In 1975, it was the first daily comic strip to win a Pulitzer Prize for Best Editorial Cartoon; prior to this, the prize had been given only to "single panel'" editorial cartoonists (IMDb 2014a).

Other than Trudeau, perhaps the most famous or successful underground artist to make the transition to mainstream success is Matt Groening. Groening grew up in Portland, Oregon, and attended Evergreen State College in Olympia, Washington, a nontraditional public university that he has called a haven for "self-disciplined creative weirdoes" (*A&E Television* 2014a). Groening never envisioned making a living as a cartoonist until he met fellow Evergreen student and cartoonist Lynda Barry, who was making a living selling her comics to underground papers (*A&E Television* 2014a). In 1973, after graduating from Evergreen, Groening moved to Los Angeles to seek work as a writer. Years of part-time work and financial struggles led to Groening's creation of his comic strip, *Life in Hell*. The underground paper *LA Weekly* printed *Life in Hell*, and soon Groening had gained quite a bit of notoriety. The success of *Life in Hell* attracted the attention of writer and producer James L. Brooks, who commissioned Groening to write a series of animated short sketches for *The Tracey Ullman Show*. Groening's characters, modeled in part on his own family, were called "The Simpsons" (*A&E Television* 2014a). And the rest, as they say, is history.

Webcomics, as the name implies, are cartoons that appear on the Internet. They may also be referred to as online comics and Internet comics.

While some cancelled newspaper comics may find their next life online, other webcomics are original strips. There are numerous websites that offer comics; one, *Top Web Comics*, provides a "Comic Ratings" site wherein they provide a monthly Top 100 with links to each of the webcomics. In June 2014, the top ranked webcomic was *Twokinds* and the second-ranked was *Grrl Power* (*Top Web Comics* 2014). Buzz Feed Comics provides a link to "42 Web Comics You Need to Read." In June 2014, the top-ranked must-see webcomic was *Nedroid Fun Times* and the second-ranked was *(@Dril)bert*, a parody of *Dilbert* (Buzz Feed Comics 2014). The sample comic strip included the "Wally" parody character using the f-word when telling the "Dilbert" parody character what he does when people fuck with him. In case you are wondering, Wally goes to the beach and takes it out on the crabs by punching their "shitty little bodies." This is definitely a version of *Dilbert* you will not find in regular newspapers.

Many members of mainstream society may have first learned about webcomics when a near-fatal stabbing that took place in Waukesha, Wisconsin, in May 2014 was attributed to the influence on its perpetrators of a horror website that featured a character called "Slenderman." Slenderman (aka "Slender Man") appears on the Internet site "Something Awful." The "Something Awful" site encourages submissions that contain references to supernatural entities, in particular photographs of paranormal entities. "'Slenderman' is a paranormal being who lurks near forests and who absorbs, kills, or carries off victims. In some accounts, he targets children" (*The Citizen* 2014). This tall, fictional, faceless character is often depicted as sprouting tentacles. He is essentially a bogeyman-type character of the sort that in various incarnations has appeared in nearly every culture throughout time.

Although most people realize that Slenderman is not real, two twelve-year-old girls in Wisconsin believed that he did exist and felt that if they killed a friend of theirs as a type of offering to Slenderman he would reveal himself to them. They also believed that such a sacrificial offering would so please Slenderman that he would take them to live with him in a mansion in a national forest, according to the criminal complaint brought in the case (News Service Reports 2014). The girls learned about Slenderman on creepypasta.wikia.com. The Creepypasta Wiki (2014) site defines a creepypasta as a "short story posted on the Internet that is designed to unnerve and shock the reader."

The two Wisconsin girls, identified as Anissa Weier and Morgan Geyser, of Waukesha, were accused of carrying out a plot to kill a Horning Middle School classmate (whose name has not been released). According to authorities, Geyser was allowed to have two friends stay overnight every year for her birthday. In 2014, Geyser celebrated her birthday on May 30 (a Friday) and invited Weier and the girl they planned to kill. Weier packed a backpack with clothes, granola bars, water bottles, and a picture of her mother, father, and siblings (in preparation for her trip with Geyser and Slenderman to the mansion in the forest). Weier told police that it was Geyser's idea to kill their friend to please Slenderman and prove that he was real, and that she was excited about the prospect of proving skeptics wrong (*News Service Reports* 2014).

On Saturday morning, while the three girls played hide-and-seek in the wooded park, Weier and Geyser unexpectedly attacked their victim with a knife, stabbing her nineteen times. Thinking they had killed her, the two girls left the scene. The victim managed to crawl out of the woods, where a bicyclist found her and called 911. She was taken to a hospital, where she underwent surgery for her wounds.

In March 2015, the two girls were officially charged with one count each of being party to attempted first-degree intentional homicide, a charge that automatically places them in adult court under Wisconsin law. Each could face up to sixty-five years in the state prison system if convicted (*Associated Press* 2015). The court heard expert testimony as to whether or not the brain of a twelve-year-old is developed enough to control their impulses, and in August 2015, the presiding judge ruled that Weier and Geyser should be held legally responsible for their actions and tried as adults.

The case prompted Waukesha police chief Russell P. Jack to warn parents in the community about evil and dangerous Internet sites accessible to children. At least one Waukesha parent said that she does not blame the creator of the Slenderman character because her own son likes to read and write Slenderman stories on the Creepypasta website. On June 2, 2014, Eric Knudsen, the creator of Slenderman, and an administrator posted on creepypasta.wikia.com an apology and a reminder, of sorts, that all stories on the site are fiction and not mean to advocate or endorse killing or other forms of violence (Anderson and Johnson 2014). Knudsen added, "I am deeply saddened by the tragedy in Wisconsin and my heart goes out to the families of those affected by this terrible act" (*News Service Reports* 2014:B-3).

Political cartoons, which appear in traditional newspapers, underground newspapers, and online, have been a staple of American history for as long as there's been political dissent; in other words, a long time. "The earliest political cartoon as we know it was published in The

Pennsylvania Gazette in 1754, depicting the then colonies as a snake in pieces, captioned 'Join, or Die,' a call to rebellion against the British. The cartoonist was that jack-of-all-trades, Benjamin Franklin" (Moir 2011:8). The use of political cartoons was an especially powerful way to reach the largely semiliterate populace of the time (Moir 2011).

As Alan Moir has indicated, the beauty of political cartoons is that they have the capability of transforming a complex political issue into a single, potent image. "Political cartoonists gained currency during the Civil War, when artist Thomas Nast created some of the most instantly recognizable images in U.S. politics, including Uncle Sam, the Republican elephant and the Democratic donkey. Today, political cartoons remain a staple of newspapers' editorial pages" (*Public Broadcasting Services* 2011). PBS (2011) argues that while it's unlikely that political cartoons will disappear anytime soon, their heyday is over and their influence have waned because of competition from TV and the Internet.

Nonetheless, political cartoons have the ability to "cause trouble" because of their content. "Following the 9/11 attacks, the popular comic strip 'Boondocks' was yanked from several newspapers when it suggested that Reagan administration policies gave birth to the Al Qaeda terrorist group" (*PBS* 2011). Islamic extremists placed a bounty on Danish cartoonist Kurt Westergaard because of his political cartoons mocking Islam and depicting an image of the prophet Muhammad. Twelve of his cartoons appeared in the Danish newspaper *Jyllands-Posten* in September 2005. "The cartoons, which the newspaper said it published as a challenge to perceived self-censorship, provoked massive and violent protests in early 2006 in Muslim countries, after the drawings were reprinted by a range of Western media outlets. Islamic law generally opposes any depiction of the prophet, even favourable, for fear it could lead to idolatry" (Agence France-Presse 2010:6). Westergaard defends his cartoons and states, "We say no and won't let anyone forbid us to criticize radical Islamism. We may not be intimidated when it comes to our values" (Agence France-Presse 2010:6).

Political cartoonists have the ability to appease or offend readers with a single cartoon. They are almost always clever, maybe a little too clever at times. As Moir (2011) explains, "Cartoonists have always been a subversive lot, dovetailing with journalists over the past couple of hundred years, expanding bit by bit the role of 'free expression'" (p. 8). The authors of this text, whether we agree with a particular political cartoon or not, believe in the right of cartoonists to express themselves via their comics, and we support the idea that newspapers, traditional or not, should print them. Whenever possible, an opposing viewpoint regarding controversial topics should be presented.

Lesson Learned: Comics have the ability to entertain, enlighten, and/ or offend.

Harvey Pekar and American Splendor:
An Everyday Superhero

Comics are words and pictures. You can do anything with words and pictures.

—Harvey Pekar

When considering the status of the comic book, it was once natural to think of superheroes battling all-powerful villains, Archie and Jughead matching wits with Principal Weatherbee, or Bugs Bunny and Porky Pig harassing Elmer J. Fudd. In short, the assumption was that comic books were kids' stuff, not to be taken seriously by world-weary adults. Much has changed in the last twenty-five or so years with the rise of graphic novels, but many of these—including such seminal works as Frank Miller's *The Dark Knight*, Alan Moore and Dave Gibbons's *Watchmen*, and Ed Kramer and Neil Gaiman's *The Sandman*—still deal with superheroes, albeit in complex and ethically shaded ways. While it is the case that the comic book field has primarily dwelt in the world of fantasy, there has always been a strong undercurrent of realism as well, detailing the everyday adventures of ordinary individuals. Examples of this can be found in the works of artists such as Will Eisner, Milton Caniff, and Frank King. This realistic strain is perhaps best exemplified by the late Harvey Pekar's magnum opus, *American Splendor*.

Best known now for the 2003 film with the same title, *American Splendor* began in 1976 as a self-published yearly comic detailing Pekar's life as a file clerk at a Cleveland, Ohio, hospital. It is a chronicle of his life: his boyhood, growing up as a "greaser" in the fifties; his relationships with women, and his eventual marriages (he was wed three times, and each wife puts in an appearance in the *Splendor* issues); his reflections on politics, literature, jazz, work, and life in general. Pekar was a down-to-earth guy who tried to record things as they really happened. He was reflective without being preachy. In his story "Rip-Off Chick," for instance, he told of his on-again, off-again relationship with a woman he described as being "basically a worthless person," to which he added, "Dig me, casting stones."

One could never accuse Pekar of pandering to his audience. He did nothing to spruce up the often grim realities of his day-to-day existence. Many of the stories dealt with his money woes, his anxieties about growing old, his health issues (including several bouts with cancer), and his tendency to say the wrong thing at inopportune moments.

Yet for all their apparent harshness, one had to admire Pekar's attempts to show life as it really is: for the most part unglamorous, often tedious, but nonetheless worth living. His stories remind one time and again of Samuel Beckett's famous words, "I can't go on/I'll go on." It is the meaningfulness of simple pleasures which really comes across in these tales. For example, in one of them, Harvey—who constantly portrays himself as a diehard cheapskate—comes across a secondhand store that sells good shoes for fifty cents a pair. He's in heaven!

Pekar had a fine ear for dialogue, and some of the best stories in *American Splendor* involve his interactions with members of the working class, a segment of society that is all too seldom dealt with in literature, let alone the specialized area of comic books. It is in this manner that he expanded the comic book field, showing what it is capable of doing, and pointing out new horizons, which fellow authors and artists might capitalize upon. The comic book can detail a credible, realistic story without resorting to the hero (and Pekar *is* a hero in these tales) having to attain mystical powers or supernatural strength. Pekar's honesty, his eye for details, and his sympathy for the human condition places him in the same category as Mark Twain, Stephen Crane, and Henry Miller. And the fact that it is by no means ridiculous to place a comic book author in such company is due entirely to the quality and integrity of *American Splendor.*

Much praise is also due to the various artists of these works, for these stories were all collaborative efforts. Pekar—who couldn't draw—wrote them, then worked closely with the men and women who depicted, through their artwork, his autobiographical texts. Probably the best known of these artists is Robert Crumb, creator of Fritz the Cat, Mr. Natural, and other famed underground comic figures (and recently the creator of a comic-book rendition of the Book of Genesis). The two first met in Cleveland in the 1960s, and it was Crumb's wild versions of a nervous, bug-eyed Pekar that first gave *Splendor* its prominence. It is interesting to compare the different ways in which the various artists portray Pekar and his world: in some of the stories he appears quite handsome, resembling a slightly manic Ben Gazzara; while in others (particularly those drawn by

Crumb) his appearance is more akin to a raving lunatic; and in most he is much like the schlubby Everyman so ably portrayed by Paul Giamatti in the film version of *American Splendor*. The film nicely demonstrates this confusion when Joyce Brabner (later to become Harvey's third wife) is about to meet him for the first time and wonders which, if any, of the artistic renditions she's seen most accurately depicts the flesh-and-blood version she's soon to meet.

The lesson one learns through reading *American Splendor* is that life is far more complicated than one can imagine, and that the simplest events can have unexpected profundities—which James Joyce referred to as "epiphanies." As the comic strip and the movie based upon it ably show, Pekar's life was unpredictable, but then so are all our lives. One of the constant themes of the work is personal identity: who was "Harvey Pekar"?

There were many levels to Pekar's personality which went beyond that captured by his work—as may be witnessed in the story (well depicted in the film version) called "The Harvey Pekar Name Story." In it, Pekar reflects on the fact that for many years there was *another* Harvey Pekar listed in the Cleveland phonebook, someone he was not related to or connected with in any way. Soon a third man with the same name, the son of the "other" Harvey Pekar, appeared. For years he wondered who they were and what they did, but he never followed up on this. Then, within six months, both of the other Harvey Pekars died. "Although I'd met neither man, I was filled with sadness. 'What were they like,' I thought. It seemed that our lives had been linked in some indefinable way." He is nonplused to see, a few years later, yet another Harvey Pekar listed in the directory. "What kind of people are these? Where do they come from, what do they do? What's in a name?" he reflects. And then he asked the ultimate philosophical question: "Who *is* Harvey Pekar?" which is followed by a panel—masterfully drawn by Crumb—of *our* Harvey Pekar reflecting wordlessly upon this.

Thanks to *American Splendor*, we can all better appreciate our own such Pekaresque moments.

Lesson Learned: Comic books aren't just for kids.

Look, up in the Sky!: The Continuing Legacy of Superman

In 2014, a copy of *Action Comics No. 1*—famous because it marked the first appearance of Superman—sold for $3,207,842 on eBay. Interest in the Man of Steel has never flagged since his first appearance in June

1938. While Kryptonite may someday bring about his ultimate demise, for more than seventy-five years now, Superman has fought evildoers, rescued innocents in distress, and made the world a safer place for democracy. He is a true popular culture phenomenon.

It's safe to say that almost everyone knows who Superman is. Since his initial appearance, he has appeared not only in a continuous series of comic books (including ones detailing his youthful adventures as Super-boy with his dog Krypto), but also in a multitude of television series (including *The Adventures of Superman*, starring George Reeves, *Lois and Clark: The New Adventures of Superman*, and *Smallville*); movies (from cartoons made by the Fleisher Studios in the early 1940s and shown in movie theaters, to live-action serials made in the late 1940s, followed by 1978's *Superman*, with Christopher Reeve, and its various sequels, to more recent films such as 2006's *Superman Returns*, 2013's *Man of Steel*, and 2016's *Batman v Superman: Dawn of Justice*); a Broadway musical (*It's a Bird . . . It's a Plane . . . It's Superman*, which originated in 1966 and is often revised on stage); and countless references in popular song (such as the Kinks' 1979 "(Wish I Could Fly Like) Superman," Laurie Anderson's 1981 "O Superman," The Crash Test Dummies' 1992 "Superman's Song," to Eminem's 2002 "Superman").

Perhaps the ultimate pop culture homage to the Man of Steel is the fact that he regularly appeared in episodes of the ultimate popular culture sitcom, *Seinfeld*. Jerry Seinfeld himself has often remarked about his love for Clark Kent's alter ego, and even appeared in a series of commercials for American Express with the visitor from Krypton, entitled "The Adventures of Seinfeld and Superman." It has often been claimed that every episode of *Seinfeld* has a reference of some sort to Superman. While this is a continuous source of debate on various websites (see http://www.seinfeldscripts.com/seinfeld-superman.html for details), it is certainly true that one of the classic *Seinfeld* episodes (#137, "The Bizarro Jerry") is a direct homage to The Bizarro World, a place found in the D.C. Superman comics of the 1960s, where all the characters are polar opposites of their equivalents on earth. Marilyn Monroe, for instance, is hideously ugly on Bizarro World. In the *Seinfeld* episode, Elaine meets a group of people who look like her friends Jerry, George, and Kramer, except that their characters are diametrically opposite: they are kind, considerate, literate, and not at all self-centered. Jerry is amazed to learn about his alter ego:

JERRY: So he's Bizarro Jerry!

ELAINE: [pause] Bizarro Jerry?

JERRY: Yeah, like Bizarro Superman. Superman's exact opposite, who lives in the backwards Bizarro world. Up is down. Down is up. He says "Hello" when he leaves, "Good-bye" when he arrives.

ELAINE: [pause] Shouldn't he say "Bad-bye?" Isn't that the opposite of "Good-bye?"

JERRY: No. It's still a goodbye.

ELAINE: Uh, does he live underwater?

JERRY: No.

ELAINE: Is he black?

JERRY: Look, just forget it already. All right?

Whereas nearly everyone knows of Superman, very few of us know who his creators were. Unlike Charles Schulz and *Peanuts* (or even Harvey Pekar and *American Splendor*), most people would be hard-pressed to come up with the names of those who brought Superman into existence. Jerry Siegel and Joe Shuster, two boyhood friends from Cleveland, Ohio, originated the concept in 1933 while still in high school. Siegel came up with the plots, and Shuster did the artwork. They ended up selling the rights for $130 to Action Comics, and shortly after the superhero became popular, they were forced out. While they made a few attempts, both together and independently, to come up with another superhero to rival their original (including Funnyman, a professional comedian who uses jokes to paralyze his villainous enemies) they were unsuccessful, and they spent much of the rest of their lives in poverty, struggling to survive, while their cartoon progeny generated billions of dollars for others. When the Christopher Reeve *Superman* films came out, fans who discovered that Siegel and Shuster were still alive and in bad straits successfully petitioned for them to get some money from the film studio, but it was only a tiny reflection of the ultimate gross from the films.

Perhaps in Bizarro World Siegel and Shuster are receiving the recognition that is due them; however, in this world, sadly, they are still basically forgotten. Interestingly enough, a fictionalized version of their lives, entitled *The Amazing Adventures of Kavalier and Klay*, written by Michael Chabon, won the National Book Circle Award in 2000, and a film version has been in the works for several years.

While his creators may be obscure and unheralded, Superman himself lives on. New comics are coming out; new movies are in the works; computer games are being created; and websites thrive. The many TV shows are still available for viewing, and some lucky one of you might well find another copy of *Action Comics No. 1* in your attic someday. When it comes to popular culture, no one is more popular than the visitor from Planet Krypton.

Look, up in the sky! Is it a bird? Is it a plane? You know who it is!

Lesson Learned: Despite his 1992 DC Comics storyline death, Superman lives. And, as we, his loyal fans know, nothing can kill the Man of Steel.

8

Books and Popular Culture

In this chapter, we take a look at a variety of books, including children's books, best-selling books, and banned books. Writing has been around since as early as the seventh millennium BCE. Prior to the invention of the printing press, it took a long time to create a book. Monks spent years writing out the Bible, one copy at a time. Then a fellow named Gutenberg came along in the late 1400s and revolutionized the world with his amazing printing press. Soon every person who could read could own a Bible or any other book—unless, of course, it was on a list of forbidden works, in which case owning it could cost one more than just the price of the volume; it could cost one one's life.

The publishing industry has contributed mightily to popular culture. Some works, such as Harriet Beecher Stowe's *Uncle Tom's Cabin* (discussed later in this chapter), not only were best-sellers, they were eventually adapted into other popular culture media, in radio, television, film, and play versions. Some books, such Mario Puzo's *The Godfather*, are, arguably, better known through their film adaptations than in the original printed editions.

As the recent *Harry Potter* series of books have proven, children—with the right encouragement and the right sort of books to choose from—can be the most eager audience of all. We begin this discussion of books and popular culture by looking at some children's book writers, from the best known (Dr. Seuss) to lesser known (would you believe Crips gang founder Stanley "Tookie" Williams?), and the relatively new craze of popular culture celebrities penning books for kids.

We then explore the phenomenon of banned books from ancient times to the present, and the fact that some of the most beloved and important works in literature were once forbidden entities.

Access to books has always been an issue, going back at least to the time of Gutenberg. Today many people purchase books over the Internet, chiefly through Amazon.com, although such access can be fraught with peril, as several contemporary authors are finding out.

For a long time now, there has been talk about "the death of publishing." But, with an estimated two million books printed each year, the rumors of book publishing's death—to paraphrase Mark Twain—are greatly exaggerated. We are happy that *Lessons Learned from Popular Culture* is helping to keep alive the drive to sustain book publishing.

Dr. Seuss on the Loose

Even though he died in 1991, in 2014 Theodor Seuss Geisel astonished the publishing world with a "new" collection of stories. Better known to the world as the beloved children's book author known as Dr. Seuss, Geisel (1904–1991) was both a master of rhyme and a talented artist. His 2014 *Horton and the Kuggerbug and More Lost Stories* was not in fact a "new" book at all, but rather a collection of previously published but long forgotten works that had appeared originally in *Redbook* magazine in the 1950s. Geisel's biographer Charles Cohen had discovered these pieces, dealing with some of Dr. Seuss's most famous characters and places— Horton the Elephant, the Christmas-hating Grinch, and Mulberry Street, as well as newly discovered characters such as the Kuggerbug, a mean little creature who loves to tap dance on Horton's nose. "The stories," Philip Sherwell writes, "feature his distinctive free-flowing rhyme in its anapaestic tetrameter. 'He climbed and he climbed and he clum and he clum,' he writes of one character, displaying his playful use of tenses and language" (Sherwell 2014).

A gifted cartoonist as well, Seuss's poetic skills were legendary—he had the ability to use simple rhymes that nonetheless stayed permanently in one's head. Millions of people have had the experience of reading one of his classic works, such as *The Cat in the Hat, Horton Hears a Who,* or *Green Eggs and Ham* when they were children and still remember them by heart decades later. And most parents have had the pleasure of reading these stories again, this time to their own children (and grandchildren).

As Amy Graff points out, "Seuss has been delighting children with his extraordinary imagination, made-up words, zany characters and silly rhymes ever since publishing *And to Think That I Saw It on Mulberry Street* in 1937. The release of this book was a miracle of sorts as the manuscript was rejected by 27 publishers" (Graff 2014). Just when he was about to give up, a former college classmate who had gotten a job as a children's book editor saved the day. And the rest is history.

While he eventually wrote almost fifty books for children, many people do not know that this was not Theodor Geisel's original vocation. He began his career as a commercial illustrator (creating such memorable ads as "Quick Henry, the Flit!" for a brand of insect repellant, which became a national catchword) and a political cartoonist. During the Depression era he created many political cartoons for the liberal New York newspaper *PM*, most of which attempted—in as humorous a way as possible, given the subject matter—to alert Americans to the growing danger of Adolf Hitler and Nazism, and encourage them to begin preparing for eventual war against the fascist powers. This advocacy of preparedness went against the Isolationism that predominated in America at the time. Having only recently experienced the horrors of World War I, most Americans were in no mood to contemplate going to war again, and many—including such stalwart figures as the national hero Charles Lindbergh—urged their fellow citizens to stay out of European affairs. Lindbergh, in fact, downplayed the horror stories being told about the Nazis, and even accepted a medal from Hitler's righthand man, Hermann Goering. Geisel took it upon himself to use his cartooning skills for an explicitly didactic purpose—to awaken Americans to the realities of the Nazi regime, and to appeal to their inherent sense of decency by showing them the outrages occurring in Germany and the lands being occupied by Hitler's regime. After the United States entered the war in December 1941 Geisel joined the Army and became the head of the First Motion Picture Unit of the United States Army, creating cartoons that were used to boost the morale of the armed services and the general public.

After the war's end, Geisel—now known primarily by his pen name, Dr. Seuss—devoted the rest of his long career to producing the children's books for which he is famous. But his commitment to public advocacy, while not as obvious as his work for *PM* or the First Motion Picture Unit, nonetheless remained an important part of his career. For instance, his most famous work, *The Cat in the Hat*, came about in part in response to a growing national concern over childhood illiteracy. He took it as a personal challenge to see if he could write, using the simplest language possible, works that young people—as well as their parents, who would of course be reading these works aloud to their children—would genuinely enjoy. And just as in his political cartoons for *PM*, there is a sly, subversive wit in many of his books, such as when the Cat in the Hat continually goads the goody-goody goldfish for being too rulebound and stuffy, and creates havoc in the house, only to bring everything to a nice resolution in the end. *Horton Hears a Who*, another beloved tale, has been interpreted by many as a call for toleration and a criticism of mob mentality—the very sort of issue that had concerned Geisel during the prewar years when he confronted Hitler's rise to power and the techniques used by fascist regimes to destroy individuality.

One can perhaps read too much into such interpretations, and no doubt most people delve into Dr. Seuss's works for the sheer fun of them, not to find hidden political messages. The power of Dr. Seuss's writing comes from the combination of his sheer love of language and his wild and whimsical drawing style. How many parents have thrilled to narrate his daring rhymes while teaching their children how to read, and how many children have delighted in the lovable characters that came from his pen?

Dr. Seuss was—and remains—a genuine popular culture phenomenon. His books have sold millions of copies and been the basis of countless movies, television specials (including the beloved perennial holiday classic, *How the Grinch Stole Christmas*), audio recordings, and even a Broadway musical, *Seussical.*

And amazingly enough, yet another previously unknown work came to light and was published in 2015: *What Pet Should I Get?* As *Entertainment Weekly* described it: "In October 2013, Random House art director Cathy Goldsmith got a phone call. There was a 'box full of something' at the home of the late Theodor Geisel—a.k.a. Dr. Seuss—in La Jolla, Calif., and his widow Audrey thought Goldsmith might like to see it. . . . It turned out to be a nearly complete manuscript, written and illustrated, of a never-before-seen book. *What Pet Should I Get?* follows a brother and sister through the titular decision, from cats and dogs to fantastic Seussical creatures like the Yent (it sleeps under a tent)" (Biedenharn 2015). It seems to have been written sometime between 1958 and 1962, and thus is vintage Seuss. And at least two more books based on recently rediscovered materials are likely to be published. "A box full of something," indeed.

There aren't many authors who have brought joy to millions of people by "reappearing" more than twenty years after death.

Lesson Learned: Learning can be fun and not a bad time if you follow Dr. Seuss and do it through rhyme.

Stanley "Tookie" Williams: A Controversial
Nobel Prize–Nominated Author of Children's Books

In the world of street gangs, no gang is larger than the Crips. The Crips are one of the four recognized "nation" gangs in the United States. A nation gang is one that has extended its presence across the country (the definition includes that the gang be located in at least thirty of the fifty states), and the Crips meet this requirement. (Note: The Crips can also be found in Canada and some Central American countries, but their primary operations are within the borders of the United States.) There are four nation gangs in the United States: Crips, Bloods, People, and Folks. The People and the Folks are based in Chicago, the second most notorious American city for street gangs, and the Crips and Bloods are based in Los Angeles, the street gang capital of the world.

The Crips originated from the tough streets of South Central Los Angeles in the early 1970s. Interestingly, it was the FBI's crackdown on the Black Panther Party (BPP) in the late 1960s that directly influenced the formation of the Crips. Founded by Huey P. Newton in Oakland, California, the BPP was a progressive political organization that attempted to help the black community. The BPP was created in the wake of the assassination of black leader Malcolm X, on February 21, 1965, and the massive urban uprising in Watts, California, which lasted six days in mid-August 1965). The BPP created a Free Breakfast for Children at a Catholic church in the Fillmore district of San Francisco. The program was so successful it spread to every community where the BPP had chapters. One of these chapters was located in Los Angeles. This Southern California chapter was founded in 1968 by street gangster Alprentice "Bunchy" Carter (Black Panther Party 1999). Bunchy Carter was known as the "Mayor of the Ghetto" and was the former head of the five thousand–strong Slauson Gang (Delaney 2014).

In Los Angeles, police and city leaders tried to calm the nerves of the citizenry following the Watts riots. The federal government had the greater problem of trying to calm the citizenry of the entire nation, as by the end of 1967 there had been more than one hundred major rebellions in the African American neighborhoods of cities across the nation that had followed the Watts riots. The Vietnam War had escalated by this time, further stirring up the climate of discontent in the country, which television news exacerbated by reporting every bit of urban unrest that occurred in the cities of the United States.

While the Free Breakfast Program, along with other social programs created by the BPP, had the overt intention of helping poor black families, it also had the covert intention to make the government look inept in their ability to provide assistance to the needy. The government also wondered how the BPP raised the money needed to run their programs. Consequently, the FBI and the Los Angeles Police Department deemed the BPP as a threat to national security (Chambliss 1993). To combat the perceived threat of the BPP, the federal government quickly copied the party's free breakfast program for children in poorer school districts. At the same time, the government and law enforcement were working on a way to bring the BPP to an end.

As a point of interest, Bunchy Carter had begun to attend UCLA, and on January 17, 1969, he was gunned down at Campbell Hall on the UCLA campus—some say by the FBI, others say by rival gang members in the BPP. Huey Newton was assassinated in 1989 after serving time in prison. (As an interesting bit of popular culture relevancy, while Newton was in prison the expression "Free Huey" became a popular rallying cry at black gatherings and protests.)

The South Central black youths who were too young to join the BPP but who admired the party included among their number Raymond Lee Washington and Stanley "Tookie" Williams. Both Washington and Williams had established their own vicious street gangs and inevitably they crossed paths. Rather than fight each other, they decided to merge their gangs into one super gang, and thus, around early 1970, Washington's Baby Avenues gang and Williams's gang joined up in an organization that came to be known as Avenue Cribs. Before long, Cribs was changed to Crips. During the first few years of the 1970s, the Crips challenged the other neighborhood gangs to either join them or die. Most of these local street gangs happily agreed to merge with the rapidly growing Crip gang. In the summer of 1972, the much larger Crip gang came across the Piru Street Boys of Compton. The Piru Street Boys found other gangs who hated the Crips and convinced them to join Piru. The Piru Street Boys gang would change their name to The Bloods to signify their commitment to one another. By the mid-1970s, the Crips and Bloods had been formed, primarily because of their shared distrust of local law enforcement the government, following the BPP crackdown.

Both Williams and Washington were imprisoned during the 1970s. Washington was released in the late 1970s and was shot dead during a drive-by shooting on August 9, 1979. In 1981, Williams was sent to prison after being convicted of four murders and two counts of robbery and sentenced to death. He was sent to San Quentin and awaited his execution while on Death Row (*A&E Television* 2014b). Although authorities

believed that Williams was still running the Crips from prison, he was trying to turn his life around and make amends for the chaos that his actions
had created. During the twenty-five years of his incarceration before he
was finally executed on December 15, 2005, Williams had plenty of time
for self-reflection. He had never thought the gang he'd helped to create
would spread across California, let alone the entire country. He regretted
the legacy that he had created—black on black homicide—and wanted to
extend an olive branch to youths through his writings, and particularly
through children's books (Delaney 2014). And while it seems today that
nearly every celebrity believes that he or she can author a distinctive children's book, Williams's stories were truly unique, and they were anti-gang.

Although children's books are, ostensibly, easy to write because of
their limited number of words (artwork is as important as, if not more
important than text) and straightforward content, Williams had to to
increase his limited vocabulary. Among his writings were "My Letter to
Incarcerated Youth, No. 1," an open letter posted on "Tookie's Corner," a
website that he regularly updated with his newfound words of wisdom
(Williams 1997a). In this letter, Williams warned youths in juvenile halls
and youth detention centers to straighten out their lives so they would
not end up dying in prison like him. In his letter, "The Apology," Williams (1997b) apologized for creating the Crips. He also video recorded
a message to be sent to youth everywhere.

In September 1996, the Rosen Publishing group PowerKids Press
published Williams's eight children's books as a series. These books all provide an anti-gang message. They have been distributed to libraries across
the nation and throughout many parts of the world. The series includes
such titles as *Gangs and the Abuse of Power*, *Gangs and Self-Esteem*, *Gangs
and Violence*, and *Gangs and Your Friends*. The books gained instant attention around the world and were so highly acclaimed that in 2001 he was
nominated for a Nobel Peace Prize by Marjo Fehr, a member of the Swiss
Parliament (Delaney 2014). Fehr wanted the members of the Nobel Prize
Committee to set aside their feelings about Williams the co-founder of
the Crips street gang and instead consider the positive influence his books
and Internet project ("Tookie's Corner") had on children in encouraging
them to resist gang life. It was the first time that a man on death row
had ever been nominated for the prize.

Many in the general population, in the law enforcement community,
and among those negatively affected by street gang life did not like the
idea that the Nobel Peace Prize, the prestigious award associated with
dedication and brilliance in pursuit of world peace and human rights,

was now associated with a notorious gangbanger who started the first nation gang (Severson 2001).

In 2002, Williams was nominated for the Nobel Prize for Literature. In total, he was nominated five times for the Nobel Peace Prize and once for the Nobel Prize for Literature (Robinson 2005). He did not win any of these nominated awards. However, in 2005, Williams did win an Outstanding Character of America Award and a President's Call to Service Award from President George W. Bush for his efforts to inspire volunteerism in the United States (*Jet* 2005).

Williams attempted to persuade California governor Arnold Schwarzenegger to grant him clemency that the evidence presented against him for the murder of four persons in 1979 had falsely led to his conviction. Schwarzenegger did not buy Williams's explanation and he was executed on December 13, 2005, in San Quentin State Prison.

Lesson Learned: If you are the founder of the notorious street gang, the Crips, even though you go on to gain critical acclaim for writing children's books while on death row, if the governor is known as the "Terminator," you can expect to be terminated.

Celebrity Children's Book Authors

As the first two sections have shown, children's book authors come from varied origins—from political cartoonists such as Theodor Geisel to gang leaders like Tookie Williams. And since we are dealing with popular culture, it's probably not surprising that, in recent years, some noted children's book authors have been pop celebrities themselves. Since they already have name recognition, parents who are already fans might well be predisposed to purchase these writers' works. In the highly competitive world of children's books, celebrity-penned stories stand out. Best-selling recent authors include such movie and TV stars as Jim Carrey, Katie Couric, Gloria Estefan, Ricky Gervais, Jessica Lange, Steve Martin, Julianne Moore, and Weird Al Yankovic, as well as athletes like Women's World Cup soccer winner Alex Morgan and NBA player Adonal Foyle.

The actor Jason Segal, known for his roles in the TV series *How I Met Your Mother* and such adult-themed films as *Forgetting Sarah Marshall* and *Sex Tape*, is one of the latest stars to venture into this lucrative realm. He has co-written a children's book with Kirsten Miller, entitled *Nightmares!* According to *Entertainment Weekly*, the book, which "centers on a group of kids trying to save their town from fear itself," was inspired in part by his own life. Segal "draws on his own childhood fears. 'I had terrible night terrors when I was a kid,' says Segal. 'I had a strange recurring nightmare of witches eating my toes, which I did use in my book. They didn't want all of me, just my toes" (Lee 2014). This will be the first of a series of such books, published by Random House. Segel, by the way, has become his own pop culture phenomenon. In addition to appearing in a hit television show and several successful films, he has been involved in several ventures that appeal primarily to children. He voiced the character Vector, the villain in the 2010 animated feature *Despicable Me*. He also helped to revive the Muppets film franchise by appearing in and co-writing the 2011 movie *The Muppets,* the first Muppets theatrical release in twelve years. He even has a Muppet figure based upon himself, the character Walter, who "plays" his brother in the film. As Renee Dale writes, "Jason Segel is no doubt your favorite kind of multitalented person. He acts, writes, sings and navigates varied entertainments with an unassuming touch. He's amiable. He's large. He gives the impression of 'Hey, I'm just trying out some stuff because it makes me happy, and maybe it'll make you happy too!'" (Dale 2014). This is certainly the case with his book *Nightmares*—for all its chills and thrills, the tale of Charlie Laird confronting his various fears is ultimately a delightful read, which parents can easily trust will satisfy their children's cravings for a good bedtime story.

It should be noted that children's books with a "weird theme" based upon nightmares, even those penned by otherwise mild-mannered celebrities, are nothing new. Many beloved children's stories of old were written by individuals who were, to put it mildly, off-putting. Danish author Hans Christian Andersen (1805–1875), creator of the Ugly Duckling, the Little Mermaid, the Tin Soldier, and the Little Match Girl, had a reputation for being himself an Ugly Duckling—a gawky, socially challenged maladroit who had difficulty relating to people or understanding how he was perceived by them. For instance, while he befriended Charles Dickens when visiting London in 1857, and Dickens welcomed Andersen into his home, things grew frosty when—like a character from one of his own stories—Andersen became "The Guest Who Wouldn't Leave." At first, Dickens was happy to have the author—whose works were loved by Dickens's children—in his home, but as days turned to weeks, and gentle questions about when he was planning to move on became not-so-subtle hints that he was no longer welcome, things became uncomfortable. As Dayla Alberg relates, "After he finally left, Dickens wrote on the mirror in the guestroom: 'Hans Andersen slept in this room for five weeks—which seemed to the family AGES!'" (Alberg 2008). While Andersen remained oblivious to the ire he had created, "[t]o the Dickens family it was eternal torment. Dickens's daughter, Kate, would later recall that Andersen 'was a bony bore, and stayed on and on.' He was, she added, 'a social blockhead.' Andersen never quite understood why Dickens ceased to answer any of his letters" (Alberg 2008).

But there may have been more to Dickens's desire for Andersen to vacate his premises than merely weariness of his company. For Andersen had a decidedly creepy persona, which some literary critics speculate may relate to the disturbing themes found in his seemingly innocent stories. As Simon Tait points out, "Andersen was tall with a slightly effeminate appearance, a long nose and close-set eyes, which might have alarmed Dickens's many children at first—he had 10, with eight or nine of them at home in 1857," adding further that "what is to be made of Andersen's request—subsequently denied—that he should be shaved by one of the older Dickens boys each morning? He had tortuous unrequited sexual yearnings for both boys and women, including the singer Jenny Lind and the son of a Danish patron, but he never married and, later, resorted to brothels" (Tait 2005). Whether or not Dickens was repulsed by Andersen's unsettling character or whether he just was fed up with having to feed another person in such a large household remains an open question.

Whatever the truth may be, it does seem that—like other noted children's authors, including Lewis Carroll, Roald Dahl, and Maurice Sendak—Hans Christian Andersen was able to draw upon his own personal demons, and his own rejections, as the basis of his beloved creations. Having a dark edge, as Jason Segel can attest, can actually be beneficial when writing books for children.

It should be pointed out that not everyone is enamored of the current craze for celebrity children's book authors. British writer Tom Lamont, for instance, was incensed by the fact that Segel's *Forgetting Sarah Marshall* co-star, the controversial comic Russell Brand, had ventured into this area. For him, this was the last straw. Lamont writes: "I'll express this in short sentences. Stop it, celebrities. Go away, celebrities. John Travolta has written a children's book. [English model and television personality] Katie Price has written a children's book. Frank Lampard, Katie Price's former kiss-and-tell, has written a children's book. Some that I've read are good; others as sluggish as the career lull that inspired them" (Lamont 2014).

If Lamont is nonplused by Russell Brand penning a book for children, what must he think about *Gus and Me: The Story of My Grandad and My First Guitar*, by none other than the Rolling Stones' perpetual Satanic Majesty Keith Richards? Fresh on the heels of his best-selling tell-all autobiography *Life* (a work definitely not safe for children), Richards's surprise followup book is aimed directly at the under-ten audience. Based on his recollections of his grandfather and the influence he had on Richards's own love for guitars, he has kept it in the family by having his daughter Theodora Richards do the artwork.

Ultimately, whether celebrities take Lamont's advice or not, it will be the public that decides if such books become long-lasting classics, like the works of Dr. Seuss, or forgotten works decaying in old attics or, even worse, put on shelves in restaurants for purely decorative purposes. For any author, that would be the worst nightmare of all.

Lesson Learned: If you want to be a successful children's book writer, it helps to be a little "off."

Banned Books:
You Can't Read These Books, Because I Said So

The concept of banned books is quite fascinating; after all, authors took the time to write them and publishers printed them, so why can't the public read them? Who decides whether or not a book should be banned? On what basis is a book banned? Are books banned only in societies with a repressive ideology? And, are books still banned in the twenty-first century or is this a holdover from the past, when people were less enlightened than they, supposedly, are today?

We will answer the last question first: books are still banned today, and, clearly, a large number of people and governments are not especially enlightened. In 2012 alone, there were 464 attempts made to ban books in the United States. Among the popular books banned in recent years have been the *Harry Potter* and *Twilight* series. These novels were censored because they seemingly promoted "unchristian magic" (Brunner 2013). The calls to ban these books have not been limited to nations with repressive governments but, instead, reflect the attitudes of close-minded people who feel threatened by any ideology other than their own. For example, in the United States, Religious Right factions, led by the Christian Coalition, want the Harry Potter novels banned because they're about wizards and witches. Some members of the Christian Coalition are divided about whether the *Twilight* novels should be banned, because on the one hand they are pro-abstinence, but on the other hand they are pro-vampires and encourage teen marriage, which goes against family values (Mantyla 2010).

In addition to specific groups (the Christian Coalition), governments have led the charge to ban books. In some cases, repressive governments ban books that go against official ideology, or to control the flow of information available to citizens. On the other hand, governments that otherwise are not categorized as repressive might ban certain publications because the contents contain potentially dangerous information (e.g., books that explain how to make bombs or carry out terrorist attacks) that might harm innocent citizens.

Individuals possess the power to ban books from the eyes of specific readers. For example, parents may forbid their children to read certain books or other published materials. They do this for a variety of reasons, including the idea that their children are too young to be exposed to specific topics (e.g., pornography or violence) or because the reading material may contradict their own socioreligious philosophies. Books assigned or made available in public schools may be targeted by parent groups or individual parents because they find something offensive in the contents. For example, a parent at West Marion High School in Foxworth, a rural Mississippi town, complained to the school superintendent that the book *Fahrenheit 451* was offensive and should be banned. The offensive phrase that upset the parent was "God damn." The book was removed from the required reading list shortly afterward. It is interesting to note that *Fahrenheit 451* is a futuristic tale of a society in which all printed materials are banned. The title is a reference to the temperature at which paper starts to burn (*Banned Books and Authors* 2011; Delaney 2012a).

Thus, books may be banned for any number of reasons ranging from a complaint by an individual or group about the contents of specific books to policies issued by a government opposed to the political content of the book or fear that it constitutes a threat to public safety. Borgna Brunner (2013) provides us with a list of famous banned books, and the given reasons they were banned:

1. *Anne Frank: The Diary of a Young Girl*: Banned because it was "too depressing"

2. *Blubber*, by Judy Blume: The characters curse and the mean-spirited ringleader is never punished for her cruelty.

3. *Bony-Legs*, by Joanna Cole: Deals with subjects such as magic and witchcraft

4. *The Chocolate War*, by Robert Cormier: Offensive language

5. *Harriet the Spy*, by Louise Fitzhugh: Teaches children to spy, talk back, and curse

6. *A Hero Ain't Nothin' but a Sandwich*, by Alice Childress: Anti-American and immoral

7. *In the Night Kitchen*, by Maurice Sendak; Nudity: Mickey loses his pajamas during his fall into the kitchen.

8. *A Light in the Attic*, by Shel Silverstein: Contains a suggestive illustration that might encourage children to break dishes so they won't have to dry them

9. *Sylvester and the Magic Pebble*, by William Steig: The characters are all shown as animals; the police are presented as pigs.

10. *Confessions of an Only Child*, by Norma Klein: Use of profanity by the lead character's father

That certain books can be banned because their contents are deemed by one person, one group, or one government as offensive in some manner is controversial in nations such as the United States that grant their citizens rights and privileges related to free expression. In the United States, the First Amendment of the Constitution guarantees our right to free speech, including the right to read and write books that might be considered by some to be harmful in some manner. But the First Amendment does not ensure that books will not be banned, and truth be told, a number of Americans think that it is perfectly acceptable to violate this amendment under certain circumstances.

Alex Knapp (2013), a *Forbes* magazine contributing author, wrote an article about five banned books that he believes people should read. They are listed below:

1. *Our Family Tree: An Evolution Story*, by Lisa Westberg Peters. This is a book written for children that is beautifully illustrated but it was banned because it explains evolution so clearly that even a child can comprehend it (Knapp 2013). Because some adults still cannot understand evolution, they might want to read this too.

2. *The Curious Incident of the Dog in the Night-time*, by Mark Haddon. The book is banned in several school and public libraries. It is written in the first person from the

perspective of a teenager with autism and describes his struggles to understand the people around him.

3. *Dialogue Connecting the Two Chief World Systems*, by Galileo Galilei. This book is not generally banned now, but it was when it was written because Galileo defended the Copernican model of the solar system, where the earth moves around the sun rather than the opposite, as the church taught.

4. *Zhuangzi* (named for its author). A philosophical text on Taoism, banned at different times in China because of its content.

5. *The Epic of Gilgamesh*. An epic poem from Mesopotamian era, often considered the world's first great work of literature. It has been challenged and banned in schools in the United States by parents who object to some of its depictions of sexuality (Americans are much more prudish than the Babylonians were).

This list was compiled by Alex Knapp; you will have to read the books for yourself to get the true impact of their contents. You might also want to do an online search of other banned books to read. Or, you could ask your local librarian for suggestions on banned books to read. Librarians, like college professors, after all, certainly encourage people to read, and that includes banned books. In 1982, the American Library Association launched its National Banned Books Week (this occurs during the last week of September each year) in an effort to publicize our right of free expression and our freedom to read, emphasizing those books deemed dangerous by government and special interests (Delaney 2012a).

As educators, the authors of this book, like Alex Knapp and American Library Association, encourage adults to read materials that are banned, if for no other reasonthan to judge for themselves whether or not the material they contain is offensive. Furthermore, reading "forbidden" materials generally expand the critical thinking abilities of the open-minded. When it comes to children, reasonable adults should take into consideration the content of reading materials and the maturity level of the underaged reader.

Lesson Learned: Do yourself a favor, read a banned book and find out what all the fuss is about.

Amazon is Banning Books:
They've Crushed Authors and Publishers
and Want Even More Money

In theory, authors and publishers have a symbiotic relationship, if the book sells, both the author and publisher make money. Authors are generally happy to receive a contract from a publisher, as this means they have found a venue to broadcast their printed words to the public. Presuming that we speak on behalf of all authors, we are confident that authors are also happy to receive a royalty check from the publisher. Unfortunately, most authors—especially academic authors—generally get a small percentage of a book's sales revenues—anywhere between eight and fourteen percent, of the *net*. It is the author's creative mind and hard labor that produce a book, and yet authors receive the smallest portion of the profit.

Publishers will counter that they have to pay an editor to copyedit a book, pay the marketing department to promote the book, pay workers who pack and ship the book, and so on. Publishers also claim that they work on a small profit margin, which is why they have increasingly passed on costs to authors. For example, it has become common for authors to have to pay for indexing the book, a task generally, and historically, covered by the publisher. The publisher's marketing department has also increasingly asked authors to take over the chore of promoting the book (e.g., provide a list of professors who might order the book for their classes, provide selling points for the book—the publisher should read the book and create their own selling points—and identify awards that might be available for that book).

Authors have other issues with publishers. For example, when an author tries to contact a specific person at the publishing house (e.g., the assigned editor, or an acquisitions editor), it might take days or weeks to reach someone who can make a decision. Conversely, when a publisher sets a deadline for an author, the author is expected to respond immediately. For example, a publisher might send chapter proofs and editing comments/suggestions to an author on Monday and expect a return by Friday, ignoring the fact that these authors generally have full-time academic jobs and/or other projects in the works.

In short, publishers generally hold the power over authors. The authors of this book could write a book just on their experiences with publishers, but then again, no one would publish it. We can share one story, however. We once had a signed contract with a publisher (that we will not name here), delivered the manuscript on time, and were placed in a state of limbo waiting for the book to be published. The publisher ignored us; we kept trying to reach him. After a year—yes, a year—the publisher copied us on a generic mass e-mail to authors announcing that the company had been sold to another press. In other words, while we had worked in good faith with the publisher, the opposite was not true. The publisher was trying to keep costs down (e.g., by not spending money on books that were under contract but not yet published) in order to make the company look more profitable in the eyes of potential buyers. Once the new publisher took over, it was under no legal (although but one might think ethical) obligation to publish our book. And they did pass on it, because they had other books in their catalog on the same topic. Unless you are a published author, you might have never considered these, and other, details when it comes to publishing.

Authors and publishers do share one common problem, that is, they both only make money on the initial sale of a book. If the book is resold as a used copy the author and publisher, oddly, do not receive any percentage of that sale. College bookstores are especially the bane of academic authors and publishers, as they buy and resell books from students repeatedly, making more money than either the author or publisher (not to mention that they are profiting from college students). College bookstores should, at the least, be made to provide a percentage of a book's sale directly to the author. In an effort to maximize their profits, college bookstores seek out used copies of books instead of ordering new copies from the publisher, at the expense of those who have actually put in the labor and creative vision behind the book.

In mid-2014, authors and publishers found another common problem—Amazon, the online site that, among other things, sells books (they account for around 50 percent of all book sales around the world). Authors and publishers have found Amazon to be a problem for years as the e-retailer has taken on the role of the college bookstore, not only buying used copies of books but buying large quantities of new books from their publishers and selling them at a discount rate. The latter practice can be blamed at least in part on publishers' cooperation. Authors have no say in this matter, which returns them a smaller royalty. Amazon offers used copies for sale alongside new copies and many shoppers opt to buy the used, thus denying the royalty away to the author. In 2014, however, Amazon decided that they wanted/deserved more money. We agree that Amazon deserves to profit from shipping and handling their merchandise, but that is all they deserve. They did not write or publish the books, so why should they receive any profit from the books?

In their attempt to earn more money from selling books, Amazon decided to challenge the Hachette Book Group. As Valby (2014) explains, the confrontation reached its peak on May 22, 2014, when Amazon stopped accepting preorders for Hachette books (including U.S. imprints Little, Brown & Company, Hyperion, and Grand Central). "Customers suddenly were denied the option of clicking 'Add to Cart' on upcoming works from J. K. Rowling and Michael Connelly and were shown a 'Currently Unavailable' box instead. This on the heels of earlier reports that the site was delaying delivery of some Hachette books for weeks" (Valby 2014:17). Amazon wanted a bigger cut of Hachette's revenues, and one might say that the online company has been using blackmail as a negotiating strategy. The publisher, understandably, has refused to cave in to Amazon's demands. On May 23, 2014, Hachette chief executive Michael Pietsch stated that his company requires a deal that "best serves our authors and their work, and that preserves our ability to survive . . . as a strong and author-centric publishing company" (Valby 2014:17).

As a smoke screen, Amazon countered that Hachette is part of a $10 billion media conglomerate and thus able to afford to let Amazon take a larger percentage of the profits. Undoubtedly Hachette authors would like a larger share of the profits, too; get in line behind them, Amazon.

As noted at the beginning of this story, authors, on occasion, have their own problems with publishers, but because the relationship between them is basically symbiotic, they have joined the cause on Hachette's side and made it known that they regard Amazon as their enemy. "Hachette's best-selling author Jeffery Deaver—who calls Amazon's negotiating tactics 'repugnant, distasteful, and tawdry'—has seen his novel *The Skin Collector* become part of feud's collateral damage" (Valby 2014:18). As to Amazon's claim that if they were given a greater percentage of Hachette's profits they would pass the windfall on to their customers, Deaver asks, "Do we really believe that whatever money they save because of the deal with Hachette or any other publisher is going to be passed on to customers?" Another Hachette author, James Patterson, who has pledged to give $1 million of his own money to independent bookstores across the country, also chimed in on the Amazon issue. "[Amazon] wants to control bookselling, book buying, and even book publishing, and that is a national tragedy" (Valby 2014:18). Meanwhile, authors continue to want their fair share of the profits of their labor.

Stephen King has joined the feud, comparing the impasse between "heavy-handed" Amazon executives and Hachette to the traffic jam caused in September 2013 by the notorious, apparently politically motivated closure of two lanes on the New Jersey approach to the George Washington Bridge. King (2014) writes, "What makes it dismaying is how little recourse the publishers have, because Amazon has come to dominate the business of selling books. In a sense, it's like a hoodlum in the protection racket strong-arming one small-business owner so that all the other owners on the street—we could call it Book Street—will fall into line. If Hachette renegotiates contractual terms (which are unclear) in a way that's favorable to Amazon, chances are good that the rest of the publishers will have to fall into line" (p. 18).

Stephen Colbert, the host of *The Late Show* (having replaced David Letterman in September 2015), also joined in the feud with Amazon. During a skit on the June 4, 2014 episode of *The Colbert Report*, he opened a package from Amazon to reveal his middle finger directed at Amazon. He then put his other hand under the package (which had a hole in its bottom) and "flipped the bird" with both hands, proclaiming, "Hey, Amazon, customers who enjoyed this also bought this." (If you missed this on TV, you can find it on YouTube). Colbert ended his rant against Amazon by warning its CEO, Jeff Bezos, "Watch out Bezos, because this means war." Colbert, himself an author with Hachette and negatively affected by Amazon, encouraged his viewers to protest against Amazon and cleverly suggested that people put stickers on their books that read, "I didn't buy it on Amazon" (Kastrenakes 2014). The stickers can be downloaded from his website (although people are on their own turning the download into a sticker).

Publishers could cut out Amazon completely by not selling any books to them. You might ask how, if Amazon doesn't sell the books, will customers purchase them? The answer, of course, is simple; the customer goes to the website of the publisher instead. If the publisher finds the increased volume of orders overwhelming they can hire people to work in their warehouse and cover these new costs with shipping and handling fees.

A mass revival of bookstores would be a nice way to bring customers face to face with books again. We mentioned earlier that Hachette author James Patterson was giving away $1 million to support independent bookstores, and it might be noted that other successful authors have opened their own bookstores. *Diary of a Wimpy Kid* author Jeff Kinney, whose books have sold more than 100 million copies worldwide, is opening his own bookstore in Plainville, Massachusetts; Ann Patchett runs Parnassus Books in Nashville; and Larry McMurtry is the longtime owner of Booked Up, in Archer, Texas (*The Citizen* 2014). While these authors are doing their part to try to keep bookstores open, it is unlikely we will see the return of large chain bookstores.

Lesson Learned: If we're not careful, Amazon will refuse to sell this book. Or, they might decide to sell it only at a discounted rate—which is great for the reader but not so good for the authors or publisher.

The Book that Started the Civil War: Harriet Beecher Stowe's Popular Classic

In this chapter, we've talked mostly about recent best-selling books. But it's good to reflect on books that not only sold well in their own times but have continued to do so long after their authors' demise. One of the most popular novels of all time, and certainly one of the most influential, is Harriet Beecher Stowe's classic diatribe against slavery, *Uncle Tom's Cabin*, originally published in 1851–52 and never out of print since that time. Stowe, none of whose other many writings were ever popular, touched a nerve with this particular work, which raised the consciousness of millions of readers not only by making them aware of the horrors of slavery, but also by bringing to life the many characters impacted by this "peculiar institution." So powerful and so successful was the book that printing presses operated night and day to meet the demand.

While Abraham Lincoln's supposed quote upon meeting Stowe shortly after the Civil War began ("So you're the little woman who wrote the book that made this great war!") is almost surely apocryphal, it nonetheless captures the strong feelings that the book evoked in its time, and which it continues to arouse in modern readers. Viewers of the 2013 Academy Award–winning motion picture *12 Years a Slave*—a film based on the nonfiction book of the same name, which was published in 1853, one year after Stowe's book—can attest to the horror that seeing slavery depicted in all its manifestations can still inspire, 150 years after the abolition of the practice. Imagine, then, the effect Stowe's work had on contemporary readers, at a time when four million people languished in slavery in the Southern United States. Stowe touched a nerve with her immortal story, although it was at times unwieldy in its writing style. As John William Ward writes in his afterword to the Signet Classic edition:

"Its immense, incredible popularity puts a problem to both literary and historical understanding. For the literary critic, the problem is simply how a book so seemingly artless, so lacking in apparent literary talent, was not only an immediate success but has endured" (Ward, 1966:480). In many ways, the book succeeds in spite of itself—its various characters took on the roles of archetypes, and became immortal in their own right. Ward continues: "More importantly, if one of the tests of the power of fiction is the way in which a novel provides images that order the confusing reality of life, then *Uncle Tom's Cabin* ranks high. Uncle Tom, little Eva, Simon Legree, Topsy who just growed—these are characters who now form part of the collective experience of the American people" (Ward, 1996:480).

Like many other best-selling works (including, ironically enough, Margaret Mitchell's 1936 *Gone With the Wind*, which takes a much more romanticized view of antebellum Southern plantation life), the reason for *Uncle Tom's Cabin's* continued popularity remains mysterious. The earnestness of Stowe's writing must have something to do with it. To quote from the noted historian David McCullough: "The book had a strange power over almost everyone who read it then, and for all its Victorian mannerisms and frequent patches of sentimentality much of it still does. Its characters have a vitality of a kind comparable to the most memorable figures in literature. There is a sweep and power to the narrative, and there are scenes that once read are not forgotten" (McCullough 1992:44). To use a popular term, *Uncle Tom's Cabin* is a page turner.

Yet, while it is easy to read, it is by no means a simple book. For instance, while it might be assumed that the novel, written by a Northerner living in the slave-free state of Ohio, was nothing but a denunciation of the Southern slave-holding states, this is by no means the case. Orville Vernon Burton, in his book *The Age of Lincoln*, makes an important point in this regard. "Stowe," he writes, "did not demonize southerners. They too were helpless victims of a sinful system. The villain in the story is Simon Legree, a Yankee dealer in slaves who owns a plantation in Louisiana. Because of his love for money, Legree puts aside all morality for the sake of gain. In a warning to her northern readers, Stowe portrays Legree without one iota of Christian compassion. He is the embodiment of mammon-worship" (Burton 2007:66).

When it comes to popular culture, perhaps no character in the book is as well-known as "Uncle Tom" himself, the title character who has come to exemplify subservience. The term *Uncle Tom* has been used to denigrate African Americans who seem to accept second-class (or worse) status in society, and who refuse to criticize the white power structure. This type of character is brilliantly parodied in Quentin Tarantino's 2012 Academy

Award Winning film *Django Unchained* where Samuel L. Jackson, playing the role of Samuel, a fiercely loyal house slave on the Candyland Plantation, defends his master Candie rather than side with the abolitionist Django. Samuel is the epitome of an Uncle Tom in the subservient sense, and audiences cheer when he ends up getting gunned down by the vengeful Django, whom he had earlier betrayed.

And yet, for those who read Stowe's novel, it is surprising to find that the Uncle Tom depicted there is anything but subservient. He is a heroic figure, who refuses to accept that he is a "lesser being" and who fights against being a slave at every turn. His inherent dignity is in fact the key to the novel's success—readers then and now can identify with his struggle for freedom and his refusal to knuckle down to domination. The novel ends on a tragic note, when Tom sacrifices his life so that others can escape from slavery. But he dies knowing that he has lived a truly virtuous life, and he can die content in the knowledge that his enslavement never harmed his inner sense of self-worth.

Why, then, the popular misconception about Uncle Tom? Blame it on popular culture. Stage versions of the novel, starting shortly after its publication and going on for many years afterward, took great liberties with the plot. In these popular representations—some of which were filmed in the early days of motion pictures—Tom was indeed depicted as the passive, unassertive, and downtrodden character personified by the negative term *Uncle Tom.* McCullough notes: "The book is also rather different from what most people imagine, largely because it was eventually eclipsed by the stage version, which Mrs. Stowe had nothing to do with (and from which she never received a cent), and which was probably performed more often than any play in the language, evolving after a few years into something between a circus and minstrel show" (McCullough 1992:44–45).

How sad that Stowe's noble character in many ways came to symbolize the very opposite of what she had intended. As McCullough further points out: "That Uncle Tom would one day be used as term of derision ('A Negro who is held to be humiliatingly subservient or deferential to whites,' according to the *American Heritage Dictionary*) she would have found impossible to fathom, and heartbreaking. For her he was something very close to a black Christ" (McCullough 1992:45).

However, there is an easy remedy that will restore Uncle Tom to his rightful place as a strong, forceful, and noble character, and one that Stowe no doubt would surely encourage. All you have to do is read the book.

Lesson Learned: Uncle Tom was no "Uncle Tom."

9

Fads, Fashion, Technology, and Trends and Popular Culture

In this chapter we take a look at the interrelated topics of fads, fashion, technology, and trends as influences on popular culture. In many ways, popular culture thrives upon these social phenomena in order to stay relevant and connect with large audiences.

Fads are cultural phenomena that seem to arise spontaneously and engulf large groups of people. They are collectively followed, usually for brief periods of time, primarily because they are deemed to be popular—few people want to be left out of these exciting mass movements. Disco dancing in the 1970s, for instance, was a fad that seemed to sweep the nation almost overnight (albeit with some vociferous opponents making themselves known and refusing to don leisure suits and boogie on down), with such related phenomena as the film *Saturday Night Fever* (which made a legend of its star, John Travolta), and the accompanying multimillion dollar soundtrack, which rejuvenated the careers of the Bee Gees. In fact, it's impossible to think about the 1970s without referencing disco. (Or, for that matter, another '70s sensation, the Pet Rock.)

But most fads, including disco, eventually fade away, as people grow tired of them, start to question their relevance, or—as is more likely the case—start to look for a newer fad that will supplant them. In the first story below, we look at such a temporary fad, "the Ice Bucket Challenge," which dominated social media throughout the summer of 2014 but then quickly disappeared as it, if you'll pardon the expression, ran out of steam.

Some fads, though, seem to survive for the long haul, including words that begin as slang (often to confuse those who aren't hip to the events they refer to) and end up entering the language. We look at several recent such additions to the dictionary and their connection to popular culture.

Many people claim that one trend from the early 2000s that has survived into the present is a culture of shamelessness. This is perhaps a furthering of what Christopher Lasch referred to in 1979 (as the disco craze was beginning to fade) as "A Culture of Narcissism." More and more people seem to be "letting it all hang out," releasing photos and sharing information on social media of the most highly personal nature, seemingly without caring if they becomes public knowledge. Whether this is a temporary fad or a permanent state of affairs remains to be seen.

But surely, connected with this trend toward shamelessness is the obsession most of us have with so-called smart phones (ironically, one of the last things most of us do anymore is use our phones to talk on—how twentieth century that is!). But are smart phones actually making us smarter, or might they be causing us to do dumb things such as walk into walls or get hit by cars?

And speaking of cars, a new fad looming on the horizon—something we've been expecting for decades now—are cars that can drive themselves. Perhaps soon enough we can get into our cars and text on our phones without any fear, since we don't need to watch the road—the car will do the driving for us. Whether or not that is something to anticipate with joy or with fear will be explored in the final story of this chapter.

Ultimately, the authors hope that they can help start a new fad of finding lessons in popular culture, but whether we'll be the new Disco Daddies remains to be seen.

The Ice Bucket Challenge

In the summer of 2014 a strange and unexpected popular fad spread across the United States and a number of other nations (including Australia, Brazil, Canada, Germany, India, Mexico, New Zealand, the Philippines, and the United Kingdom). It consisted of people purposely pouring buckets of freezing cold ice water over their own heads (or having someone else do it to them). While it was a very hot summer, pouring a bucket of ice cold water over one's head would seem a drastic thing to do to avoid the heat, if only because the extreme temperature change might shock the body. But as Shakespeare would say, there was method to their madness. For the purpose of such public dousing was not to keep cool but rather to raise money for charity, in this case to help eradicate amyotrophic lateral sclerosis (Lou Gehrig's disease).

How did such an action connect with charity? Simple. Before the dousing, the person involved publicly challenged, via social media, three other people to do the same thing. The challenged persons then had twenty-four hours to complete the challenge (publicly and recorded, of course) or donate one hundred dollars to the ALS Association. Most people heeded the challenge *and* donated to the ALS Association.

With regard to how the challenge originated, *Sports Illustrated* reported that "[i]t has become a phenomenon thanks in part to Pete Frates, a former Boston College baseball captain who has become a minor league celebrity since being diagnosed with ALS in 2012. Frates' involvement led to a flurry of donations to the ALS Association, which received more than $1 million [that week]; the same time period last year brought in less than $10,000" (*Sports Illustrated* 2014:18).

The Ice Bucket Challenge soon crossed over from a minor fad to a genuine popular culture sensation, as first hundreds and then thousands of individuals rose to the challenge. It received a firestorm of attention on Facebook and other social media outlets, and was wildly reported on TV new shows and sports radio programs, by late night comedians, and on countless Internet blogs. A host of major celebrities made it a point to take the challenge, including Gwyneth Paltrow, Charlie Sheen, Justin Timberlake, Lady Gaga, Tom Cruise, Simon Cowell, and, of course, Kim Kardashian. Very quickly it was easier to name celebrities who *hadn't* taken the challenge than those who had. Even former president George W. Bush rose to the occasion.

Not everyone was eager to join in, however. Radio personality and shock jock Howard Stern, for one, was against it from the beginning, even warning that it might ultimately lead to someone's death. (And, in fact, Tony Grider, a forty-one-year-old firefighter in Campbellsville, Kentucky, did die in August 2014 from injuries sustained after getting too close to a power line when he had the water dumped on him.) But, after being challenged by both Jennifer Aniston and Matt Lauer, he relented, then nominated Barbara Walters, Mark Consuelos (husband of Kelly Ripa), and the late Casey Kasem.

It was a good-natured feelgood event, and an excellent example of the so-called bandwagon effect. This is a phenomenon whereby people feel compelled to join a crowd simply so that they won't be left out. The term originated in nineteenth-century American political campaigns, when bands were featured in parades supporting political candidates. Spectators were encouraged to climb aboard the bandwagon as a show of support. This relates to the psychology of collective behavior; as Aristotle said long ago, we are social animals, and it is difficult not to feel compelled to join a crowd, and unpleasant to stand alone. In the case of the Ice Bucket Challenge, not only was it a fun—if temporarily freezing—experience, it was a chance to bond with others, as well as promote oneself on social networks. And best of all, it was for a worthy cause. It was estimated that by the end of the summer more than $115 million dollars had been raised for the ALS Association, an astonishing sum of money (Worland 2014). Who could possibly raise any objections? Surely, eradicating Lou Gehrig's Disease is a cause everyone can get behind.

However, like many previous fads, this one could not be sustained. As quickly as it arose, by summer's end it began to fade. Not only did it rapidly seem to become "yesterday's news," there were those who started to raise serious objections to both the fad and the cause for which it stood. Emily Steel of the *New York Times*, for instance, wrote: "There has been a backlash. Some have criticized the campaign for so-called slacktivism, where people will click and post online for social causes with little actual impact on the cause. 'There are a lot of things wrong with the Ice Bucket Challenge, but the most annoying is that it's basically narcissism masked as altruism,' said Arielle Pardes, a writer for *Vice*. On Slate, Will Oremus urged people to take the 'no ice bucket challenge' and just donate the money" (Steel 2014).

Some celebrities not only refused to take the Ice Bucket Challenge, they criticized its purpose. Pamela Anderson, for instance, a noted animal rights advocate, protested that the search for an ALS cure funded by the Ice Bucket Challenge would involve research on rodents and primates. " 'Mice had holes drilled into their skulls, were inflicted with crippling illnesses, and were forced to run on an inclined treadmill until they collapsed from exhaustion. Monkeys had chemicals injected into their brains and backs and were later killed and dissected,' the former *Baywatch* star writes on Facebook, citing recent tests reportedly funded by the group" (Nudd 2014). Defenders of the ALS Association objected to these claims, and cynics couldn't help but point out that by refusing to take the challenge, Anderson was able to get her name in the news. But her protest did mark a shift in perspective, and more negative reports began to appear.

Various Twitter accounts started to claim that, for every dollar raised, only twenty-seven cents went for research, the rest going to pay for the salaries of the board of directors of the organization. This too was immediately disputed, but such accusations began to take away the feelgood sheen of the fad. Dan Diamond of *Forbes* magazine defended the ALS Association. "Unlike certain celebrity fundraising phenomenons," he writes, "the donations are headed to a good place: The ALS Association is a highly respected charity. Charity Navigator gives the association four stars—its best rating—and the organization is trying to be transparent and proactive" (Diamond 2014). But he also observed that the amount of money was raised so quickly and unexpectedly that ALS Association representatives couldn't state how exactly they were planning on allocating it. And, more to the point, a practical question began to be asked by more and more people. "Several observers have raised an important, if queasy question: Will all these donations really make a difference?" (Diamond 2014).

Furthermore, there were many who, while desiring that Lou Gehrig's Disease be eradicated, wondered if the Ice Bucket Challenge might be taking away donations from other worthy causes. Could there be a finite capacity for generosity? How many individuals, to avoid being shamed, gave a donation to the ALS Association that they might have otherwise given to a charity they were more committed to?

The Ice Bucket Challenge has a *Seinfeld* connection, too. It is similar to another worthy cause that people were encouraged to support in a public way, namely, by wearing a red ribbon to indicate support for research to eradicate AIDS. In "The Sponge" (episode #119), Kramer enters a race that is raising money for AIDS research. While he is a wholehearted supporter of the cause, he doesn't feel that he needs to wear the ribbon to prove it. The following scene ensues as he arrives to sign up for the race:

KRAMER (to organizer at desk): Uh, Cosmo Kramer?

ORGANIZER: Uh . . . okay, you're checked in. Here's your AIDS ribbon.

KRAMER: Uh, no thanks.

ORGANIZER: You don't want to wear an AIDS ribbon?

KRAMER: No.

ORGANIZER: But you have to wear an AIDS ribbon.

KRAMER: I have to?

ORGANIZER: Yes.

KRAMER: See, that's why I don't want to.

ORGANIZER: But everyone wears the ribbon. You must wear the ribbon!

KRAMER: You know what you are? You're a ribbon bully. (He walks away.)

ORGANIZER: Hey you! Come back here! Come back here and put this on!

Kramer proudly joins the race, but is soon accosted by those around him, who demand to know why he isn't wearing the ribbon. When they ask him if he's against AIDS he insists that he is, but he just doesn't want to wear the ribbon. Eventually he's taken into an alley to receive some "Ribbon Justice" and the crowd demands he put it on or face the consequences. "This is America!" he yells. "I don't have to wear anything I don't want to wear!"

So there you have it. While most people love to be part of something that does great good, no one likes to be bullied. Sometimes you just don't want to wear the ribbon, or have a bucket of ice cold water poured over your head, no matter how worthy the cause might be. Like many fads, the Ice Bucket Challenge ultimately "kicked the bucket."

Lesson Learned: Sometimes you have to pour icy water on a trend no matter how well-intended.

Language, Slang, and New Words: Influenced by Popular Culture, Technology, and the Internet

Language refers to a set of abstract symbols that can be strung together in an infinite number of ways to express ideas and thoughts. Some languages, such as English, are nearly universally spoken, while others, as in the case of Native American dialects, are localized and specific to their own cultures. Interestingly, within a given society regional variations of the language may be so distinct and unique that one has to wonder if it really is the same language. If you have traveled in the United States and visited different areas, you have no doubt witnessed what is called "regional linguistics."

Language tells us a great deal about what is important and relevant to a culture. As technology alters the world in which we live, it changes our perceptions, thoughts, and symbolic interpretations of the world (Krug 2005). Developments in technology, as well as changing cultural values, lead to the creation of new words, which helps to explain why hundreds of new terms are added to dictionaries every year (Pyle 2000). With the growing importance of the Internet, our culture has been further altered by technology. Katy Steinmetz (2014) states that most of the new words added to the 2014 *Merriam-Webster Dictionary* "speaks to some intersection of pop culture, technology, and the Internet."

If we use the total number of words spoken by a culture as a measurement of changing cultural values and norms and technologies, we might conclude that English-speaking people participate in a dynamic world. According to the Global Language Monitor (GLM), the English language, as of June 2009, contained more than one million words. GLM estimates that the millionth English word, "Web 2.0," was added to the language on June 10, 2009. Web 2.0 refers to the second, more social generation of the Internet (Shaer 2009). Like most new words, it is the product of popular culture. Words that are no longer used in popular culture tend to be viewed as outdated and as a result generally elicit a negative response. For example, most people today would chuckle at outdated 1960s slang words such as "bookin'" (going really fast), "fab" (fabulous), or "fuzz" (police).

The use of slang words, like regional linguistics, further complicates effective communication between people who speak the same language. Members of a particular social class or profession often modify formal words into a form of language known as "slang." Slang refers to the informal usage in vocabulary and idiom that is characteristically more metaphysical, playful, elliptical, vivid, and ephemeral than ordinary language (*Dictionary.com* 2014). Slang fits the needs of the people who use words repeatedly in ways that are a little off centered from their dictionary definition. For example, the dictionary defines the word *fuzz* as a fluffy or frizzy mass of hair or fiber, or the outer layer of a peach, or when used as an adjective (*fuzzy*) it means unclear—our memory is kind of fuzzy on the details. But in the 1960s, it was common among certain subcultural groups to refer to the police as "the fuzz." In the 1970s, if someone said, "I need some hits off that bong so that I can get wasted," you knew that person was a pot smoker. Thus, the use of slang words helps to identify people as belonging to certain social groups.

Every year, and sometimes more than once a year, new words are added to well-established dictionaries such as *Merriam-Webster* and *The Oxford English Dictionary*, to reflect changes and advancements in technology and popular culture. Not everyone is happy that popular culture has such an influence on the dictionary. As described in *The Guardian* (2014), while adding new words may represent an excellent publicity opportunity for dictionaries, it is also "a form of gentle social-media trolling, provoking sticklers to charge that lexicographers who allow 'twerk' into the dictionary are literally destroying the English language as we know it." Whether the source is popular culture (e.g., "twerking" and "bromance"), technology ("connectile dysfunction," defined as the inability to establish a connection, especially with a cell phone), or new world realities ("IED," the abbreviation for "improvised explosive device" of the kind that has become common in the wars in Iraq and Afghanistan), dictionaries will continue to add new words for as long as humans exist and use language to communicate.

In May 2014, 150 new words were added to *Merriam-Webster Dictionary*. Listed below is a sampling:

- Auto-Tune (2003)—to adjust or alter (a recording of a voice) with software or other audio-editing software, especially to correct sung notes that are out of tune.

- Baby bump (2003)—the enlarged abdomen of a pregnant woman.

- Catfish (2012)—a person who sets up a false social networking profile for deceptive purposes.

- Crowdfunding (2006)—the practice of soliciting financial contributions from a large number of people especially from the online community.

- Digital divide (1996)—the economic, educational, and social inequalities between those who have computers and online access and those who do not.

- E-waste (2004)—waste consisting of discarded electronic products (such as computers, televisions, and cell phones).

- Fracking (1953)—the injection of fluid containing chemicals into shale beds at high pressure in order to free up petroleum resources (such as oil or natural gas).

- Hashtag (2008)—a word or phrase preceded by the symbol # that clarifies or categorizes the accompanying text (such as a tweet).

- Selfie (2002)—an image of oneself taken by oneself using a digital camera especially for posting on social networks.

- Social networking (1998)—the creation and maintenance of personal and business relationships especially online.

- Spoiler alert (1994)—a reviewer's warning that a plot spoiler is about to be revealed.

- Turducken (1982)—a boneless chicken stuffed into a boneless duck stuffed into a boneless turkey.

- Tweep (2008)—a person who uses the Twitter online message service to send and receive tweets.

- Unfriend (2003)—to remove (someone) from a list of designated friends on a person's social networking Web site. (Source: *Merriam-Webster Dictionary* 2014; Steinmetz 2014.)

Notice that, following each word, we added a date. This is the date that the word was first documented in use. That words may exist long before they reach the dictionary is a testament to the fact that dictionaries respond as much to what has already occurred in society as to what is occurring. Language, slang, and new words are indeed the products of, and influenced by, popular culture, technology, and the Internet.

Lesson Learned: If people use words often enough, they will eventually find their way into the dictionary. And once that happens, the concept of "a rose by any other name would smell as sweet" will not be applicable to such words as "Catfish"—for a catfish is not always a catfish.

The Culture of Shamelessness Meets the Culture of Public Shaming: If Everything Is Shameless, Can There Be Shameful Behavior?

In his book *Shameful Behaviors* (2008), Tim Delaney puts forth the notion that there is a growing culture of shamelessness in both the United States and many other nations in the world. This idea is supported by his contention that people are engaging in behaviors today that in the past would have provoked embarrassment, shame, and a diminished sense of self. In the past, people would have done almost anything to avoid shameful behavior, for fear of private or public ridicule. Instead, today the culture of shamelessness brings with it an attitude of not caring what others think of one's behavior no matter how shameful it may be. In addition, people are willing to shame themselves publicly, especially via social networking sites.

While self-shaming is not the focus of this short story, we should elaborate a little bit on its meaning. People who shame themselves are, in effect, challenging the cultural norms that dictate a certain level of self-control, self-regard, and attempts to avoid being ridiculed by others. Self-shamers freely engage in behaviors that should cause shame, but they do not experience the expected shame. Getting drunk in public and making a fool of oneself is an example of self-shaming. Sure, it seems like fun at the time to be the "life of the party," but the reality is, people are laughing at you and not with you. Other examples of self-shaming include singing karaoke at a crowded bar even though the singer completely lacks singing ability; dressing in a ridiculous Halloween costume; dressing inappropriately in social situations that dictate certain attire (e.g., wearing tattered clothes at a formal gathering); exposing oneself in public; participating in a "reality TV show" and dramatizing every mundane aspect of life as if it's a big deal; admitting to watching a reality show that focuses on self-shamers; and a willingness to do almost anything for "fifteen minutes of fame." Self-shamers argue that such activities give them thrills and that the attention they receive, good or bad, outweighs the value of acting appropriately for one's age or attaining full acceptability within the greater community.

Self-shaming sometimes overlaps with public shaming. For example, Johnny Knoxville and his crew enjoy making fools of themselves (self-shaming) on film and showing the footage via *Jackass* movies for the world to see, often resulting in ridicule by mainstream society (public shaming). Then again, in this culture of shamelessness, many people find humor in the *Jackass* antics, and Knoxville is laughing (whether in private or public) all the way to the bank.

Public shaming is not a new phenomenon in society. In reality, public shamings have a long history in nearly all cultures. During America's colonial era, people were modest, hard workers who went about their business without drawing attention to themselves. They had a strong sense of community and adhered to prevailing codes of conduct dictated by the moral climate of the times. Puritan society also encouraged "traditional" family values whereby men and women married—and stayed married until "death do they part"—and raised a family together. Although some people have cheated on their significant others throughout history, such indiscretions were generally kept a secret, to avoid public humiliation. This was the case in the Puritan days of the seventeenth century, as described by Nathaniel Hawthorne in *The Scarlet Letter* (1850) in which Hester Prynne is publicly shamed and forced to wear a patch of fabric in the shape of an "A," signifying that she has committed adultery. This scarlet letter indicated that she had sinned, for which her punishment included public ridicule and scorn. Imagine if, in contemporary society, everyone who ever cheated on their significant other had to wear a scarlet "A"; there wouldn't be enough people to represent the "good and moral" community to condemn the act of adultery committed by others.

So we have moved on, and cheating on a lover, while still very painful to the victim, is so commonplace today that society looks for other forms of behavior to condemn publicly. Public shaming as a form of judicial punishment for criminals has come into vogue in recent years. Judicial public shamings are an example of formal shaming. A formal shaming is one conducted by an organization, social institution, or the government. Formal shamings may be conducted in public (e.g., a thief is ordered by a judge to stand in front of the store he or she stole from wearing a sign that states, "I am a thief and I stole from this store") or a slightly more private arena (e.g., a court martial). In the case of a court martial, proceedings are conducted behind closed doors, but there have been high-profile cases that involve public disclosure of the identity of the defendant.

First, they represent attempts by those in authority to enforce group norms or law. When punishments are served in public (e.g., wearing a sandwich board that reads, "I stole from this store"), attention is drawn to specific instances of norm violations. The second purpose of a formal shaming is to send the message to would-be norm violators that certain behaviors are unacceptable. It is hoped that, if made to serve a punishment in public view, the violator will feel shame and his or her sense of self will be negatively impacted.

The judicial system, the formal institution designed to interpret laws and assign punishment for those who break them, has increasingly opted to employ public forms of shaming as punishment, rather than incarceration. In the past decade or so, there have been numerous cases of judicially imposed public shamings. Here are a few examples:

- A drug user in Florida had to place an ad in the local newspaper that read, "I purchased drugs with my two kids in the car" (*USA Today* 2004).

- A man who stole mail in California was made to wear a sandwich board outside a post office that read, "I stole mail. This is my punishment." After he complained that his punishment was cruel and unusual, the Ninth U.S. Circuit Court of Appeals upheld the shaming and ruled that the unusual sentence was for the purpose of rehabilitation and not just a form of public humiliation (Egeiko 2004).

- In 2005, Tennessee passed legislation requiring convicted drunken drivers to wear orange vests reading, "I am a Drunk Driver" while performing twenty-four hours of roadside trash pickup (Redhage 2006).

- In September 2006, police broke up a toga party at the University of Massachusetts. James Connolly, the host of the party, was charged with underage drinking, making too much noise, and having a keg without a license. As part of his punishment, Connolly was made to wear his toga in front of the police station (*The Economist* 2006).

- In November 2006, the *Tennessee Tribune*, an African American weekly newspaper, took a page from *The Scarlet Letter*, by affixing an "A"—for apathy—onto the names of individuals who didn't cast ballots during the August primary in an attempt to "shame them into voting" on Election Day.

- In Cleveland, Judge Pinkey Carr sentenced a man named Richard Dameron, who had threatened a police officer, to stand outside a police station wearing a sign that read, "I apologize to Officer Simone and all police officers for being an idiot calling 911 threatening to kill you. I'm sorry and it will never happen again." To give the sentence a personal touch, the judge hand-lettered the sign herself (*Sentencing Law and Policy* 2013).

- In 2012, a different Cleveland judge gave a woman the choice of going to jail or spending two days standing on a street corner with a sign reading, "Only an idiot would drive on the sidewalk to avoid a school bus." The woman chose to hold the sign (Morrison 2014).

- The judicial system has been assisted by the media in a variety of ways in their effort to shame perpetrators of crime, including covering shameful punishments. For example, when people are arrested and charged with a criminal offense, the name, age, and address, of the accused is likely to appear in the local newspaper, on radio news, and/or on the televised news. However, seldom is the same coverage provided if the charges are dropped against the accused.

- The judicial system also utilizes social networking sites to shame people who have broken the law. Listed below are a few examples:

- In Boston, men who miss child support payments have found their photos displayed on subways and buses. In London, parents who fail to pay child support are "named and shamed" on the Internet (Shipman 2006).

- Police in Evesham Township, a small town in New Jersey, shame drunk drivers by posted their photos on the town's Facebook page (Dugdale 2010).

Although the present-day United States is as about as far removed from colonial American values and norms as we can possibly be, we are as willing today as we were then to shame people publicly. So far, we have merely taken a glimpse into the world of formal public shamings. However, thanks to the Internet and the desire of others to serve as unelected, self-appointed judges, there are plenty of people outside the judicial ranks that are publicly shaming others. These types of shamings are known as informal shamings.

Informal shamings are attempts to alter the behaviors of a targeted person or persons who have violated key social norms or expected codes of conduct. Informal shamings contain elements of moral indignation, shame, and stigmatization, in an attempt to compromise the victim's self-identity and self-esteem. Informal shamings may be conducted by anyone in any given social environment. For example, a lover scorned may choose a public setting to voice displeasure toward a cheater's actions. Calling someone a liar in front of a group of people and then backing up the claim with corroborating evidence is another type of informal shaming that anyone is capable of performing. But, it is the willingness to shame others in cyberspace that best represents an example of informal public shaming. Again, it is informal in that the shamers have no official capacity to call someone out, that is, they are not representatives of a social institution or a government official.

Surfing the Internet yields any number of examples of people who take pleasure in publicly shaming others. For example, in 2010, Matt Binder started a Twitter blog (@MattBinder) titled "Public Shaming." On his website, Binder retweets people's complaints about welfare, food stamps, etc. and then follows up with previous tweets of theirs that makes them look hypocritical/dumb/etc. If the target of his public shaming deletes the offending tweet, Binder posts a screenshot that he has taken, just in case he feels the need to re-shame.

There are times when friends shame each other, either purposely or inadvertently, by posting compromising or unflattering photos online. It is common to be "tagged" on Facebook in a photo taken with a group of friends, and there are times when those being tagged prefer that the photo not be posted, or at the very least that the tag line be removed. (It should be noted that a tagged person can notify Facebook that they have not given their permission to be tagged and request that the tag be removed.)

We have reached the point of absurdity when it comes to public shaming, as a number of people now post shaming photos of their pets online. We found one site (Mashable 2014) that included such photos and corresponding messages as:

- "While you clean my tank, I will see-saw on your Power Bar then pee when you come to stop me"—a sign next to pet turtle.

- "I chew up headphone cables when people are not around"—a sign next to a pet parrot.

- "I crawl into empty slippers and take a poop so that whoever puts it on gets poop on their toes"—a sign next to a pet gerbil (we believe it to be a gerbil; we are not really sure what kind of pet this was).

- "I humped and peed on this dog without asking for his permission"—a sign next to a hamster and dog lying next to each other on a bed.

- The culture of shamelessness has merged with the culture of publicly shaming others. Is it any wonder so many people have a hard time finding the dividing line between proper and improper behavior in given situations?

Lesson Learned: Shame me once, shame on you; shame me twice and I'll get even with you on social network sites.

Smart Phones:
Making Us Look Smarter and Dumber at the Same Time

When observing the behaviors of others one cannot help but notice that many people act as though they are beyond the point of enjoying the benefits that a smart phone can bring; they not only appear lost without their phones, but some folks appear to be addicted to them. As college professors, the authors of this book have witnessed students who act as though they physically cannot survive without having their smart phones in hand "at the ready" to respond to an electronic stimulus, or to send their own words of wisdom out into the cyberworld. One cannot help but wonder, Why do people love their smart phones so much?

In simplistic terms, cellular phones whose features included such options as Web connection and apps (software application programs designed to connect directly to specific programs) are generically referred to as "smart phones." These mobile devices serve many functions and are useful in many situations. For instance, they are great for emergencies, such as when your car breaks down or you are stranded someplace and need to contact someone for help. Secondly, smart phones, can in fact, make us look smart, as any bit of information regarding nearly any topic can be found online via a smart phone. Do you need the answer to a trivial question being discussed between friends? Look it up on your smart phone. Thirdly, the more apps you have on your phone, the more specific and condensed bits of information are available to you. People tend to add apps that are important to them, some examples include the ESPN app, flashlight and compass apps, and so on (the options are nearly limitless). Travelers looking for the nearest gas station or restaurant can use an app to find it. Other benefits of smart phones include: opportunities to learn new things; a variety of better ways to communicate with other people (such as texting, calling, e-mailing, or tweeting); the ease of using several apps at the same time; global coverage; taking and posting photos; and many more.

The authors are reminded of the 1996 "The Bizarro Jerry" *Seinfeld* episode (referenced earlier in chapter 7), where George demonstrates that he knows where all the best public bathrooms are in Manhattan. After being advised by George not to use a particular bathroom, Kramer asks,

"George, why couldn't I use the bathroom in that store?" George replies, "Kramer, trust me, this is the best bathroom in midtown." Kramer starts to ask, "Wha . . . ??" when Jerry interrupts and states, "He *knows*." George says, "[Anyway], on the left—exquisite marble. High ceilings. And a flush like a jet engine." (He imitates the sound). "Ha ha!" As anyone who is often away from home or their place of work can attest, finding a safe, clean bathroom can be difficult. Some people, like George Costanza, have made a point of documenting all the best places. But smart phones weren't around when *Seinfeld* was on the air, so a public bathroom location app (or any other app) was unimaginable. We have often thought this would be a good idea and were fully willing to give George credit for it. Well, there is such an app now.

We have cited some positive aspects of smart phones. But smart phones have the ability to make people look dumb, or at the least, to foster dumb habits in people. As Steve Tobak (2013) explains, "Technology is smart. It's people who are dumb." Let's first look at motorists. Drivers, if you use your smart phone GPS for driving directions be sure to use some common sense too. When the app informs you to "turn right now," make sure there is, in fact, a road to turn onto, and don't drive into a pond, field, or office building. While there not many reports of drivers who blindly follow GPS directions that are obviously wrong, a significant number of drivers do use their smart phones while behind the wheel of a moving automobile, risking their lives and the lives of others. Such drivers fall under the category of "distracted drivers." There's a reason that driving while talking or texting is illegal in many jurisdictions—it costs more lives and property damage than drunk driving. According to the National Highway Traffic Safety Administration, driving a vehicle while texting is six times more dangerous than driving while intoxicated (Hanson 2014). The National Highway Traffic Safety Administration reported that in 2010 driver distraction was the cause of 18 percent of all fatal crashes, and the Virginia Tech Transportation Institute found that text messaging while driving creates a crash risk twenty-three times greater than driving while not distracted (FCC 2014).

Think about this the next time you see someone driving their car and operating their phone with their hand(s); picture that smart phone as a bottle of Jack Daniels (or any bottle of liquor). If you drove next to someone drinking from a bottle of Jack, you would be concerned. You should be just as concerned if you drive next to someone who is driving and using his or her smart phone. Such behavior is the farthest thing from being smart.

Let's turn our attention to pedestrians and their dumb and/or annoying habits. Some people are so caught up by their tiny smart screens that they are oblivious to the world around them. They literally run into other people, walk into traffic, or step directly into mud puddles. And this phenomenon is not restricted to Americans and their obsession with smart phones. Many people around the world are just as detached from the real environment outside their smart screen worlds. A photo recently reposted on Facebook showed a sign in a European office building that warned: "IN CASE OF FIRE: Please leave the building before posting it on social media." The warning included the universal symbol for fire beside a stick person holding a bright red phone that was ringing. If we have reached the point where people have to be warned to leave a burning building before posting a message about it, humanity may be in trouble.

Pedestrians engrossed by their digital smart phone worlds multitask by walking while texting, a chore more challenging than chewing gum and walking at the same time. Add some inclement weather, such as a snow storm or a windy rainstorm, and the challenge increases. Often, pedestrians on their smart phones bump into, or almost bump into, each other. In larger cities we can add into the mix bicycle messengers on their smart phones weaving through traffic consisting of cars and pedestrians. Pedestrians walking with smart phones have become the new menace in New York City, at least from one reporter's perspective. "Smart phones have replaced tourists as New York pedestrians' biggest headache. We used to disdain people from out of town when they wandered slowly on the sidewalks, looking skyward at tall buildings and muttering as we walked by with purpose. Now we're the menace" (Bauder 2011). So we've gone from people looking up at tall buildings in large cities to people looking down at their smart phones, not only in these same large cities but also in small cities, suburbs, and rural areas. Everywhere, it seems, people are looking down and walking right past everyone else.

Face-to-face conversations with friends, let alone with strangers or service people, are being replaced by "screen sniffing"—keeping one's nose buried in the screen. When pedestrians keep their heads buried in their smart devices they not only miss out on face-to-face conversations and run the risk of stepping into traffic, they make themselves vulnerable to smart phone theft. "About 3.1 million Americans had their phones stolen last year [2013], according to a just-released national survey by Consumer Reports. That's nearly double the magazine's estimate of 1.6 million mobile phones stolen during 2012" (Weisbaum 2014). Thieves appropriate smart phones in a variety of manners, but one of the most daring, and potentially most dangerous, scenarios involves the smart phone being ripped from the hands of the pedestrian who has not been paying attention to the world outside his or her screen space. (There are plenty of videos on YouTube showing examples of pedestrians having their smart phones ripped from their hands.) Thieves like to steal smart phones because it's usually easy to swipe an item from a distracted person and a phone can be turned into quick cash in the underground market. In reaction to the smart phone theft increase, the development of a "kill switch" is encouraged by users. The kill switch, essentially, makes a stolen smart phone useless.

Lesson Learned: Don't be a dumb-ass screen sniffer; look up and pay attention.

What's Trending? Everything from the Latest Clothing Fashions to Greeting Styles

Popular culture has a great deal of influence over many aspects of life, including the types of clothes that are fashionable, styles of dance, and greeting patterns. With the advent of advanced communications technology the latest social trends spread to the masses quicker than ever before. The masses are even told what the latest trends are, via the social networking cues "What's trending," or "Trending now." Facebook and Twitter are among the social network sites that utilize a "trending" prompt to indicate topics or articles that generate the biggest buzz detected among posts and tweets. (AOL uses the term *buzz worthy* to highlight "the latest news that matters to you.") Treading topics include a wide variety of subjects including the latest news in sports, entertainment, and world events. If you happen to make a post on one of the current hot topics, you will see a message indicating that your topic is trending.

In the world of fashions and fads, there is always something trending. Many people feel the need to keep up with the latest trends and fashions while others are less inclined to follow along with them. How we react to trending events has a great deal to do with the socialization process. The socialization process defines developmental changes brought about as a result of individuals interacting with other people. Socialization is a lifelong process that begins in infancy with messages received and lessons taught by parents, guardians, and other significant family members and extends through one's lifetime, reflecting the influence of close friends and peer groups, education (teachers and schools), employers, the government, and the mass media. Mass media today, and their influence on the public's perception of such matters as fads, fashions, and trends in contemporary society, play a greater role in socialization than at any other time in human history.

Mass media have influenced a number of aspects of popular culture, including the latest dance styles. In 2013, pop star Miley Cyrus caused a stir at the televised annual Video Music Awards show, held in Brooklyn. Dressed in provocative attire, Miley sang and danced on stage with Robin Thicke. At one point, she shook her booty in Thicke's face, to the delight, or chagrin (depending on your taste in dance), of those in the theater and the viewing audience at home. The dance of choice for Cyrus was "twerking." According to the *Urban Dictionary* (2014b), twerking involves the act of moving/shaking one's butt/ass/buns/buttocks in circular, up-and-down and side-to-side motions. It is considered a slutty dance, derived from strip clubs. At the present time, twerking is a popular culture dance style that is trending and seems to resurface at some of the oddest social events. For example, twerking made an appearance in front of the Seattle Symphony at Benaroya Hall when Seattle's Sir Mix-A-Lot joined the symphony orchestra on stage and performed "Baby Got Back" during a June 2014 performance. Sir Mix-A-Lot invited women to join him on stage, and about two dozen enthusiastically did so (Wyatt 2014). Images of the women twerking were disturbing enough but to see the Seattle Symphony performing behind them was quite the scene. As reported in *Entertainment Weekly* (2014), "We're not sure who's more desperate."

In the long run, twerking is likely to remain popular with only a limited number of people in specific social environments such as strip clubs and weddings or when someone has had too much to drink.

Twerking is not the only popular dance style to have trended recently and then quickly all but disappeared. Consider, for example, the "Gangnam style" dance craze made popular by South Korean musician Psy. Released in 2012 as a video song and dance routine, "Gangnam Style" became the first YouTube video to attract a billion views (Gruber 2012). By mid-2014, the number had surpassed two billion. The song has a catchy beat and it is fun to listen to, but like most fads, although popular for a time, it was destined to disappear. The phrase "Gangnam Style" refers to a lifestyle associated with the Gangnam District of Seoul, a trendy and hip upper-class area that Psy studied while he was trying to come up with an idea for his sixth studio album. And although the dance reflects a distinct, trendy style, the video is filled with odd characters that are anything but representative of high culture.

In the mid-1990s, Los del Rio released an album, *A mi me gusta* (1994), with a breakout song titled "Macarena" about a woman with the same name. "Macarena" became a huge hit when released internationally (in 1995 in the United States) because of the dance it inspired. It was nearly impossible to escape this dance craze in the 1990s; nearly every wedding reception, as well as numerous other social events at which people danced. featured this catchy beat song. For the most part, dancing the Macarena is now a thing of the past; it certainly is no longer trending.

In another example, in 1962 Little Eva released a popular song (it went to Number One in the charts) with a dance to go along with it, "The Loco-motion." The term *loco-motion* means movement that starts after all movement has ceased, and is usually associated with driving an automobile. As a dance, the loco-motion resembles a version of the samba in which everyone places their hands on the person in front of them and the whole line "chugs" along to resemble a train, thus causing locomotion (*Urban Dictionary* 2014c). The lyrics of the song encourage people to join and do the loco-motion, and they describe the dance moves:

> Everybody's doin' a brand new dance now
> C'mon baby do the loco-motion . . .
> [Skip ahead in the lyrics]
> You gotta swing your hips now
> Come on baby, jump up, hmmm jump back
> [Skip ahead in the lyrics]
> Now that you can do it
> Let's make a chain now
> Chug-a-chug-a motion like a railway train now . . .
> Move around the floor in a loco-motion . . .
> Do it holding hands if you got the notion . . .

From their youth, the authors remember the Grand Funk Railroad version of "The Loco-motion," and like Little Eva's, their version of this catchy tune reached Number One on the U.S charts. To add to the distinction of the song, in 1988 Australian singer Kylie Minogue's version of "The Loco-motion" climbed to Number Three on the *Billboard* charts. "The Loco-motion," while not a popular dance style today, remains the only song to reach *Billboard*'s Top Five in three different decades. It is also ranked #359 in *Rolling Stone* magazine's "Top 500 Greatest Songs of All Time" (*Rolling Stone Music* 2014).

It seems as though nearly every decade, starting in the 1920s, has had dance styles that were trendy:

- 1920s: Charleston, Black Bottom
- 1930s: Jitterbug, Lindy Hop
- 1950s: Waltz, Fox Trot, Rhumba
- 1960s: Twist, Monkey, Mashed Potatoes
- 1970s: Hustle, Bus Stop
- 1980s: Break dancing, Pop dancing
- 1990s: Rave, Hip Hop, Macarena

And while all of these dance styles still exist, they no longer carry the buzz they once held. Rest assured, somewhere out there, someone is creating the next dance trend.

Clothing styles are subject to the same trending forces as dance; that is to say, there will always be something that is currently in style and countless of examples of styles that are now out of vogue in the fashion world and yet remain identified with at least some portion of the population. Styles of shoes, pants, dresses, and handbags are prime examples of "must have" items for the fashion conscious, and yet, before long, anything in style now will soon be out of style. What's trending now is merchandise from Michael Kors (men's and women's apparel and handbags); coach bags; gladiator-style shoes; yoga pants; floral print and bold print pants; tribal design clothes; Patagonia (designer outdoor apparel); Longchamps (hand bags); Vineyard Vines (preppy men's and women's clothing; and Jack Rogers shoes.

Listed below is a sampling of popular fashions by decade, starting with the 1900s (Fact Monster 2014):

- 1900s: tight collars; lots of lace; corsets for tiny waists; skirts with trains; narrow shoes for both men and women; feathered hats for women; upswept hair

- 1910s: trench coats; narrow "hobble" skirts; draping blouses for women; Middle Eastern patterns; V-neck sweaters; bows on shoes and sneakers (worn only for sports)

- 1920s: cloches (close-fitting hats) for women; baggy flannel trousers for men; long, wide coats; costume jewelry;

drop-waist "flapper" dresses; T-strap shoes; sheer stockings; bobbed hair

- 1930s: patterned sweaters; one piece wool bathing suits; long, flowing gowns; sandals; fox fur collars; hats worn at an angle; shoulder pads; wide overcoats for men; rectangular wristwatches

- 1940s: rolled-up blue jeans; narrow "drainpipe" trousers; matching skirts and sweaters; halter tops for women; sleek evening dresses; the pageboy haircut for women; the "pompadour" hairstyle; baggy pull-on sweaters; Hawaiian shirts for men

- 1950s: white T-shirts; motorcycle jackets; black leotards; Bermuda shorts; pedal pushers (calf-length pants); poodle skirts; ballerina flats; full skirts with petticoats; strapless evening gowns; ponytails

- 1960s: bell bottoms; miniskirts; T-shirts with messages; pale lipstick and dark eyeliner; longer hair for men and women; the beehive hairdo; white vinyl "go-go" boots; peace signs; paisley and Indian prints

- 1970s: Western boots; lots of lip gloss and blush; T-shirts with logos; denim; legwarmers; pants suits (women had almost always worn dresses until the 1970s); earthtones; leotards with wraparound skirts; the Afro hairstyle

- 1980s: frills on collars and hems; bright vests and shirts for men; "power suits" with big shoulder pads; fingerless lace gloves; long fake-pearl necklaces; tunics over leggings; big hair with lots of mousse; Levi's 501s; ankle socks; penny loafers

- 1990s: designer athletic shoes; designer sneakers; puffy jackets (the decade when *Seinfeld* introduced the puffy shirt); chain wallets; baggy pants; colored hair; bare midriffs; hooded sweatshirts; tattoos

- 2000s: low-rise pants; blazers; graphic T-shirts; bare midriffs; tank tops; bell-bottom jeans; skinny jeans

As a side note, the authors would like to share their observations about men wearing shorts. As children of the 1960s, the authors have witnessed a change in attitudes toward men wearing shorts. For starters, in the 1960s men almost never wore shorts (with rare exceptions such as British soldiers, who wore Bermuda shorts as part of their tropical uniforms), whether in public or private. The only men, or boys, who wore shorts, were athletes. Beginning in the 1970s, the fitness movement altered the public's perception of boys and men in shorts, as a new industry arose to meet the needs of runners. Older males often questioned the manhood of those males who wore shorts, which weren't considered sufficiently manly attire. By the 1990s, however, it was commonplace for boys and men to wear shorts, not only in private, but in public and at social gatherings. There was an expected backlash again by older folks who felt it wrong for men to wear shorts when dining in restaurants. The authors attended a conference in St. Petersburg, Russia, in June 1999 during the "White Nights," a period of about two weeks surrounding the Summer Solstice when the sun, essentially, does not set. It was very hot during this trip. As prudence would dictate, we brought shorts with us, but we quickly realized that Russian men did not wear shorts and that, as it had been several decades earlier in the United States, any adult male wearing shorts was looked down upon as less than a "manly" man. Today, Russian males, especially younger ones, do wear shorts. And American men, like men in most Western societies, wear shorts all the time, sometimes year-round. Still, you are not likely to see men from Islamic nations wearing shorts, as it doesn't fit their image of masculinity. Maybe if the Taliban started to wear shorts they would mellow out.

The socialization process and the mass media also influence the manner in which people greet one another. Male-female greetings are generally predicated on social norms that dictate certain behaviors in certain situations. For example, a handshake is appropriate in a professional setting or a situation in which the male and female do not know each other well (or at all) and are being introduced for the first time. On the other hand, a hug and/or kiss might be exchanged if the relationship between the man and woman is close. Women seem to have a wider range of acceptable behaviors when greeting other women. Once again, if the relationship is a professional one, or a first meeting, shaking hands would be most appropriate. Females who are close, or relatively close, to one another are likely to hug and kiss during their greeting. Nearly any form of affection is acceptable and not likely to raise eyebrows among onlookers. Males greeting one another, however, are held to trickier standards. Once again, in a professional setting or upon early introduction to one another, a handshake exhibits the proper degree of decorum. But what about men who know each other and are friends, how should they greet one another? With a simple handshake, as tradition would dictate (the handclasp accompanied with a brisk up-and-down pump), or a hug? And, if a hug is okay, is a kiss okay?

The acceptability of men hugging and kissing one another in greeting varies depending upon cultural norms. In some European nations, it is quite common for men to give one another a peck on the cheek as part of a greeting. Historically, in the United States, men simply have shaken hands; they do not kiss and they do not hug. The male reluctance to hug other men generally has had something to do with upbringing/socialization, by which straight men have been taught that if they hugged other men they might be viewed as gay. As a result, until recently most American men did not hug each other. What changed? There are a number of factors that have led to men feeling more comfortable greeting one another with physical expressions other than a mechanical, nonemotional handshake. The changing role of women has led to a corresponding change in the role of men in society; for example, while women have become more assertive and aggressive, men have learned to embrace their feminine, nurturing sides. One of the leading social institutions that has helped men to tap into their emotions is sports. After a big play or victory, athletes often hug each other, or pat each other on the back or butt. Male fans of sport, seeing this, have decided that it is okay to hug or high-five a fellow fan in reaction to a big play or victory, even if that other fan is another man.

In the past decade or so, men have started to greet one another with variations of hugs and complicated handshakes that have special meaning to them rather than simply businesslike handshakes. When males greet each other now, we have to stop and think: Do I fist-bump this person, or should I engage in a series of ritualistic behaviors that have become the trending handshake? There are times when one male will stick out his fist and the other male his hand for a shake, and this foulup is then followed by the predictable reversal by each of the original attempt at a hand greeting.

The male hug represents a whole new level of social engagement. Once again, a male approaches another male whom he knows, but he has to ascertain the situation, and ask himself "Do I know this person well enough to go in for the hug, or should I just lay back and be cool and shake hands" (while he sticks out a fist for a bump)? Chances are, if you are not sure if a hug is appropriate or not, it's better not to do it. But even if the male relationship is deemed close enough to warrant a hug, what type of hug should be engaged?

The male friendship hug is generally understood today as a sign of true friendship—we are close enough to hug it out—and it says that you are extroverted, demonstrative person (Mollod and Tesauro 2002). There are three main categories of male hugs that guys generally utilize (Brown 2005):

- The Hip Hop: Males greet with handshakes of various styles, pull themselves toward each other, then bump their inside shoulders.

- The Half-and-Half: Males greet each other with standard handshakes, then reach around each other's shoulders with their left arms and pat each other's backs.

- The Bear: Males dispense with the handshake altogether. When they greet, the left arm drapes over the partner's right shoulder; the right arm goes around the waist. The left hand usually pats the friend's back.

The male hug is trending. It is okay for males that know each other to hug during a greeting; the times have changed. Then again, the times haven't changed all that much. We suggest that American society is not quite ready for males who are friends to greet one another with a hug and a kiss on the lips. If you want to try to start that trend, here's your chance.

Lesson Learned: We all have our own boundaries despite what might be trending.

Look Ma, No Hands on the Wheel: Driverless Cars

An interesting thing to do when considering popular culture fads and trends is to look back at what people years earlier had once thought the future (now the present) would be like. One of the most popular TV cartoons of the early 1960s was *The Jetsons*, which ran in prime time on ABC from 1962 to 1963. A space-age counterpart to the then-popular *Flintstones*, it was set in the year 2062, one hundred years in the future. One of the things almost everyone who watched the show still remembers is the fact that the Jetsons got from place to place in flying cars. Surely, most viewers at the time must have thought, we won't have to wait until 2062 for such vehicles. The way technology is expanding, flying cars should be prevalent by 2012 at the latest.

Well, 2012 came and went, with no such vehicles in evidence. As Jon Orlin of TechCrunch.com lamented at the time, "As we enter 2012, shouldn't we all be traveling around in flying cars by now?" (Orlin 2012).

While flying cars might not be here yet, perhaps the next best thing is now among us: cars that drive themselves. We've already had automobiles that can parallel park without any human intervention. For those of us who dreaded having to prove we could perform this maneuver in order to get a driver's license, this is a godsend. The next step, of course, would be to let the car do all the driving. It's taking cruise control to its ultimate conclusion.

Just how might such driverless automobiles work? Justin Pritchard has an explanation. He writes: "Instead of the standard controls, the prototypes would have buttons to begin and end the drive. Passengers would set a destination. The car would then make turns and react to other vehicles and pedestrians based on computer programs that predict what others might do, and data from sensors including radar and cameras that read in real time what other objects are actually doing" (Pritchard 2014).

General Motors has announced that a genuine semiautonomous self-driving system will be available as an option for its 2017 Cadillac, which will be on sale in mid-2016. Other automakers are making similar promises. However, before such innovations can occur, the United States government will have to come up with safety standards and other regulations. The Department of Transportation's National Highway Traffic Safety Administration is already working on the details, but one should never underestimate the ability of government agencies to take much longer to do something than anyone could possibly anticipate.

One can immediately imagine the benefits of such technology. *Sports Illustrated* points out, for instance, that it can allow people otherwise incapacitated to once again get behind the wheel of a car: "Sam Schmidt never broke 100 mph but probably ran the greatest laps of his life at Indy last week. The former Indy racer (he won the 1999 Vegas.com 500) and current co-owner of the Schmidt Peterson Indy team was left a quadriplegic by a practice accident in 2000. But the SAM car (semiautonomous motorcar), a modified Corvette, allowed him to get back behind the wheel. 'I thought I'd never be able to race again, but this vehicle made it possible,' said Schmidt after his prequalifying jaunt. 'It was the most normal I have felt in nearly 15 years'" (*Sports Illustrated* 2014A).

But a very practical question arises. What if an accident occurs? Who should—will—be held accountable? As Alexa Liautaud of *Bloomberg News* points out, "While the idea of robo-cars whisking us off to our destinations may sound like science fiction, the technology exists and is largely ready for the real world. What's harder to determine is the risk associated with the emergence of these vehicles. If automakers effectively take the wheel, that puts them in the firing line for liability suits stemming from accidents. The vehicles would also be exposed to threats from hackers who could hijack cars and potentially control them remotely, turning them into mules for criminal purposes or even using them as weapons" (Liautaud 2014). That is indeed a very frightening scenario. Would you really want to be behind the wheel of a car that could be suddenly "carjacked" by someone using a remote control?

Once again, popular culture helps us to think about the implications of new technology and the impact it has on our personal freedom. For, returning again to George Jetson, it's well to remember his plaintive plea for help in the closing credits of the show. While walking his dog Astro on a moving sidewalk (a technological innovation we all became used to many years ago, at least in airports), he is suddenly caught up in the mechanism when Astro bolts to chase a cat. As he whirls around and around, with no control and no way to stop, George yells out his famous catchphrase to his wife: "Jane, Stop This Crazy Thing!" As we finally climb into our new driverless cars, we might well be echoing George's cry.

Lesson Learned: Do we really want to have our cars do the driving for us?

10

Celebrities, Comedians, and Other Ambassadors of Popular Culture

We have coined the term "ambassadors of popular culture" to signify those individuals who influence or represent popular culture. Throughout this book we have discussed representatives from every genre of popular culture, and their contributions to pop culture are relatively straightforward. But there are times when some individuals influence popular culture because of their unique style of individualism. Individualism may seem like a contradictory source of popular culture, as it's at the opposite end of the spectrum from collectivism, or mass participation in cultural events. But, individualism encourages the development and expression of each person's unique character and personality, and by affording individuals the opportunity to express themselves it opens the way for them to influence others. These individuals that help to shape popular culture are referred to here as ambassadors of popular culture and include celebrities, comedians, documentarians (documentarists), spokespersons, and opinion leaders.

Students of popular culture cannot avoid the fact that much of what it purveys often can be ridiculous, shallow, specious, and downright offensive. So it's not surprising that some of the most effective ambassadors of popular culture are professional comedians, who are geared toward looking at the world around them with a jaundiced eye, and who often see patterns of significance in some of the most unlikely sources, such as airline food, laundromats, movie theaters, and other mundane things we otherwise take for granted. It's not surprising, perhaps, that Jerry Seinfeld—a true master of observation—has been referred to so many times in this book, since his comedy routines, like the eponymous show he starred in, are vast repositories of data for anyone trying to make sense of popular culture in the late twentieth/early twenty-first centuries.

In this chapter, we will look at how some public figures (including documentary filmmakers, spokespersons, and opinion makers) not only capture the reality around them but also help shape perceptions; how three comedians—from "The Old Philosopher" (1950s) to George Carlin (1960s–2000s) up to the present-day Dave Chappelle—not only provide entertainment to the masses but also, through their trenchant observations and inspired wordplay have added to our language and made us see things a different way; how the ubiquitous Kim Kardashian, and her amazing "assets," has established a new standard for drawing attention and can rightly be called "The Queen of All Media"; and the ways in which it is becoming increasingly difficult to separate parody from actual news—today's most effective news presenters are often professional comedians, and that's no laughing matter.

Ambassadors of Popular Culture:
Attempting to Influence Others

There are a number of individuals who serve as ambassadors of popular culture. (We are using the term *ambassador* as a catchall to describe those that help to shape, or who report on, popular culture. In this manner, the authors might be viewed as ambassadors of popular culture, too.) Within his or her specific role, each of these ambassadors attempts to influence the opinion and/or shape the perceptions of others (primarily among the general public). In this short story, we will take a quick look at documentarians, spokespersons, and opinion leaders (we will look at comedians and celebrities later in the chapter).

The first category of popular culture ambassadors we will look at are documentary filmmakers, known as documentarians or documentarists. There is no shortage of documentaries in existence. Some are historically based and, every attempt has been made to assure their accuracy. There are, for example, documentaries on wars (*The Hornet's Nest, The Red Army*), famous historic figures (*Mandela, Jonestown: The Life and Death of the Peoples Temple*), historic events (*H. H. Holmes: America's First Serial Killer*), and musical groups (*Pearl Jam Twenty*). While it could be argued that documentaries that chronicle historic events attempt to influence opinions, they do not attempt purposely to shape views on popular culture, at least not in the same manner as documentaries with a point of view.

Documentaries with a point of view represent attempts by ambassadors of popular culture to persuade people to change their beliefs regarding a specific topic. Michael Moore's *Sicko*, a documentary about the highly profitable American health care industry and both its negative effect on Americans and positive effect on other nations, is an example of documentary with a point of view, as Moore, clearly, presents only those stories that support his views on the health care system. In 2012, PBS comprised a list of the twenty-five greatest documentaries of all time. Listed below are PBS's (2012) top ten documentaries with a point of view:

1. *Grey Gardens* (1975)

2. *Paris Is Burning* (1990)

3. *Hoop Dreams* (1994)

4. *The Thin Blue Line* (1988)

5. *Bowling for Columbine* (2002)

6. *Harlan County, USA* (1976)

7. *The Times of Harvey Milk* (1984)

8. *Grizzly Man* (2005)

9. *Roger & Me* (1989)

10. *Exit Through the Gift Shop* (2010)

Any "top list" will have its detractors—people who dispute the rankings—and documentaries with a point of view are certain to cause controversy. The documentarists' points of view may be challenged, but in all likelihood, they will have their supporters as well. Michael Moore, for example, has millions of followers and probably an equal number of detractors. Born April 23, 1954, Michael Francis Moore is an American documentarist, author, social critic, and political activist. He has directed and produced *Fahrenheit 9/11* (2004), the highest grossing documentary of all time (Waxman 2004; Berokowitz 2012), *Bowling for Columbine* (2002), and *Sicko* (2007), among his most famous films.

Perhaps the prototype of pop culture documentaries is *Super Size Me* (2004), by American documentarist Morgan Spurlock. In the film,

Spurlock documents his thirty-day adventure of eating nothing but McDonald's fast food from February 1 to March 2, 2003. During that time, Spurlock ate at a McDonald's restaurant three times a day, and he claims to have consumed an average of 20.92 mega joules, or five thousand calories (the equivalent of more than nine Big Macs), per day. As a result, he states that he gained 24.5 pounds. The film examines both his emotional and physical well-being over the course of his experiment, which he undertook in response to news ofthe obesity epidemic in the United States. Since its release, *Super Size Me* has been frequently cited in support of efforts to promote awareness of nutrition issues, and it was nominated for an Academy Award for Best Documentary Feature and won the 2004 Sundance Film Festival Award for "Documentary Directing" and the 2004 Writers Guild of America for "Best Documentary."

While it seems plausible that someone might gain weight and have their health compromised by eating nothing but McDonald's meals three times a day for a month, Amanda Mannen (2013), for one, has argued that no one has been able to duplicate Spurlock's experiment. Mannen also finds it hard to believe that Spurlock could possibly have eaten five thousand calories per day even if he had included dessert with every meal. The authors have not tried to duplicate Spurlock's experiment, so we cannot say for sure whether Mannen is accurate in her contention that *Super Size Me* is essentially a fake, but we do know that many athletes consume well over five thousand calories a day, so why not Spurlock? It has been well documented that Olympic swimmer Michael Phelps consumes more than twelve thousand calories per day while he's in training (*Fox News* 2008; Barclay 2012).

The next ambassadors of popular culture we will look at are spokespersons. Many corporate spokespersons are paid professionals who publicly represent organizations and businesses and attempt to paint their employers in a favorable light. They are essentially mouthpieces broadcasting the company line, and are unlikely to come from or influence popular culture. The spokespersons that fill the role of ambassadors of popular culture, on the other hand, are people such as celebrities and athletes, whose fame has been achieved in fields other than the businesses or industries they advocate. They are desirable as spokespersons for commercial advertising or marketing purposes because they are recognizable representatives of popular culture whose reputations have inspired public trust.

We are unceasingly bombarded by commercial messages via every form of media and technology, and it is the hope of advertisers that we consumers will purchase the products endorsed by spokespersons. While it is doubtful that a lifetime Pepsi drinker will switch to Coke just because of a spokesperson, some products that target specific groups of customers (unlike soda companies, which attempt to attract the masses) may benefit from certain spokespersons. For example, a gun manufacturer would have benefited more from hiring Charlton Heston as its spokesperson than from choosing Michael Moore. Whether by accident or design, some spokespersons are chosen so perfectly that they become synonymous with the products they are endorsing. With this in mind, we would like to share with you the ten highest ranking celebrities (and the products they are best known for pitching) on *Daily Finance's* (2014) list of the top twenty-five spokespersons of all time:

1. Bill Cosby (Jello)

2. Karl Malden (American Express)

3. John Houseman (Smith Barney)

4. Michael Jordan (Nike; Wheaties)

5. Orson Welles (Paul Masson Wines)

6. Florence Henderson (Wesson Oil)

7. Kathy Lee Gifford (Carnival Cruise Lines)

8. Jane Russell (Playtex)

9. O. J. Simpson (Hertz)

10. Wilford Brimley (Liberty)

It should be pointed out that in the wake of the allegations of impropriety made against Bill Cosby at the end of 2014, he lost nearly all of his major endorsement deals and his syndicated TV shows were taken off the air. (The Cosby matter had not been settled at the time of this writing.) Likewise, O. J. Simpson's association with Hertz ended with the notoriety that surrounded him following the murders of his wife Nicole and her friend Ronald Goldman in 1994, although many still recall the old lady in the Hertz commercials yelling, "Go, O. J., Go!" as he raced through an airport.

While the celebrities listed above are known as spokespersons for widely accepted products, there are some celebrities that seem willing to pitch just about any product. Listed below are the top ten celebrities who "will pretty much endorse anything," according to Donna Kaufman (2014), and their "weirdest" endorsements:

1. Heidi Klum (Yoghurt Gums Candy)

2. Jay-Z (The Duracell Powermat, a wireless phone-charging system)

3. Eva Longoria (SHEBA cat food)

4. Michael Phelps (Head & Shoulders)

5. Kaley Cuoco (Proactiv)

6. Kim Kardashian (Sketchers Shape-Ups)

7. Paula Deen (Schmitt Furniture)

8. Mike "The Situation" Sorrentino (Teen abstinence)

9. Brooke Shields (Latisse eyelash enhancer)

10. David Beckham (Meiji Almond Crust chocolates)

Our third category of popular culture ambassadors consists of opinion leaders, individuals who serve as role models for, and exert a great deal of influence over, others. Opinion leaders are not leaders in the usual sense, because they do not head formal organizations, but they are active leaders in the media. As leaders in the media, opinion leaders interpret the meaning of media messages by others and generate their own media messages. The influence of opinion leaders is derived from their informal status as highly informed, respected, or connected individuals (Watts and Dodds 2007).

Katz and Lazarsfeld (1955) state that opinion leaders, who are few in number, act as intermediaries between the mass media and the masses. Opinion leaders—such as citizens who frequently write letters to the editor of the local newspaper, newspaper editors, talking heads, and so on—have a way of influencing the beliefs and attitudes of others in such a manner that they stimulate behavioral change among their followers. A testimonial from an opinion leader can have great influence over others, especially if they testify for, or against, someone, or something, that is in their area of expertise (e.g., a medical doctor who is an opinion leader and expresses an endorsement in favor of, or refuses to endorse, a pharmaceutical company's new product).

Lesson Learned: In their own small way, the authors serve as ambassadors of popular culture, and they are happy to do so.

Words of Wisdom from "The Old Philosopher"

"L-L-L-Lift your head up *high* and take a walk in the sun with that dignity and stick-to-it-iveness and you *show* the world, you *show* them where to get off, you'll never give up, never give up, never give up"—[two drumbeats]—"that SHIP!"

—Eddie Lawrence (1919–2014)

The world of philosophy lost a true giant with the death of Eddie Lawrence in 2014. Never heard of him? Perhaps you knew him better by his moniker "The Old Philosopher." He was not a professor, or a learned scholar, or a writer of arcane tomes. He was a professional comedian, but he deserves to be remembered nonetheless for his contributions to human wisdom, since his performances made one think. Or as Friedrich Nietzsche put it, "Who among you can laugh and be elevated at the same time?"

In truth, Mr. Lawrence was not very old at the time he initiated his routine in the mid-1950s, being then in his spry thirties. But by taking on the persona of a wise and wizened codger, he was in line with the views of another great modern thinker, Andy Warhol, who began dying his hair gray at any early age, writing that "I decided to go gray so nobody would know how old I was and I would look younger to them than how old they thought I was" (Warhol 1975:23). Good advice indeed for someone like Mr. Lawrence, who made it well into his nineties and who performed as "the Old Philosopher" for more than a half-century.

It was the comedian Steve Allen, along with his friend Bob Thiele, who helped to launch Lawrence's career on a big scale. He produced Lawrence's concept album *The Old Philosopher* in 1956. In September of that year, a single from the album rose to the Billboard Top 40 chart. The timing was perfect, as it was one of the seminal works in what has come to be known as the Golden Age of Comedy Records, which included the works of such other comedic artists as Lenny Bruce, Tom Lehrer, Jonathan Winters, Nichols and May, Bob Newhart, Lord Buckley, and Shelley Berman, all demonstrating a cerebral type of humor that wore well even after several listenings.

The Old Philosopher routine soon swept the airwaves with its instantly recognizable wavery voice, at first reciting a litany of woes, with "Beautiful Dreamer" playing in the background:

Hiya, folks.

Ya say ya lost your job today?

Ya say it's 4 a.m. and your kids ain't come home from school yet?

Ya say your wife went out for a corned beef sandwich last week and the corned beef sandwich came back but she didn't?

Ya say your furniture is out all over the sidewalk 'cause ya can't pay the rent, and ya got chapped lips and paper cuts and your feets all swollen up and blistered from pounding the pavement looking for work?

Is that what's troubling you, fellow?

The tone then changes to one of great excitement and motivation. With the music now switched abruptly to "The Stars and Stripes Forever," he intones the stirring words quoted at the beginning of this section, importuning his listener to never give up that ship (or any other item of transportation for that matter).

Later albums followed, including *7 Characters in Search of Eddie Lawrence*, *The Old Philosopher Strikes Back*, *The Side-Splitting Personality of Eddie Lawrence*, *The Merry Old Philosopher*, and *The Kingdom of Eddie Lawrence*. In addition, The Old Philosopher became a regular guest on *The Tonight Show with Johnny Carson*, as well as many other television and radio programs, and his routines later became a staple on *The Doctor Demento Show*. Lawrence also had a prolific career as a cartoon voice actor and a commercial announcer, including a memorable promotion for Harry Nilsson's 1974 album *Pussy Cats*, produced by John Lennon:

Hiya, Pussycat.

Ya say ya opened up a bicycle wash and the first six customers drowned?

And they picked you up at the Wax Museum for trying to score with Marie Antoinette?

Is that what's got ya down, Pussycat?

Well rise up, and get yourself Harry Nilsson's new album *Pussycats*, produced by John Lennon. Meow and purr!

In addition to his work as The Old Philosopher, Lawrence had a varied career in other fields—as a playwright and lyricist (*Kelly*); movie actor (*The Night They Raided Minsky's* and *The Wild Party*); actor on Broadway (*Bells are Ringing*) and Off-Broadway (*The Threepenny Opera*) and TV (*Sergeant Bilko*), as well as countless voiceovers over the years. *Kelly*, by the way, which is about a con man in the 1880s Bowery who tries to jump off the Brooklyn Bridge for profit, has the distinction of being one of the greatest Broadway flops of all time, due to circumstances outside of Mr. Lawrence's control. But its cast album remains a favorite of many, and one of the songs he co-wrote for it, "I'll Never Go There Anymore" became a popular standard.

Lawrence was also an accomplished painter, having studied in Paris with the great Fernand Léger in the late 1940s/early 1950s after his tour of duty in World War II (for which he was granted a Bronze Star) ended. All in all, he was a true modern-day Renaissance Man, and someone who most definitely earned the sobriquet of "Old Philosopher."

Lawrence worked steadily over the years, but since, unlike many comedians, he didn't like to travel, he never achieved the fame that many of his contemporaries did in Las Vegas or through other public appearances. He primarily focused on producing long-playing albums, which allowed him to better address his absurdist word portraits. Perhaps the artists closest to his style are the late Brother Theodore and "Professor" Irwin Corey (who at the time of this writing is still alive and performing his syntactically challenged lectures at the age of 101, clad in his trademark tail coat and sneakers). It's not surprising that these performers made appearances on the New York City–based late night talk shows hosted by David Letterman and Conan O'Brien well into the 1990s, since the hosts clearly appreciated the wry and ironic wordplay of these unique artists.

While best known for his "Never Give Up the Ship" exhortations, another of The Old Philosopher's timeless routines consisted of advice about people one should definitely, as he says with great urgency, "Stay Far Away From." Here are a few examples:

Guys who always have change for a dollar.

People who put the garbage out in their underwear.

Dictators who paint clowns.

Anyone who'd moon a nudist.

Authorities on sex with dandruff on their shoulders.

People who say you remind them of someone but they can't remember *who*.

Anyone who'd start a Martin Bormann Fan Club.

People who swear Jack the Ripper was innocent.

Anyone who'd challenge an owl to a staring contest.

Fifty-five-year-old scoutmasters with rimless glasses.

Anyone who recites 'Invictus' during the sex act.

Watch 'em carefully—these are all people to stay far away from.

That's good advice indeed. But it's not just *what* he says, it's *how* he says it. Lawrence's routines deserve to be heard, and thankfully, the modern miracle of YouTube has made his work available in ways previously unimaginable. For those of you who are not familiar with him, please give The Old Philosopher a listen, and for those of you who *do* recall him, please revisit his work. It's guaranteed to bring back pleasant memories, as well as inspire you to keep on keeping on.

Eddie Lawrence was a pioneer in aural comedy, and philosophers in particular, who pride themselves on knowing the uses and abuses of language, should be aware of him. His pearls of wisdom remain as true today as when he first uttered them, such as this gem: "She who kisses the walrus must gargle frequently." And here's another one, which deserves a place in *Bartlett's Familiar Quotations*: "Remember, the whole world's a stage—and there's still no work." The Old Philosopher was the Eternal Optimist par excellence, whose motto could have been: "Never give up, never give up, never give up—that quip."

Lesson Learned: Many of us prefer humor that makes us laugh and think.

George Carlin and the Meaning of Human Life—Plastics!

Certainly one of the unique individuals in comedy, or any genre of popular culture for that matter, is George Carlin (1937–2008). Carlin, to put it generously, has a unique way of looking at the world, and one thing about him that's certain is that he was unlikely ever to receive any endorsement deals from pro-environmental organizations. Carlin's stand-up routines have included many slams against the pro-environmental movement. He has said such things as, "I'm tired of fucking Earth Day, I'm tired of these self-righteous environmentalists, these white bourgeois liberals who think the only thing wrong with this country is there aren't enough bicycle paths" (*Gospel of Reason* 2014). Carlin has also referred to the efforts of people trying to "save the planet" as a waste of their time. In his 1992 album, *Jammin' in New York*, Carlin says, "The planet is fine. The PEOPLE are fucked!. . . . The planet is fine. Compared to people, the planet is doing great. . . . The planet has been here for five and half billion years [and] somehow *we're* a threat?" Carlin is correct, the earth has survived five extinctions of nearly all species on the planet. The sixth mass extinction period, which is occurring now, will likely wipe out humans but the earth will be just fine. What humans should concentrate on is how to save their own species, as the planet will survive whatever humans do to themselves. And humans are doing a great number of things to speed along the sixth mass extinction process. One of the contributing factors to the sixth mass extinction that Carlin spoke of is the creation and continued use of plastics.

Carlin's classic plastics routine (available for viewing via any Internet search by typing "Carlin and plastics") includes the notion that the human creation of plastics may represent one of our crowning achievements, as plastics are used in a variety of ways and a wide variety of consumer and industrial products. Thus, from one perspective the creation of plastics has led to many human conveniences. Conversely, environmentalists are alarmed with the continued use of plastics because plastics are not bio-degradable and are responsible for degrading environments where many living species, including humans, reside. But Carlin counters the concerns of environmentalists with his notion that planet Earth will simply incorporate plastic into a new paradigm: the earth plus plastic.

Carlin states that the earth does not share our prejudice toward plastics because the ingredients for plastic come *from* the earth. Carlin goes on to suggest that the earth probably sees plastic as just another one of its children. Environmentalists would not describe plastics as a child of the earth, but rather as an invasive species. Carlin goes on to suggest (kid-dingly, one would hope) that because the earth did not create plastics, or did not know how to create plastic, it allowed humans to spawn. In other words, the planet needed humans in order to make plastic, and therefore, with this flawed logic comes the answer to humanity's age-old egocentric philosophical question: "Why are we here?" Why? Because of plastics.

There you have it, from Carlin's perspective, the reason humans are on this planet is to create plastic. Now that we have plastics, what are we going to do with them? What is the planet going to do with all the plastic items we have created that pollute the landscape, waterways, and landfills? Because humans created plastics and are the only species to benefit from them, it would be a good idea for humans to, at the very least, create biodegradable plastics. Otherwise, we risk someday being so overrun with plastics that are environment will suffer direly.

Recently, a number of companies have introduced biodegradable products made from conventional plastics to the public. However, Brenda Platt, coordinator of the Sustainable Plastics Project, has found that most products advertised as consisting of biodegradable plastic are not, in fact, biodegradable. Platt (2013) has concluded that, much like the "Going Green" movement, promoting bridgeable plastics is often simply a publicity stunt in an attempt by companies to lure environmentally conscious people into purchasing their products. Platt (2013) states that the following companies' claims about their products are unsubstantiated:

- The "Biogreen Bottle" a supposedly reusable water bottle made from LDPE, is advertised as being "100% biodegradable, recyclable and reusable," and, "BioGreen Plastic will fully biodegrade in home compost heaps, commercial composting operations, buried in the ground, buried in landfills, tilled into the soil, having been littered, etc."

- Aquamantra claims that ENSO single use water bottles made from PET are the "World's first 100% biodegradable recyclable bottle" and that "PET bottles will biodegrade in anaerobic and aerobic/compostable environments."

- Perf Go Green claims that their biodegradable plastic bags, including lawn and leaf bags, "will completely degrade and break down returning to nature in as little as 12–24 months—leaving absolutely NO residue or harmful toxins."

- GP Plastics Corporation claims that its PolyGreen polyethylene plastic newspaper bags as "100% oxo-biodegradable because they are conventional plastics with an additive, they are compatible with the existing recycle stream."

- Plant Green Bottle Corporation claims that its Revert oxo-degradable PET plastic bottles are "compatible with all current recycling streams."

- Discover claims that its PVC credit card is "biodegradable" and that it is completely "safely absorbed when exposed to landfill conditions."

Platt (2013) explains that truly biodegradable plastics are plastics that can decompose into carbon dioxide, methane, water, inorganic compounds, or biomass via microbial assimilation. Furthermore, the decomposition process must be measured by standardized tests established by individual nations' standards; in the United States, this would be the American Society of Testing Materials (ASTM), which has established definitions and parameters regarding what constitutes biodegradability in various disposal environments (ASTM International 2013). The products described above by Platt did not pass the ASTM test.

George Carlin joked that plastics represent the very reason humans exist on this planet. Most people view plastics as a modern convenience that has made everyday life simpler. Environmentalists warn that the creation of plastics and our inability to find a way to effectively incorporate biodegradable plastics into consumer use represent a contributing factor toward a compromised environment.

Lesson Learned: While humans are biodegradable, plastics are not.

What's the Deal with Dave Chappelle? He Walked Away from $40 Million?

It's difficult to become well known and financially successful as a comedian. George Carlin managed to do it, but there are thousands of aspiring comedians looking for that big break that may never come. And while the NBC show *Last Comic Standing* provides publicity for dozens of comedians, with the winner earning $250,000 and an NBC pilot development deal, there are only so many opportunities to become successful in this industry. Logic would seem to dictate then, that when a lucrative deal is offered, one should accept it and honor it. Logic is one word that generally does not appear when describing Dave Chappelle and his unprecedented decision to walk away a TV deal with Comedy Central worth more than $40 million.

So who is Dave Chappelle? Born on August 24, 1973, in Washington, D.C., Chappelle started his stand-up career in nightclubs at fourteen, while he was still in high school at the Duke Ellington School of the Arts, where he studied theatre arts (IMDb 2014b). After time spent paying his dues, Chappelle landed a deal with Comedy Central in 2003 to star in his own weekly sketch comedy show called *Chappelle's Show*. The show was hugely successful and helped Comedy Central gain widespread recognition. With two seasons under his belt and a deal that would earn him more than $50 million on the table, Chappelle did the unthinkable during the early part of the third season (2005): he walked away from his highly successful show and, as he told David Letterman on the *Late Show* (June 10, 2014), from the $40 million remaining on his contract. He disappeared for a few months, and no one at Comedy Central knew how to contact him. In 2005, he had expressed that he was unhappy with the direction of his show and cited Comedy Central network officials as the cause of the problem. In June 2014, Chappelle returned to renew his stand-up career, at Radio City Music Hall.

With a net worth of more than $800 million, Jerry Seinfeld is, arguably, the most successful comedian of all time (*Celebrity Networth* 2014). Born in Brooklyn on April 29, 1954, Seinfeld paid his dues working clubs for fifteen years trying to grind out a career as a comedian. (One of the authors, Tim Delaney, likes to remind people that Seinfeld spent one year at SUNY Oswego as a student before returning home to NYC in order to pursue his stand-up career.)

Seinfeld's big break came when he paired up with Larry David to create one of the funniest and most successful TV shows ever, *Seinfeld* (see chapter 3 for a more extensive discussion). A show about four friends in Manhattan, it aired for nine seasons (1989–1998). When the show ended its run, it was still the top show on TV and just as funny as ever. Seinfeld and David wanted to finish on top, so they decided not to have a tenth season. They certainly did not need the money, since, as *Forbes* magazine (2013) reports, "Thanks to the show's lucrative licensing deals, repeats of the 180-episode sitcom have generated over $3 billion in syndication royalties."

Although it is nearly two decades since the show last aired original episodes, Jerry Seinfeld continues to remain the top earning comedian. In 2013, he topped the *Forbes* (2013b) list of highest paid comedians, grossing an estimated $27 million from more than seventy tour dates over the previous twelve months (June 2012–June 2013) and earning an additional $5 million from other sources, for a total of $32 million. One of the other projects is his funny Internet show—*Comedians in Cars Getting Coffee*—a very funny show, free to the public, that, as the title of the show implies, involves Jerry driving one of his many vintage cars to a comedian friend's home and then driving to a coffee shop to have coffee while they shoot the breeze. The show is funny and light and generally makes you feel good to watch and learn the stories behind the successful comedians of our era.

The male-dominated list of the top ten earners among comedians collectively earned more than $201 million during the twelve-month *Forbes* accounting period. Listed below are the top ten highest earning comedians for 2013, according to *Forbes* (2013b):

1. Jerry Seinfeld: $32 million

2. Terry Fator (winner of *America's Got Talent's* 2007, five-year contract with Las Vegas's Mirage Hotel worth $100 million): $24 million

3. Russell Peters (Canadian-born, world successful stand-up): $21 million

4. Jeff Dunham (puppet ventriloquist): $19 million

5. Louis C. K. (stand-up, own TV show): $16 million

6. Kevin Hart (stand-up, movie star): $14 million

7. Larry the Cable Guy (stand-up, popular "redneck" character): $13 million

8. George Lopez (stand-up, actor, author): $12 million

9 (tie). Daniel Tosh (stand-up, own show): $11 million

9 (tie). Gabriel Iglesias (stand-up, TV and movie appearances): $11 million

While most comedians will never find their way on the *Forbes* top ten list of earners, there are far more ways for them to earn money today than decades ago. Comedians have learned to expand their stand-up routines for YouTube videos, some find online shows, and others have found their way into TV and movies. Few people, comedians or not, will ever be able to afford one of the world's largest collections of Porsches (forty-six total, including a rare Porsche 959 valued at $700,000), as Jerry Seinfeld does, but apparently a number of people can make a great deal of money making other people laugh.

Lesson Learned: If someone is willing to pay you $40 million for a couple of years of work doing what you already love to do, take it.

Being Famous for Being Famous in the Age of Social Media: Kim Kardashian's Book of Selfies

One characteristic of the current social media era is that so many people from outside of the traditional focal points of popular culture are afforded the opportunity to become famous. There are celebrities, such as Kim Kardashian, who are, seemingly, famous just because they are famous. This almost sounds like a new version of "Which came first, the chicken or the egg?," but now it's "Were you famous before you were famous, or just famous because you *are* famous?" The "famous for being famous" celebrities are often mocked by comedians, talk show hosts, and the masses, and yet, they have managed to become famous, regardless. Generally, the famous for being famous types of celebrities disappear quickly. Remember Paris Hilton? Nobody does.

As stated above, the social media era affords individuals opportunities to become famous. Creating, or becoming famous for utilizing, social trends is one way to become famous. This reality helps to explain, in part, people's fascination with taking "selfies." In 2013, Oxford Dictionaries, the online home of *The Oxford English Dictionary*, announced that its new word for the year was "selfie." Oxford Dictionaries proudly announced that "[t]he decision was unanimous this year, with little if any argument. This is a little unusual. Normally there will be some good-natured debate as one person might champion their particular choice over someone else's. But this time, everyone seemed to be in agreement almost from the start" (OxfordDictionaries.com 2013). Adding a new word to the *Oxford English Dictionary* is no small matter—it means that it has become so well established and so commonly used that it warrants this "immortalization" as a bona fide addition to the English language. And for a particular term to be deemed "Word of the Year" is a great honor indeed, let alone to be chosen unanimously by such an august body of experts. Just what exactly does this new word signify?

The Oxford Dictionaries folks define "selfie" as: "A photograph that one has taken of oneself, typically one taken with a smartphone or webcam and shared via social media: *occasional selfies are acceptable, but posting a new picture of yourself every day isn't necessary*" (OxfordDictionaries.com 2013).

Of course, people have been taking photographs of themselves since the invention of photography in the late 1880s, so in one sense there is nothing new about this. But the selfie is indeed a modern popular culture phenomenon, thanks to the common use of smart phones and their connection with social media of all sorts. As a means of showing where one is at all times, and as a way of capturing oneself in all manner of situations (including, for a growing number of shameless individuals, in various states of undress or no clothes at all), the selfie has taken over with a vengeance. Growing concern has been expressed over the appropriateness or inappropriateness of people taking photos of themselves at arm's length whenever a celebrity or near celebrity approaches, or during sporting events or solemn occasions. There are even websites devoted to selfies taken at funerals, which would seem to be the height of disrespect or bad taste—until, that is, President Barack Obama took a famous selfie on his cell phone with English prime minister David Cameron and Danish prime minister Helle Thorning-Schmidt on December 10, 2013, at the funeral of former South African president Nelson Mandela. It was the perfect way to prove the Oxford Dictionaries folks were correct in choosing "selfie" as their official word for 2013. Photographer Jason Feifer, who had previously launched a blog entitled "Selfies at Funerals," decided that this would be the right time to end the blog. He writes: "Many people interpreted funeral selfies as further evidence of millenials' self-centeredness. I didn't. Had my parents' or grandparents' generation grown up with the kind of social media tools that today's teens have, they'd have done equally embarrassing things for all the world to see. This isn't the nature of kids today; it's just the nature of kids. And anyway, when a teen tweets out a funeral selfie, their friends don't castigate them. They understand that their friend, in their own way, is expressing an emotion they may not have words for. It's a visual language that older people—even those like me, in their 30s—simply don't speak" (Feifer 2013). But President Obama, at least, seemed to speak the language of the selfie. (See Feifer's "Selfies at a Funeral" at http://selfiesatfunerals. tumblr.com, with its final message: "Obama Has Taken a Funeral Selfie, So Our Work Is Done Here.")

Author Tom Wolfe famously deemed the so-called Baby Boomers (those born between 1946 and 1964) to be the "Me Generation." Perhaps we are now living in the time of the "Selfie Generation." Indeed, even Pope Francis has weighed in on the topic. According to the *New York Times*, "[W]hen asked what he thought of the many young people who ask him to pose for selfies, he smiled, replying, 'What do I think of it? I feel like a great-grandfather!' he said. 'It's another culture.' He said a police officer in Asunción, Paraguay, a man in his 40s, had asked him to pose for a selfie. 'I told him, "You're a teenager!" It's another culture—I respect it' " (Yardley 2015). Who are we to criticize the selfie when the pope himself voices respect for it?

But not all selfies are created equal. While countless individuals are recording their mundane adventures for posterity, most of these will be soon forgotten, and even when they are posted not all that many people really care to see them. Bob Dylan once sang, "I'll let you be in my dreams if I can be in yours" ("Talkin' World War III Blues"). Maybe this should be updated to "I'll let you be in my selfie if I can be in yours."

There are some selfies that receive a great deal of attention, however, namely those posted by celebrities. Perhaps, since celebrities are used to being looked at and commented upon, this is not such a strange thing. No modern-day celebrity better fits this example than Kim Kardashian, of *Keeping Up with the Kardashians* fame.

Generally described as a "media personality," Kardashian first came to public attention in 2007, when a sex tape made with her then-boyfriend in 2003 was "leaked" and went viral—another seemingly new term that actually dates from the 1980s, according to Oxford Dictionaries, although it is only recently that the phrase "to go viral" has gone viral (Grammarphobia 2013). In previous times, such an explicit video, depicting one of the most private of personal situations, would have destroyed someone's reputation, but in this case it actually launched Kardashian's career. Her background was itself already steeped in the world of fame, as her mother Kris was married to the Olympic athlete Bruce Jenner (since 2015 Caitlyn Jenner), and her father Robert was the friend and attorney of O. J. Simpson and had been in constant view during the Simpson "Trial of the Century" in 1995.

Kim Kardashian, knowing that her naked body was being seen for free by countless eyes in 2007, did the sensible thing and posed for *Playboy* magazine in December of that year, thereby making a profit from the situation and capitalizing on her newfound notoriety. Since that time, she has been constantly in the news, with various television programs, websites, and media outlets detailing her personal life, her relationships with her equally media-savvy family, and her business enterprises. Indeed, she dominated social media in late 2014 when her bare behind was proudly displayed on the Winter 2014 cover of *Paper* magazine (and the rest of her anatomy displayed in the pages within), with the bold tag, "Break the Internet." Millions of people did indeed go to the *Paper* website to view the photos in question, and while the Internet survived, it certainly did take a pounding for a few days.

But the question perhaps most on everyone's tongue when it comes to Kim Kardashian is—just what exactly does she do?

This is not a new question in the world of popular culture. There have been a great many popular culture ambassadors who seem to be famous for being famous. One of the best-known such phenomena appeared in the early 1950s. A beauty queen from Hungary named Zsa Zsa Gabor came to the United States and, somewhat like Kardashian a half-century later, became the talk of the town thanks to her scandalous love affairs, her equally outrageous family members (including mother Magda and sister Eva), and her ability to turn up at seemingly every event where cameras were being pointed. Today, with social media, it is far easier to grab the attention of cameras, as Kardashian proves on an almost daily basis.

Media historian Neal Gabler (author of such books as *Walt Disney: The Triumph of the American Imagination, Winchell: Gossip, Power and the Culture of Celebrity,* and *An Empire of Their Own: How the Jews Invented Hollywood*) has coined the term "The Zsa Zsa Factor" to describe this phenomenon. He writes, "She had no talent save a talent for being herself, but this was quite enough to unleash such a torrent of attention that fifty years later Zsa Zsa Gabor would still be a household name, though virtually no one could tell you what she did or why she was famous. This made Zsa Zsa one of the first and easily among the most outstanding exemplars of what might be called in her honor the 'Zsa Zsa Factor' that undergirds so much of modern celebrity. It was a fame that required having to do no work to get it, save gaining media exposure" (Gabler 1998:163).

Kim Kardashian has easily outshone Zsa Zsa, and the "Kardashian Factor" has set a new standard for being famous for being famous. Indeed, Kim Kardashian more than meets our criterion (as described in chapter 1) for defining a popular culture phenomenon: "any instance when an aspect of one form of pop culture crosses over to at least six other genres of popular culture." In addition to her television programs, her domination of the press and websites (both her own and countless celebrity-obsessed others), she is referenced constantly by radio shock jocks and media experts, she has appeared in motion pictures (including the 2009 comedy *Disaster Movie,* which lived up to its title and for which she received the Golden Raspberry Award for Worst Supporting Actress), she has had relationships with famous athletes (including a seventy-two-day marriage to New Jersey Nets player Kris Humphries), and is currently wed to superstar recording artist and rapper Kanye West. There is even a "Kim Kardashian Hollywood" video game. "The mobile game—in which you network your way from nobody to A-lister—was played by nearly 3 billion minutes in its first month" (Yarm 2014). In it, Kardashian does voiceovers, chooses outfits, and has approval of the content. For after all, who knows better about rising from nobody to A-lister than Kim Kardashian? According to Frank Lee, co-founder of Drexel University's game-design program, Kardashian was an obvious and ideal choice for such a video game: "She's more like us than other celebrities. There isn't a defined talent that makes her famous" (Yarm 2014).

Not surprisingly, Kim Kardashian has another claim to fame. She is the "Queen of the Selfies." And to commemorate this title, she is conquering yet another popular culture realm, the world of book publishing. As reporter Carolyn Hiblen notes, in an article entitled "It Was Only a Matter of Time! Undisputed Queen of the Selfie Kim Kardashian to Release 352-page Hardcover Photo Book Aptly Titled *Selfish*," the book was a labor of love, dedicated to her husband. "The 33-year-old's initial idea for the photo book for Kanye was said to have been inspired by a collection of Polaroids she gave her 37-year old baby daddy for Valentine's Day" (Hiblen 2014).

Taking Polaroids would seem to be an old-school way of capturing oneself—that's how many of us had to do it before the age of smart phones, blogs, and social media. Taryn Ryder, of, appropriately enough, *Yahoo! Celebrity* website, writes: "Apparently, the inspiration for the photo album came from a Valentine's Day gift she gave to Kanye West. When Kim couldn't figure out what to give the rapper for the romantic holiday, she decided to make him a book filled with Polaroid shots (of herself), because 'all guys love it when a girl sends them sexy pics.'"

And to cap it all off, the famous wax museum Madame Tussauds has a new attraction: a wax replica of Kim Kardashian taking a selfie with a fully functioning camera, which visitors can pose with. Now *that's* taking the selfie to a whole new level.

Leave it to Kim Kardashian to come up with a way to capitalize—both literally and figuratively—on the selfie craze. Perhaps Oxford Dictionaries should consider adding as their next word of the year "Kardashianize"—meaning "to conquer all the realms of popular culture."

Lesson Learned: Not many of us are famous enough to publish a book of selfies; then again, few of us are so vain as to try.

The Daily Show: Getting News from Comedy

One of the most common conundrums in modern-day popular culture is the question: Is it real or it is a hoax? Thanks to the speed of worldwide communications, the prevalence of programs such as Adobe Photoshop (which allows anyone to alter photographs in ways almost impossible to detect), and the increasing number of parodic websites such as *The Onion*, *The Daily Currant*, and *Funny or Die*, it is increasingly difficult to differentiate between actual news stories and outrageous spoofs (in part because many real events are hard to believe). Emmett Rensin of *The New Republic* notes that major news media such as *The Washington Post*, *The New York Times*, and *USA Today* are reporting as actual events items that originally emanate from bogus sources. He writes: "Our domestic media, at least, had an excuse. While it takes a particularly keen immunity to irony to fall for an *Onion* article these days, *The Daily Currant* is a fake-news site of a different stripe: one entirely devoid of jokes. Whether this humorlessness is intentional or not—the site's founder contends his critics don't have a sense of subtlety—the site's business model as an ad-driven clickbait-generator relies on it. When *Currant* stories go viral, it's not because their satire contains essential truths, but rather because their satire is taken as truth—and usually that 'truth' is engineered to outrage a particular frequency of the political spectrum" (Rensin 2014).

While this may cite a case of deliberate deception, there are many other examples of sites offering stories that are openly meant to be understood as satirical or ridiculous, but which nonetheless are taken seriously. Mark Twain, upon learning that a newspaper had printed his obituary, famously wrote that, "the report of my death is an exaggeration."

Like Twain, many modern-day celebrities can make such a claim. In the summer of 2014, for instance, rumors began to spread that the beloved television legend Betty White had passed away. Given that she was in her early nineties, that was not an unlikely possibility, but it turns out that the basic for this information was an obvious play on words on a satirical website called *Empire News*. The headline for the story read "Actress Betty White, 92, Dyes Peacefully in Her Los Angeles Home." The tongue-in-cheek article then went on to report that White had stopped going to the hairdresser and was now dying her own hair at home. The article even contained a fake quote from her manager saying, "Betty has often told me she feels it is relaxing and soothing to dye her own hair, peacefully in her home, where she can laugh and enjoy time with her animals" (see http://empirenews.net/actress-betty-white-92-dyes-peacefully-in-her-los-angeles-home). While not the funniest story ever written, this "White Lie" can be easily detected by anyone reading the piece in its entirety. But since more and more of us just scan headlines these days (and also since correct spelling no longer seems to be stressed as it once was), it's not surprising that readers could confuse "dyes" with "dies" and immediately start to spread the word on social media. *The Empire News* site has a disclaimer at the bottom of every page, stating that it is "a satirical and entertainment website. We only use invented names in all our stories, except in cases when public figures are being satirized. Any other use of real names is accidental and coincidental" (*Empire News* 2014). But how many people, forwarded such an item, would think to click on the word *disclaimer* at the bottom?

Unlike in previous times, today many people get their information about the world around them not from newspapers, radio reports, or television news programs, but rather from quickly perusing websites. Given that, the prevalence of unquestioned misinformation, fallen-for hoaxes, and undetected deliberate deception is all too real.

Younger people, in particular, often report that what they know about the news comes to them from, of all things, comedy shows, in particular *The Daily Show*. Given that this particular program deliberately looks like a network television news show, one might speculate that viewers are fooled into thinking its reports are true. But that is certainly not the case—the show has been on the air since 1996 (and was hosted by Jon Stewart from 1999 to 2015), so its distinctive set, its particular format, and roving "reporters" have long been recognized as a spoof. The irony, though, is that the show assumes a familiarity on the part of the audience with the goings-on of the real world, which, in fact, many of its fans might not actually have. One has to wonder how funny a parody can be when people don't know what is being parodied in the first place.

The Daily Show is by no means the first popular culture program to have made fun of current events. *That Was the Week That Was*, for instance, was a satirical news program hosted by David Frost (who, ironically enough, later became a genuine news program host and is famous for a series of interviews he conducted with former president Richard Nixon, the basis for the play and film *Frost/Nixon*), which appeared on BBC TV in the United Kingdom from 1962 to 1963, and then on NBC in America from 1964 to 1965. Other such parodies have included *Not Necessarily the News*, which appeared on HBO from 1983 to 1990 (and was itself based on a BBC2 program of the same name that appeared from 1979 to 1982). And "Weekend Update" has been a regular feature on *Saturday Night Live* since that show began in 1975.

What makes *The Daily Show* phenomenon different (and to some extent the same held for its companion show *The Colbert Report*, which ran from 2005 to 2014) from other shows is the fact that, even though it is known to be a satire of the news, it is still watched by a great many people in order to learn *about* the news. Jon Stewart, much to his own often-stated horror, was considered by many to be a reliable, respectable broadcaster, akin to such previous figures as Edward R. Murrow, Walter Cronkite, David Brinkley, or Harry Reasoner. As Jason Easley from the

Politics USA website makes clear, Stewart was one of the most trusted figures in America. He writes: "Jon Stewart's *The Daily Show* is one of the smartest news based programs in the country. Stewart's ability to blend information with satire, and the fact that his loyalty is to the joke, has built a great deal of credibility with his audience" (Easley 2014). A recent report from the Brookings Institute indicates that Stewart was more trusted than such real news channels as MSNBC. Easley adds: "It speaks volumes about the state of MSNBC, and the media in general, that the most trusted name in news for many Americans is a guy who anchors a fake newscast" (Easley 2014).

Perhaps in a time when it is increasingly difficult to differentiate between what is true and what is contrived, this is not so unexpected a phenomenon. In fact, as Gerald Erion points out in his contribution to the book *The Daily Show and Philosophy*, the noted media critic Neil Postman predicted just such a thing long before *The Daily Show* existed. Postman, Erion writes, felt that television is by its very nature geared toward entertainment, and any news that isn't deemed to be "entertaining" will likely be underestimated or ignored, in order to hold the viewer's attention. "Consequently, Postman writes, 'Americans are the best entertained and quite likely the least well-informed people in the Western world'" (Erion 2007:11). *The Daily Show*'s effectiveness, in fact, is often predicated on its making this point evident, by showing the ways in which news is trivialized in order to make it entertaining. It exposes the mechanisms behind the day-to-day operations of legitimate news sources. "*The Daily Show*," Erion continues, "is clearly doing more than just 'fake news.' It's also offering deep satire that relies on its audience's appreciation of the substance of Postman's thesis, that television has a significant and sometimes adverse influence on the news content it reports" (Erion 2007:13).

Indeed, it is this audience awareness that helps to better explain the reason why *The Daily Show* remains such a trusted source for information. Unlike *The Daily Currant* or *Empire News*, for instance, *The Daily Show*'s "reporters" are not hoping to fool anyone into thinking that what they are saying is true—they are, instead, trying to get people to think about what does constitute "the truth" in an age where everything seems manufactured. *The Daily Show* is using popular culture to critique popular culture, a daring feat of expertise. It trusts its audience to get the joke. And, as Erion notes, Postman himself, in his book *Amusing Ourselves to Death*, written in 1985, perhaps unwittingly foresaw just such a possibility, ten years before *The Daily Show* originated. Erion writes; "In the final chapter of *Amusing Ourselves to Death*, Postman describes a then-hypothetical but subversive anti-television program that's eerily similar to *The Daily Show*. According to Postman, this program would serve an important educational purpose by demonstrating how television recreates and degrades news, political debate, religious thought, and so on. He writes: 'I imagine such demonstrations would of necessity take the form of parodies, along the lines of *Saturday Night Live* and *Monty Python*, the idea being to induce a national horse laugh over television's control of the public discourse.' In the end, Postman rejects the idea of such a show as 'nonsense,' since he thinks that serious and intelligent televised discussion could never attract an audience large enough to make a difference" (Erion 2007:15).

Perhaps Postman, a rather unamused critic of popular culture, underestimated the power of humor in helping us to better understand ourselves and our world.

Lesson Learned: Separating parody from reality is getting harder and harder.

11

Sports and Popular Culture

Sports. For billions of people around the world, sports are a passion, a following, a way of life. We are especially reminded of this every four years during the FIFA World Cup Championship games when an estimated three billion people globally watch at least some of the games. *Futbol*, or soccer, as it's known in the United States, is the world's most popular sport, so it is understandable that the World Cup is the most watched sporting event. The Summer and Winter Olympics are another reminder of the worldwide impact of sports.

When used in the plural form, "sports" refers to the wide variety of sporting activities that people play around the world. When "sport" is used in the singular, it refers to the social institution, as in "sport is one of the most important social institutions in the world." As a major social institution, sport reflects the mores, values, and general culture of a society, and it extends into a multitude of other social institutions, including politics, economics, family, community, religion, art, international diplomacy, and especially the mass media and popular culture.

Sports and popular culture have a great deal of overlap. Sports are aired live on the radio, on television, and via streaming videos; movies with a sports theme are quite popular; there are songs about sports and great athletes; sports bars are increasingly popular venues to congregate in; comics and cartoons depict sport characters; a large number of books have been written on sports; sports exist in the virtual world (fantasy sports leagues); and sporting events are often the site of fads and trends. In short, sports are a part of every aspect of popular culture, and the fans eat it up.

In this chapter, we have three stories involving sports fans, including our first story, which describes our love affair with tailgating, a unique

American phenomenon; a story on fantasy sports, another popular culture phenomenon given a huge boost by cyber technology; and a story to remind people that if they attend a live sporting event, they may be captured by the camera in compromising or embarrassing situations. The other three short stories involve social situations connected with sports, including NFL player Michael Vick and his controversial involvement with dog fighting; a look at diverse forms of surfing; and a look at a very popular sports film that reminds us: "There's no crying in baseball."

Tailgating American Style:
Eating "Trunk Meat" in a Parking Lot

When we described the topic of "tailgating" to a mutual friend and colleague, he—obviously clueless as to the popularity of this tradition—gasped in horror: "You mean you eat *in a parking lot?!*" He obviously was not a popular culture aficionado.

For millions of Americans, one of their favorite activities leading up to a football game (or a car race) is the tailgate party. This is especially true if one's favorite team is likely to lose, or has a losing tradition, because participants can say, "Well, at least the tailgate party was fun even if the game was not." What's the allure of the tailgate party? It combines many of the things we love the most, the outdoors, food and beverages, and time spent relaxing and laughing with family members, friends, and strangers. Tailgating, then, provides us with an opportunity to bond in a communal matter with other, like-minded folks.

Tailgating American style at sporting events represents a type of secular sentiment that helps to bond fans together in collective action where ritualistic behaviors are the norm. Similar to staging any gala, or party, there is a great deal of planning involved for the host of a tailgate party. First and foremost, the host and guests must agree on a designated meeting spot, which is generally a parking lot outside the stadium. Some fans pay to park in reserved lots, and this makes the meeting place much easier to coordinate. When people park scattered away from one another it is harder to form that caravan experience of open trunks containing food, beverages, and other necessities. Also, when they are scattered, people have to carry their food items to a designated spot, although with the advent of cell phones it's a lot easier to find fellow tailgaters in the vast sea of parking lots than it was in the past. We can thank technology for making it easier to find someone in a parking lot.

It is advisable to create a checklist of items needed to bring to the tailgate party; this is especially true if you are the host with the grill. A grill is at the top of the list, and making sure that you have enough charcoal and lighter fluid or a backup tank of propane for the gas grill is very important. The next obvious item on the list is the main food item. We allow for breakfast food and lunch/dinner food distinctions. Morning tailgates entail breakfast foods such as bacon, sausage, eggs, pancakes, and so forth for the grill. Morning tailgaters may also wish to bring lunch foods such as burgers, dogs, steak, chicken, pork chops, ribs, and so on. The host will always bring enough food to feed most people but it is important to designate food and beverage responsibilities to guests, even if it's a simple request to "bring your own."

The host is also expected to bring silver or plastic ware, including cooking utensils, eating utensils, napkins, paper towels, plates, bowls, seasoning mixes (e.g., salt, pepper, Tabasco sauce, etc.), trash bags, and so on. The host may also request guests to bring backup supplies, such as paper towels or plates. In the authors' decades of experience in tailgating we have found that it is common for the host and regular guests to keep bulk supplies of these items in the trunks of their cars throughout the tailgate season, replenishing supplies on a regular basis. It is a good idea to bring a number of chairs, too, as some people will want to sit, but that is also their responsibility; after all the grill master is too busy grilling and running the tailgate to sit down.

A wide range of food and beverages is the norm. Snacks and main course items are the minimum necessities for a tailgate. Beer, wine, alcohol, soda, juice, and water are normal beverage items. Some people like vegetarian food; you might want to bring your own veggie foods, though, as tailgating seems to attract people with the need to revisit their primal beginnings and nothing says primal beginnings quite like meat on a fire, especially a fire that one has created oneself. Still, this is a communal event, so a good host will always make sure there are food items that will please everyone. Submarine sandwiches are always a hit with partygoers. Salads, baked beans, and other appetizers, such as chicken wings served with side dishes, are always welcomed. And don't forget the desserts. Multiple, decadent desserts are especially welcomed at tailgate parties.

Most tailgaters will also spruce up their party area with tables with team colors for the tablecloths. Other items that signify the team you are cheering for should also be proudly displayed in the tailgate area. A host or guest with the team flag and flagpole adds a great touch—fly those colors proudly! Tailgaters may transform themselves into face painters, and team jerseys and team colors are appropriate clothing items. Be sure to lay that peer pressure on heavy to keep your tailgaters in line with the proper tailgating decorum.

Tailgating at football games lasts for hours. Most people arrive four or five hours before kickoff (depending on when the parking lots open). Tailgaters need something more than food and drink; they need games to play and music to listen to. A number of fans will bring televisions with them, usually to watch pregame shows or highlights from games played earlier in the day (if applicable). Many tailgaters bring a football with them, and friends toss the ball back and forth. Other people bring tailgating games with them, such as ladder ball, corn toss (or bean bag toss), washer pitching, and, of course, a drinking game favorite, beer pong.

So there we have it, all the elements of a tailgate. With all this information at hand, we can define tailgating as a party that centers around a group of people who meet at a designated spot, usually a parking lot, before a football game, for the purpose of consuming large amounts of food (usually grilled) and beverages, playing games, enjoying each other's company, and getting psyched for the game ahead.

Football games are the principal domain of tailgating. However, it is common to tailgate before car races and before or after lacrosse games. The cool thing about collegiate lacrosse tailgates is that fans tailgate with the players and their families *after* the game. When it comes to football and car races, it is highly unlikely the fans will tailgate with the players or drivers. Tailgating for football is most common because there are so many college and professional games every week. Then again, it's the one game a week nature of football and the limited number of home games on any team's schedule that makes each game critical, and therefore each tailgate. That football is played in the fall also makes it conducive for tailgating, at least compared to basketball and hockey. Tailgating for baseball is not common and generally it's because Major League Baseball forbids stadiums from allowing tailgates, plus, there are eighty-one home games, and who's going to tailgate before all of them?

We have already identified some of the overlaps between popular culture and tailgating—fans bring TVs and radios and check their smart phones and iPads for data. In addition, TV coverage of the game will always reference the tailgaters, especially at college games, and local news coverage is likely to show highlights that include tailgaters. Other elements of popular culture related to tailgating include the many cookbooks written on tailgating. And although this is not as common as one might think, there are films and TV shows that describe or reference tailgating. One such TV show is *The Simpsons*.

In the "Any Given Sundance" episode of *The Simpsons* (2008), Homer Simpson and family are headed to Springfield Stadium, where arch rivals Springfield University and Springfield A&M will meet on the gridiron. It is early in the morning and most of the family members are quite sleepy, but not Homer, He is wide awake and excited about the prospect of tailgating. While driving to the stadium, Homer holds a pennant (a commemorative flag generally used to show allegiance to a particular team) that reads "Tailgating" in one hand and one that reads "Is Fun" in the other hand. Homer is psyched to tailgate. Bart, harshing Homer's mellow, says aloud, "Why are we arriving so early? The game does not start for hours." Homer laughs at his son's complaining and states, "We're not here for the game. The game is nothing. . . . The real reason we Americans put up with sports is for this. [The Simpsons have arrived at the parking lot.] Behold, the tailgate party! The pinnacle of human achievement. Since the dawn of parking lots man has sought to stuff his guts with food and alcohol in anticipation of watching others exercise." Homer continues his praise of tailgating and explains that eating "trunk meat" is a glorious thing, especially for men. Trunk meat refers to the food packed away in the trunk to be grilled. Calling it "trunk meat" may not make it sound appealing, but it is what it is.

Homer, perhaps summing up the general sentiment of all tailgaters states, "What could be greater than eating and drinking for hours in a drizzly parking lot?!" We agree, Homer, nothing is better, except maybe tailgating in blizzard conditions on the shores of Lake Erie in Cleveland in December, but that's Delaney's cross to bear, as a Browns season ticket holder. Hot chili from the grill seems to taste good when tailgating in the cold in a parking lot in midwinterlike conditions. Tailgating in sunny seventy-degree weather sounds a lot better.

Lesson Learned: Don't let anyone tell you differently: food and beverages taste better when consumed in a parking lot as part of a football tailgate.

Fantasy Sports: What Does It Say When Someone Is a Loser in His Own Fantasy World?

We know that billions of people around the world love sports, either as participants, spectators, or fans. Few social institutions can claim such a widespread community of adherents. Many sports fans and spectators think that they know more about the games and athletes than the professionals who play sports, the executives who run leagues and teams, or the analysts who provide expert insight on such topics as upcoming player drafts, game strategies, interpretations of the rules, the accuracy of officials' calls, even whether or not a game should have been played in extreme weather conditions, and more. Until recently, anyone who wished to complain about the results of games and the decisions made by the athletes, managers, coaches, and owners had no recourse but to voice their opinions to those unfortunate persons within earshot. Thanks to the Internet, though, today people can air their grievances throughout cyberspace, including directing their comments to complete strangers in distant places.

In addition to providing a forum for those who think they know more about sports than the professionals do, we can also thank, or curse, the Internet for providing fantasy sports leagues. Fantasy sports leagues are an aspect of virtual reality (see chapter 12). Virtual reality is a made-up environment that, while it exists in the cyber sense of existence, is based on a modified or fantasized version of the real world. As it pertains to fantasy sports leagues, the Internet, via a plethora of media outlets that provide seemingly never-ending amounts of data and statistical analysis, provides the opportunity for people from all walks of life, with all categories of skills and all levels of sports knowledge to participate in fantasy sports leagues. In essence, they are given a chance to "put their money where their mouths are." The leagues provide opportunities for the "know it all" sports fan and the novice alike to can compare their sports strategies with one another and measure their effectiveness against the outcomes of real games played by real people on real teams.

Fantasy sports leagues, also known as rotisserie, roto, or owner simulation leagues, have become a pop culture phenomenon, with more than 41.5 million Americans participating in 2014—a figure that represents 14 percent of the total U.S. population (Fantasy Sports Trade Association 2015). Participants in fantasy sports leagues act as owners of sports franchises and draft players for their teams. The draft order is set by the fantasy league organizer, or commissioner, and the owners draft players (from the rosters of real teams) until their rosters are filled. In some fantasy leagues, the draft is conducted auction style, meaning that owners can bid on the players they want to draft. The fantasy league that allows auction style drafting sets a dollar amount limit during the auction. The draft continues until all the owners have full rosters.

Owners draft starters and a limited number of bench players that can be substituted in case a real-life player is out of commission (e.g., injured or suspended) or when the owner plays a hunch and starts a bench player instead of a starter. When an owner decides to go with a bench player, he or she is either relying on a gut decision or has examined real-life data that indicate that the bench player generally outperforms the usual starter against that week's opponent. This is one way fantasy owners can show that they really do know something about sporting contests. Fantasy winners and losers are determined by using real-life statistics of players on a game-by-game basis. Each fantasy owner receives a certain number of fantasy points based on the performances of real-life players. For example, a football player earns points for the fantasy owner if he scores a touchdown, recovers a fumble, makes an interception, kicks a field goal, and so on. Because the fantasy sports league has a built-in data analysis system, points are tallied automatically. Fantasy owners not only know their own accumulated score but keep track of the number of points earned by their opponents as well.

One of the odd things about fantasy sports is that real-life sports fans who participate as owners of fantasy teams cheer for the performances of their fantasy players and root for the real-life success of these players. In this regard, what might be good for one's fantasy team may come at the expense of one's real-life team. Thus, one's loyalty to a real team can be compromised when he or she must cheer for the success of real-life rivals in order to earn fantasy points in a virtual reality world. It is this contention between fantasy and reality that stops most true fans from joining a fantasy league. To do both, to cheer for a real-life team while pulling for a fantasy team's success, is a conflict of loyalties waiting to happen, unless the owner drafts only players from his or her real-life preferred team. But that would pit a team with a roster of regular players against an all-star team, and such a proposition is generally a losing one.

Despite the built-in conflict that real fans face when they opt to participate in fantasy sports, make-believe leagues are now a multibillion-dollar online industry. With football as the unchallenged number one sport in the United States, and the National Football League (NFL) as the favorite sports league, it comes as no surprise that the favorite sports fantasy league—with nearly twenty-six million online participants in 2012—is professional football (Subramanian 2013). While fantasy football leagues are the most common, nearly all major team sports lend themselves to fantasy play. Baseball, basketball, hockey, and auto racing are among the other common sports amenable to adoption by fantasy sport leagues. Even individual sports such as golf and tennis have fantasy sports appeal.

When the Internet became available to the masses, it was only a matter of time before online fantasy sports leagues would be developed,

but the idea of picking players and running contests based on real statistics preceded it by decades. "Conventional wisdom holds that fantasy
sports were officially born in 1980 when a group of baseball fans including
magazine writer and editor Dan Okrent founded Rotisserie League Baseball over lunch at a Manhattan restaurant called La Rotisserie Franchise"
(Frost 2006:1). However, as Sam Walker, author of *Fantasyland: A Season
on Baseball's Lunatic Fringe* (2006) explains, Rotisserie-style baseball was
"only the live birth" of fantasy sports. In fact, according to Walker (2006),
the concept of fantasy sports leagues dates back to 1960, when Harvard
sociologist William Gamson started the "Baseball Seminar" where he and
his colleagues would form imaginary rosters that earned points based on
major league players' final statistics, such as their batting averages, runs
batted in, earned run averages, and total wins. Participants anted up $10
each in those early days to play in the first fantasy baseball league. Gamson (currently professor of sociology at Boston College) still participates
in what is now called the "National Baseball Seminar."

Fantasy sports leagues have grown quite a bit from their sociological roots in classrooms and local pubs. Participants across the nation and
around the world are connected to the virtual world of fantasy sports
leagues. That the number of participants continues to increase is a testament to the joy, or addiction, that they find as owners of fantasy sports
teams. And when one considers that it is likely to cost at least $1 billion
to purchase a real franchise, plucking down $20 to $100 for the right to
own a fantasy sport team makes a kind of sense. Subramanian (2013)
provides us with five additional possible explanations for the growing
popularity of fantasy sports leagues:

1. Participation by Women: Fantasy sports leagues are not
   the exclusive domain of males; instead, it is estimated that
   women comprise 20 percent of the total number of fantasy sports participants. The number of women playing in
   fantasy sports leagues is expected to continue to increase.

2. Fantasy Users Continue to Play Year after Year: Nearly 80
   percent of current fantasy sports participants expect to be
   playing a decade from now, and 40 percent indicate that
   they will continue to play until they die. Thus, current users
   are likely to keep on playing indefinitely.

3. The Youth Revolution; While current fantasy owners will
   continue playing as they age, more and more younger folks

are joining the ranks of the fantasy sports world. The fastest growing demographic is under-eighteen players.

4. Fantasy Sports, but Real Money: As mentioned earlier, the fantasy sports leagues are make-believe, but the money that someone can win as champion of a league is real. The producers of fantasy sports products and services are cashing in on nearly the nearly $2 billion this industry generates.

5. Rise of the Daily Game: Like the lottery, the fantasy sports industry seeks to take as much money as possible from the masses. The industry realizes that professional sports seasons last five or six months, on average, and it's hard to sustain the attention of working folks or the adult parents of young children for that long because of their work and maintenance needs. As a result, the new big thing in fantasy leagues is the one-day fantasy sports league where players can join a league, draft a team for that day, and at the end of the day the league dissolves itself (and payouts are made). In this manner there are immediate winners and losers.

While the authors understand the appeal of participating in a fantasy sports league, we have to wonder about the millions of losers. After all, just like real-life sports where there is only one champion, each fantasy sports league has one winner, and the rest are losers. What does that say about someone who is a loser in their own fantasy world? It's kind of sad, isn't it? Then again, that's life. There are big winners and a mass of players just hoping for a nugget of gold every now and then.

Lesson Learned: Fantasy sports leagues give people a chance to fail in their fantasies and not just real life.

Caught by the Camera at a Sporting Event for the Whole World to See: "Hey buddy, they got a new invention. It's called a napkin."

Spectators at sporting events take certain assumed risks. For example, at a baseball game one might get hit by a home run or foul ball or even occasionally a bat that slips out of the batter's hands. At a sporting event that is televised, a camera might record your actions and behaviors. This includes the now-common practice of focusing on spectators during such promos as the "kiss cam" or in response to stadium prompts for spectators to dance or smile for the cameras. On many occasions, the camera scans the crowd looking for people doing silly things that on-air announcers may comment on. In instances such as these, spectators may have no idea that they are on the air and might be photographed doing something embarrassing.

Such was the case for a New York Yankees fan who was caught sleeping in the fourth inning during the April 13, 2014, night game between the Boston Red Sox and the host Yankees. The ESPN broadcast's camera spotted Andrew Rector with his head tilted and eyes completely shut, prompting on-air announcers Dan Shulman and former major league player John Kruk to make a series of comments. Surprised to see a fan sleeping during a Red Sox-Yankee game, especially so early in the game, Kruk began the dialogue by saying, "It's only the fourth inning!" Shulman asked, "Did he sleep through the [Carlos] Beltran homer? I mean forty-five thousand people stand up and cheer, and he sleeps through it?" Kruk answered, "I think it would be tough to, but he seemed pretty comfortable. It didn't look like he just started to sleep" (Mongelli, Li, and Golding 2014).

The announcers also made fun of the sleeping fan's large girth, with Shulman asking the heavy-set Kruk, "Not a cousin? Not a relative?" "No, I don't think so, but you never know," Kruk replied. "I didn't get a good look at him because of the head tilt. But, I mean physically we could be, yeah" (Mongelli, Li, and Golding 2014). The game moved on and the attention directed toward the sleeping fan ended. Most people viewing the game likely responded with laughter and smiles, if they reacted at all, and like the game itself, they moved on without giving the incident any further thought.

One of the authors, who did not watch the live broadcast of the game, but instead saw the highlights of the game on ESPN's *Sports Center* the next morning, found it odd that ESPN would include the sleeping fan in their highlight package of the game. But then again, *Sports Center* is known for a low-quality production of highlights of the previous day's sporting events. But that's a conversation for another time. The sleeping fan being made fun of on the air reminded *Seinfeld* fans such as ourselves of the episode where the George Costanza character was caught eating ice cream and making a mess of himself.

In the *Seinfeld* episode "The Lip Reader," Jerry and George are sitting in the bleachers watching a tennis match. It is a hot day and George decides to go to the concession stand and purchase some ice cream. Meanwhile, back at Jerry's apartment, Kramer is watching the tennis match on TV and we hear the announcer's commentary, "And that is it. The match to Ms. Natalia Valdoni. Coming up next, men's singles, but for now let's stop a minute and take a look at our beautiful tennis center backdrop." It is common for TV announcers during televised broadcasts such as this to make transitions from the primary subject (in this case the tennis match) to a secondary subject (spectators in the stands). It was true when this 1993 *Seinfeld* episode first aired and it was still true in 2014 when a Yankee-Red Sox game analyst transitioned to a fan asleep in his seat.

Kramer starts to laugh and says aloud, "Hey, hey, it's George," when he notices that the camera has caught George eating an ice cream sundae. His face is covered in ice cream and fudge and when he takes another bite of the sundae it drips around his mouth and onto his shirt. The camera shows a close-up of George's face covered with ice cream and melted fudge. The announcer says, "Holy cow it's a scorcher. Boy, I bet you that guy can cover a lot of court. Hey buddy, they got a new invention. It's called a napkin. We'll take a station break and continue with more . . ." George is oblivious that he has been on the air, that is, until the next day when he learns that he was mocked on national television.

At Jerry's apartment the next day, Jerry and Kramer are joined by Elaine. Elaine says, "Hey, you know a friend of mine from work said that she saw George at the tennis match on TV yesterday." Kramer responds, "Yeah, yeah, me too. Yeah he was at the snack bar eating a hot fudge sundae. He had it all over his face. He was wearing that chocolate on his face like a beard and they got in there real nice and tight. And he's [Kramer imitates George lapping up ice cream]." Meanwhile, George is at Monk's coffee shop with his girlfriend Gwen. George is shocked to hear his girlfriend break up with him.

GWEN: I'm sorry, George.

GEORGE: I don't understand, things were going so great. What happened? Something must have happened.

GWEN: It's not you, it's me.

GEORGE: You're giving *me* the "it's not you, it's me" routine? I invented "it's not you, it's me." Nobody tells me it's them not me, if it's anybody it's me.

GWEN: All right, George, it's you.

George is confused. Gwen's breaking up with him seems to have come from out of nowhere. He decides to go to Jerry's apartment and try and figure things out. Jerry acknowledges that he thought things were going great between Gwen and George. Jerry asks George if he has any idea why she broke up with him.

GEORGE: She tried to give me the "it's not you, it's me" routine.

JERRY: But that's your routine.

[Kramer enters Jerry's apartment]

KRAMER: Hey, George, I saw you on TV yesterday.

GEORGE: Really? At the tennis match?

KRAMER: Yeah, you were at the snack bar eating a hot fudge sundae.

GEORGE: Get out of here. I didn't see any cameras there.

KRAMER: Oh, the cameras were, vroom, there. The announcers, they made a couple of cracks about you.

GEORGE: Cracks? What were they saying?

KRAMER: That you had ice cream all over your face. They were talking about how funny you looked.

GEORGE: Maybe Gwen saw it. Maybe that's what did it [led to the breakup].

KRAMER: Well I'll tell you, it wasn't a pretty sight.

GEORGE: She must have seen me eating it on TV.

JERRY: So, she sees you with hot fudge on your face and she ends it? You really think she would be that superficial?

GEORGE: Why not? I would be.

Just then, Jerry's phone rings. Jerry's parents have called to tell him they saw George on TV from their retirement home in Florida. George cannot believe that seemingly everyone he knows saw him be humiliated on TV by sports announcers. "This is a nightmare," George proclaims. "Kramer, how long was I on?" Kramer replies, "it felt like eight seconds." George counts one-one-thousand, two-one-thousand, three-one-thousand and realizes how long eight seconds really is when you're being mocked on national TV. Elaine walks into Jerry's apartment and opens her conversation by saying to George, "I heard you really inhaled that thing. Did anyone tape it?" George is convinced that not only was he humiliated by the announcers, causing him great shame, but he also lost his girlfriend because she was too ashamed to be seen with him.

While the George Costanza incident involving shame and ridicule made public was make-believe, the incident involving Andrew Rector, the Yankee fan who fell asleep during a game, was real. We are not sure if he lost a superficial girlfriend like George did, but Rector does claim to have been disgraced to the point that he is suing Major League Baseball Advance Media, ESPN New York, the New York Yankees, Dan Shulman, and John Kruk for $10 million, claiming defamation of his character (Machir 2014). Rector admits that he "briefly slept" while attending the April 13 game but believes he was subject to an "unending verbal crusade" against him with their "vituperative utterances" redistributed on the MLB website the following day (Machir 2014). A video of Rector sleeping at the game also appears on YouTube, making him the possible target of more abuse.

We have already shared the actual comments made by Shulman and Kruk. In Rector's suit filed with the Supreme Court of New York State, County of Bronx, which was riddled with typos and improper grammar, claims are made that the broadcasters used such words as "stupor, fatty, unintelligent, and stupid" to describe Rector. Rector also claims in his suit that Kruk insinuated that he knows "neither the history nor the understood the beauty or rivalry between the Boston Red Sox and New York Yankees." MLB, ESPN, and the announcers contest Rector's claims regarding the words used on the air to describe him specifically and all accusations of slander in general.

While spectators should be free from harmful comments made by announcers that might be considered slanderous or lead to a relationship breakup, attending sporting events comes with the inherent risk, or opportunity, of being shown, and described by announcers, on air.

Lesson Learned: When attending a sporting event, stay awake and always use plenty of napkins.

Michael Vick and Dogfighting

Determining whether an activity should be considered a genuine sport can be a bone of contention (if not a sport in itself). The authors define *sport* as "institutionalized, structured, and sanctioned competitive activity beyond the realm of play that involves physical exertion and the use of relatively complex athletic skills" (Delaney and Madigan 2015:13). By this criterion, such activities as American football, rugby, tennis, and hockey obviously qualify; other activities, such as golf, chess, poker, and competitive eating (all of which are now regularly found on various sports-related broadcasts and websites) are suspect. And what about an activity that is beloved in many parts of the world, and whose best-known figures are revered as heroic athletes—professional bullfighting? In popular culture—especially in the writing of Ernest Hemingway and in many movies filmed in Spain or Mexico—there is a romantic identification with the matador swinging his cape to provoke the enraged bull. But animal rights advocates consider this to be a case of animal cruelty pure and simple, rather than a sport to be watched with pleasure.

While one might still see a televised bullfight on a sports network, at least outside the United States, there is a related activity you will surely never see on such shows, namely, dogfighting. It is highly unlikely that many people consider this a sport but it received a great deal of attention in 2007 when it was learned that Michael Vick, the quarterback of the Atlanta Falcons NFL football team, was involved in an interstate dogfighting network. Before this news broke, Vick had received mostly positive media attention, as one of the first African American quarterbacks and as someone who had risen from poverty and danger in a crime-ridden area of Virginia to achieve tremendous wealth and success due to his athletic prowess. Almost overnight, his reputation was shattered, and he soon was under indictment on federal charges.

Vick ended up serving twenty-one months in prison. Seemingly contrite, after serving his term he was reinstated by the NFL and has since played for the Philadelphia Eagles, the New York Jets, and the Pittsburgh Steelers. But controversy still follows him, years later. As Matthew Bershadker, president and CEO of the American Society for the Prevention of Cruelty to Animals (ASPCA), writes: "Vick is free to do as he pleases both on the football field and off. But one thing he can't do is absolve himself of his direct participation in horrific and fatal animal torture and abuse. . . . Michael Vick was fully involved in a six-year pattern of illegal activity that included dogs being savagely electrocuted, drowned, and beaten to death. We fully acknowledge Vick has 'done his time' and even participated in some public outreach, but that does not erase the crime" (Bershadker 2014).

Clearly, the Michael Vick dogfighting controversy touched a nerve. Why was this so controversial, given that other NFL players (as well as athletes in other sports) have been involved in what seem to be greater crimes, including assault and battery, rape, and even murder? Football, after all, is a brutal sport, and one might expect that brutal behavior—including animal abuse—might not be altogether unexpected among those who play it. Still, there is something viscerally disturbing about dog fighting.

Many people, of course, have dogs as pets and feel as close—or even closer—to them as they do to their fellow humans. Others, particularly members of animal rights groups, feel that humans should never treat other animals as merely means to their own ends, such as winning bets or killing for pleasure. ASCPA spokesperson Bershadker makes another important point, though. He writes: "Dog-fighting represents the ultimate betrayal of the unique relationship that exists between humans and animals. Manipulating a dog's desire to please its owner to perpetuate a life of chronic and acute physical and psychological pain is the most horrific form of animal abuse. . . . Every American should look at dog-fighting as more than just a crime, but as a deep stain on our national character" (Bershadker 2014).

The philosopher Immanuel Kant (1724–1804) made a similar point. Such abuse is not only a form of cruelty toward other animals, he held, but also a moral affront to our very concept of what it means to be human. We harm all humanity when engaging in such acts, because they are beneath us as moral beings.

While one might think that betting on animals fighting would be a topic unlikely to be found in popular culture, once again, *Seinfeld* was willing to tread upon such delicate turf. In the episode called "The Little Jerry," Jerry accidentally bounces a check at a bodega run by a man named Marcelino, and is shamed to see the check publicly displayed. Not wanting to be exposed as a scofflaw, Jerry offers to make good on the amount, but Marcelino insists that he be made an example of and refuses to remove the bounced check. Kramer, meanwhile, has come into possession of a rooster who he thinks resembles Jerry (thereby naming him "Little Jerry" in his friend's honor). Marcelino, who runs an illegal cockfighting contest, is impressed when he sees Little Jerry and tells Kramer that, if he sells him to Marcelino, he'll take down the other Jerry Seinfeld's bounced check.

Not understanding the realities of the situation, Kramer makes the deal and goes to tell Big Jerry.

JERRY: Kramer, cockfighting is illegal.

KRAMER: Only in the United States.

JERRY: It's inhumane!

KRAMER: No, Jerry, it's not what you think it is.

JERRY: It's two roosters peckin' at each other!

KRAMER: What?

JERRY: Yeah!

KRAMER: Well, I thought they wore gloves and helmets, you know, like *American Gladiators*.

JERRY: No Kramer, Little Jerry could get hurt.

KRAMER: Yeah, well, I left him with Marcelino!

(Jerry shrugs and holds his hands out.)

KRAMER: My Little Jerry! (Runs out.)

Luckily, it all works out for Little Jerry when Kramer bursts into the cockfight to rescue him, although Kramer is viciously pecked by Little Jerry's huge and skilled opponent when he enters the ring.

It seems clear that the Michael Vick dogfighting affair will not soon be forgotten, and offers us all a lesson on the ways in which such activities not only harm animals but harm human beings as well. Arthur Schopenhauer (1788–1860), one of the first philosophers to take the topic of animal rights seriously, once visited the site of a battlefield, and was appalled to see the vast number of dead and dying horses there. He reportedly said that if humans want to kill themselves, then go ahead, but leave the horses out of it.

Lesson Learned: Cruelty to animals is no sporting matter.

Surfing USA and Beyond

Thanks to the Beach Boys and their various imitators, the sport of surfing has become in many ways almost as American as apple pie and Chevrolet. Movies such as *Gidget* (1959), *The Endless Summer* (1966), *Point Break* (1991), *Blue Crush* (2002), and *Soul Surfer* (2011) exemplify this American theme. "Surfing USA" may not literally be true, but especially when summer is upon us, it seems that it's everywhere.

It is impossible to determine the exact origins of surfing, although most would agree that it has Polynesian roots. Ben Finney and James D. Houston, in their history of surfing in Hawaii, note that "early sources tell how the sport was bound up with the traditional religion, sexual practices, and the system of social classes. Surfing feats and romantic encounters in the surf were celebrated in song and legend. Board builders followed sacred rituals, and at least one temple was solely dedicated to surfing. The privileged chiefs as well as people from all levels of society took part" (Finney and Houston 1996:13). Surfing, from its very beginning, was intimately connected with popular culture, so it's no wonder that it is embedded in the popular culture of the United States.

In 1898, Hawaii was annexed as a United States territory. A growing number of American tourists began to travel to Hawaii, looking for sun, sandy beaches, and something a little exotic. At the same time, an early "traditionalist" movement began in Hawaii. This movement represented the first of many attempts among native Hawaiians to revitalize traditional Hawaiian culture. Hawaiians cite the formation of the Waikiki Outrigger Canoe Club in 1908 and the example of one of its earliest members, Duke Paoa Kahanamoku (known as "The Duke"), as major influences encouraging the native desire to reestablish surfing on the Hawaiian Islands.

Historian Michael Beschloss writes: "Duke Kahanamoku, who won a total of five swimming medals in the Olympics from 1912 to 1924, probably did more than anyone else to bring the sport of surfing from his native Hawaiian Islands to the United States mainland. Almost in reverse, he also played a substantial part in the Americanization of old Hawaii" (Beschloss 2014).

Beschloss notes that, sadly, after he moved to Southern California, Kahanamoku "was not immune from racial prejudice. Arriving once with fellow swimmers to a restaurant in Lake Arrowhead, California, he was told 'We don't serve Negroes' " (Beschloss 2014).

Surfing is popular on the East Coast as well as the West, from Florida north to Long Island, New York. Surf competitions net champion-caliber surfers large sums of money. And although it seems obvious that surfing has geographic restrictions—an ocean is almost always necessary—the influence of this sport extends beyond coastal areas. According to Surf Industry Manufacturers Association, surfing is a $7.5 billion industry in the United States, and every state is home to at least one surf shop. And in fact, while we understandably think of Hawaii, California, and Florida as the surfing capitals of America, there are some unexpected places where the sport is practiced. Would you believe, for instance, Houston, Texas, and Buffalo, New York?

In Galveston, Texas, "super tanker surfing" is all the rage. The Houston ship channel in Galveston is the busiest such channel in the United States, with twenty supertankers traveling through the waters daily. These 95,000-plus ton vessels (including oil tankers, car carriers, and storage container ships) create gigantic waves. Unlike reef surfing, with its shore breaks that last four or five seconds, tanker waves can last as long as ten minutes. Utilizing precision timing, surfers follow the tankers in motorboats, leap off, and catch a wave. There are even human-made wave machines that allow surfers to ride waves almost indefinitely.

Even when tankers are not creating waves for them, Houstonians from all walks of life love to surf—even those who walk on four legs. Charles Schulz, creator of *Peanuts* (discussed in chapter 7) was himself an avid surfing devotee and often drew Snoopy "hanging ten" on a giant wave. He'd be happy to know that Galveston now has a "surfing dog competition." Heather Alexander writes: "The brain child of the Ohana Surf and Skate shop, the watery spectacle is in aid of the Galveston Island Humane Society. Four shelter dogs got out for the day to join the crowd of regular pet owners who came along to enjoy the fun. Many had never been on boards before and instructors were on hand to make sure there were no doggie 'wipe outs'" (Alexander 2014).

But surfing in the USA doesn't only take place in warm weather places in the summer. Brave Buffalonians shout "Kowabunga" in the dead of winter. When there are gale force storms over the Great Lakes, particularly brave surfers from Cleveland to Detroit to Chicago are likely to be found battling the elements. The late Magilla Schaus, a firefighter in Buffalo, New York, braved the waves during many Western New York winters by organizing a surfing contest on chilly Lake Erie. The gales of November never came too soon for him. "The winter is the best time for me," he claimed. "When the weather starts changing, then the fair-weathered surfers go away. . . . On the ocean they say, 'A surfer leaves nothing behind but his footprints in the sand.' A Great Lake surfer leaves nothing behind in the sand—or the snow" (Higgins, 2005:B-21). Schaus died in 2009, and in his honor his friends have started an annual Gales of November/ Magilla Schaus Memorial Surf Contest. Shortly before his death in 2009, he was quoted as saying: "Surfing in this part of the world is like living at the bottom of a trap door. I know surfers from across the planet and the Great Lakes" (Delaney and Madigan 2009:62).

As Schaus rightly pointed out, surfers can be found across the planet, often in places almost as unexpected as Buffalo, New York. The authors of this book, for instance (who have witnessed surfing culture in such traditional places as Redondo Beach, California, Honolulu, Hawaii, and Manly Beach, New Zealand), were amazed to come across a dedicated surfer in, of all places, Tramore, Waterford County, Ireland. Originally from Australia, the surfer asserted that the waves of Waterford were the longest and strongest he had ever experienced. As BBC Travel writer Catherine Le Nevez, in a piece entitled "When Irish Eyes Are Surfing," asserts: "Pods of surfers bobbed on their boards, watching eagle-eyed as white-capped waves rolled in and paddling fervently for sea-sprayed ride towards the beach. Due to its notoriously inclement weather, Ireland isn't known for being a prime surfing destination. But low pressure systems in the Atlantic actually stir up ferocious winds—which create huge swells. Without any landmass to impede them, these swells land along the Irish coast, resulting in waves that can reach up to 12m high. With 3,171km of crenulated coastline, plenty of reef, beach and point breaks fringing the coast and opportunities for beginners and seasoned pros alike, the sport is riding a wave of recent popularity—all set against a backdrop of spectacular Irish scenery" (Le Nevez 2014).

Faith and begorrah, surfing is everywhere, it seems. Have you heard?—surfing's the word!

Lesson Learned: People are catching waves all over the world.

There's No Crying in Baseball

As pointed out throughout this book, the term *popular culture* has different meanings for different people, not unlike the term *sport*. It generally is used to describe areas of the culture that people participate in or have positive feelings about. It relates to people's everyday activities. Sports are activities that, indeed, countless numbers of people choose to engage in. But in addition to people participating in sporting activities, it is important to note that sports is also something that countless numbers of people choose to *watch*, as spectators at live events and viewers of motion pictures and television.

Sports films represent one of the more entertaining forms of popular culture. As Randy Williams writes, "From passion (*The Cup*) to cynicism (*North Dallas Forty*), from fantasy (*Field of Dreams*) to culture clashes (*Mr. Baseball*) and racism (*The Jackie Robinson Story*), and from celebrating our need for heroes (*Knute Rockne: All-American*) to questioning it (*Cobb*), sports movies have covered a broad range of topics as an allegory of the human condition, an insightful window on society, and we are passionate about them" (Williams, 2006:xi).

ESPN.com (2005) came up with a list of the twenty-five best sports movies, as chosen by a panel of experts. They were:

1. *Hoosiers*

2. *Raging Bull*

3. *Field of Dreams*

4. *Bull Durham*

5. *Caddyshack*

6. *The Natural*

7. *Chariots of Fire*

8. *Jerry Maguire*

9. *Seabiscuit*

10. *Remember the Titans*

11. *A League of Their Own*

12. *Eight Men Out*

13. *White Men Can't Jump*

14. *Major League*

15. *Tin Cup*

16. *61**

17. *The Hurricane*

18. *The Color of Money*

19. *Finding Forrester*

20. *The Rookie*

21. *Ali*

22. *Bend It like Beckham*

23. *Cobb*

24. *Rudy*

25. *Searching for Bobby Fischer*

One can quibble with some of the selections (is chess, the subject of number 25, really a sport, for instance?), but no doubt that was the purpose of this list, since ESPN thrives on heated debate, and few topics are more likely to get a debate going than what constitutes a great film.

While football remains the most popular sport in America, it's interesting how many of the films on this list deal with baseball (hockey, by the way, gets short shrift—where's the classic 1977 film *Slap Shot*, for instance?). Perhaps there is something about the nature of baseball that makes it particularly amenable to depiction in narrative film.

Number 11 on the list is 1992's *A League of Their Own*. It deals with such important themes as economics (how to keep baseball alive during wartime), family (the sibling rivalry between two sisters on opposing teams), and class status (players from a rural setting coming into conflict with big city players). And it especially deals with gender issues: *should* women play baseball and is their style of play identical to or different from that of men?

The film is a fictionalized account of the real All-American Girls Professional Baseball League (AAGPBL), which was founded by chewing gum magnate and Chicago Cubs owner Philip K. Wrigley in 1943, and which lasted until 1954. Wrigley was deeply worried that, with most of the young men in America off to fight in World War II, baseball would fade from the public view until after the war's end and might not be able to recoup its losses. Wrigley, along with other baseball executives, decided to found an all-female league in order to keep baseball in the public eye. *A League of Their Own* has a similar plot. Candy manufacturer Walter Harvey (Garry Marshall—the brother of the film's director Penny Marshall) starts an all-female league during the war and announces a national talent search, with tryouts in Chicago. Two sisters from a farm in Oregon, Dottie (Geena Davis) and Kit (Lori Petty), become the star pitcher and catcher, respectively, of the Rockford Peaches. Dottie's husband is fighting overseas, and she is initially reluctant to leave the farm, but her baseball-loving sister convinces her to do so. Other recruits include a gruff third baseman (played by Rosie O'Donnell), a sexy center fielder (played by Madonna) known as "All the Way" Mae, and a second base player (Megan Cavanaugh) who is talented but not considered attractive enough by the scouts initially to be invited to play. When Dottie and Kit refuse to join the team because of this, an exception is made—but the importance of "sex sells" is brought home again later, when they see the skimpy costumes they are expected to wear. "What do you think we are?" one of them exclaims, "ballplayers or ballerinas?" This is further hammered home when, in addition to team practice, they are also required to go to charm and beauty school.

Tom Hanks, in the role of coach Jimmy Dugan, a former ballplayer who is initially opposed to the entire idea of the league, which he considers to be a publicity stunt and not worthy of his expertise. In the film's most famous line, he bawls out an outfielder (Bitty Schram), who breaks down in tears. "Are you crying?" he yells out. "There's no crying in baseball!" He is further disgusted when, in order to get publicity for the new league, the players are encouraged to perform antics such as catching balls while doing splits (which lands them on the cover of *Life* magazine). Sharing the sexism of the times, Dugan does not take the women players seriously, until he begins to see that their genuine talent and love for the game matches his own.

Another theme of the film is the different ways in which the characters view the game's role and position in their lives. All of them they understand that being in the league is giving them new opportunities (a montage sequence includes a newspaper headline stating that they have traded "oven mitts for baseball mitts"), but they are ambivalent about what this means to them. "Penny Marshall uses her baseball game sequences to show how sport, even for most of these women, was not all-encompassing. We see not only the women's relationships with each other, their manager, their owner, and the media but, more importantly, their confusion and internal struggles caused by suddenly finding themselves in transition. Now they have new roles, new opportunities that go against the images and principles fed to them all their lives about staying at home and caring for the family" (Williams 2006:107).

Dottie, although she is both the star player and the sex symbol of the team, quits baseball as soon as her husband (played by Bill Pullman) comes back from the war. At the end of the movie, a now-aged Dottie is reunited with her sister (who earlier in the film had been traded to another team and became her great rival) at the opening of a women's section at the Baseball Hall of Fame and Museum, in Cooperstown, New York. Dottie's daughter is proud of her mother's achievement, and the movie makes it clear that much has changed since the war era in terms of women's sports. (Many of the women shown in the final scene had been actual members of the AAGPBL.) *A League of Their Own* is an entertaining film, but it nonetheless depicts a formerly little-known part of baseball's history, and connects it to the ongoing drive for women's equality in sports and society in general.

Perhaps the theme that comes across most clearly in *A League of One's Own*, as well as in most of the other films on the ESPN list, is sportsmanship. While he lived long ago, the ethical writings of the Ancient Greek philosopher Aristotle (384–322 BCE) still have relevance to the present day, particularly when we try to understand the meaning of the term *sportsmanship*. For Aristotle, the purpose of ethical training was to help human beings achieve personal excellence, what he called *eudaimonia* or "self-fulfillment." Since we are by nature social animals, such fulfillment can only occur within a communal setting. One judges an individual by the way in which that individual excels, and one judges a community by the role models it holds up as citizens who best express that community's ideals. To win by cheating, or by disparaging an opponent's abilities, or by excessively violent acts, would not be the mark of a worthy character.

Good sportsmanship, therefore, is intimately connected with good moral character. And it's perhaps not coincidental that Aristotle was a great admirer of the theater and wrote a classic work called *The Poetics*, which dealt with the ways in which artistic works can help people develop their moral nature appropriately. He, too, would have likely been an admirer of motion pictures that demonstrate the power that sports has to shape our lives. Such depictions allow us to release otherwise harmful emotions, which, if acted upon directly, might hurt us (for instance, hitting someone in anger) but which can be equally harmful if we keep them bottled up. *Catharsis*, to use Aristotle's term, is the means by which artistic works let us experience strong emotions in a vicarious manner—such as rooting for a favorite team though one is not actually participating on the field, or losing one's sense of disbelief when engrossed in an emotional film. So, while there may be no crying in baseball, shedding a few tears in the darkness of a movie theater is nothing to be ashamed of. When it comes to sports and popular culture, the best advice is—Play Ball!

Lesson Learned: We can learn a lot about sportsmanship from sports films.

12

Virtual Reality and Popular Culture

Throughout this book, we have discussed the role of technology and our increasing reliance on the virtual world as a source of communication, news, sports, entertainment, and general information. Cell phones, social network sites, video games, and make-believe virtual worlds such as fantasy sports leagues are a part of our contemporary realities. That these computer-simulated worlds are not based on face-to-face encounters means that we have increasingly retreated to virtual realities. Virtual reality itself, then, can be defined as technology that allows users to interact with a computer-simulated environment.

Our fascination with the virtual world has not developed overnight, even though for older folks it may seem that way. For nearly two generations, people have become increasingly habituated to an electronic world. The use of computers and online devices in business and private life is the standard, not the exception. The ease of accessibility to the cyberworld provides users with opportunities to socialize in a virtual setting and to access information instantly. Virtual reality gives individuals an opportunity to transcend the real world by creating a fantasy world (Delaney 2012).

In this chapter we will discuss a wide variety of virtual realities including display technology, digital cloning, and holograms; the increasingly growing popularity of video gaming and the specific phenomenon of "swatting"; street gangs and gaming; Facebook and the creation of communities of "friends," which exist only in the virtual world; the virtual monetary system based on bitcoins; and the growing concern over accessing the digital assets of loved ones after they die in the real world.

Popular culture and virtual reality are the best of friends, and whether we like it or not, more and more of our lives are being spent in virtual worlds.

Virtual Reality, Display Technology, Digital Cloning,
and Holograms: Who Needs Reality When the
Virtual World Can Be Controlled by a Console?

A growing characteristic of contemporary society is virtual reality. Virtual reality refers to technology that allows users to interact with a computer-simulated environment. Typically, people rely on display technology to utilize computer-simulated environments. "A display is a computer output surface and projecting mechanism that shows text and often graphic images to the computer user, using a cathode ray tube (CRT), liquid crystal display (LCD), light-emitting diode, gas plasma, or other image project technology. The display is usually considered to include the screen or projection surface and the device that produces the information on the screen" (Rouse 2005). The display screen is typically referred to as a *monitor* when packaged in a separate case. The display is the most-used output device on a computer, and it provides instant feedback by showing you text and graphics as you work or play (Tyson and Carmack 2014). The clarity of the image being projected is influenced by display technology resolution. Resolution is based on the number of individual dots of color, known as pixels, contained on a display. "Resolution is expressed by identifying the number of pixels on the horizontal axis (rows) and the number on the vertical axis (columns) such as 800x600. Resolution is affected by a number of factors, including the size of the screen" (Tyson and Carmak 2014).

In computers without a separate monitor, the display is integrated into a unit with the processor and other parts of the computer. In some cases, the processor and other parts of the computer (e.g., notebook computers) are integrated into a total unit. Displays and monitors are also sometimes called video display terminals (VDTs) (Rouse 2005). Most people use the terms *display* and *monitor* interchangeably.

As Rouse (2005) explains, the defining characteristics of computer display devices include color capability, sharpness and viewability, screen size, and projection technology. Most computers provide color display; some smaller computers use a less expensive monochrome display. The image sharpness of a screen is based on the dot pitch—the size of an individual beam that penetrates to light up a point of phosphor on the screen. Screen sizes vary considerably, according to the computer device. Desktop screens of today are larger than many TV screens of the past, and for good reason, as many people stream TV shows and movies on their computer screens. Cell phones were once valued based on how small they could be made (an early goal was to make sure the phone could fit into a pants pocket); later, larger screens became the vogue. *Projection technology* refers to the manner in which graphics and text are delivered (e.g., CRT, LCD, or 3-D; wired or wireless).

This quick, basic review of display technology was made available to introduce the relationship between virtual reality and simulated environments. Simulated environments, accessible as visual experiences via display technology, are utilized by a variety of social institutions, organizations, groups, and individuals. The medical community uses virtual medicine to train surgeons and to experiment, virtually, with new, radical procedures before subjecting humans to untried treatments. The field of psychology also utilizes virtual reality to treat people who suffer from phobias. Engineers use virtual reality in testing a wide variety of designs to gauge their functionality before proceeding to implement their construction in the real world.

Hollywood has increasingly employed virtual reality in filmmaking. Among their newest tricks is "digital cloning," which was used, for instance, in the blockbuster film *Maleficent* to affix "pixie-perfect" human faces on tiny animated fairies. The surreal technique of digitally cloning human faces onto animated characters is the creation of Paul Debevec who heads up the University of Southern California's Institute for Creative Technologies. Debevec is reinventing the way movies are made by digitally cloning actors so perfectly that the "digital puppet has every skin pore, fine crease and the ability for any little twitch or bulge or buckle of skin that the real person would've had" (*CBS News* 2014a). In order to achieve digital cloning more than six thousand computer-controlled LEDs and fifty cameras are used to capture every nuance of the subject. "The key to creating believable virtual humans is how the computer measures both light reflecting off the surface of the skin and penetrating beneath it. The result is a perfect digital clone that can be inserted into any scene" (*CBS News* 2014a). Digital cloning techniques were also used in *Gravity* and *Avatar*. The lead actors were scanned to create lifelike images for digital stunt doubles.

Digital cloning is used for more than making movies. Debevec has teamed up with USC's Shoah Foundation to scan Holocaust survivors so their stories will live long after they are gone. The virtual technology used to create these clones has advanced to the point where the clones appear in life size and in 3-D and can be seen without 3-D glasses. In 2015, the Shoah Foundation and its partners successfully debuted a fully interactive display of Holocaust survivor Pinchas Gutter at the Illinois

Holocaust Museum and Education Center. The virtual Gutter appears as a hologram and provides a first-person narrative of his experiences surviving five concentration camps.

While Hollywood often generates big profits from its blockbuster films, the industry itself was not responsible for the funding that enabled the development of digital cloning. Instead, it has been funded by the Department of Defense, to produce virtual reality training for the armed forces (*CBS News* 2014a). The military uses virtual reality to train pilots, parachutists, and combat soldiers. Soon, they may add cloned personnel to their drones. The possibilities are nearly endless, and a bit scary.

Holograms, at least in concept, have been around for generations. But only recently have we seen holograms so freely inhabit the real world. We just described how Hollywood and the military use, and plan to use, them but holograms are also being used for entertainment, in music videos and even live concerts. A hologram of Tupac Shakur performed on stage at the 2012 Coachella music festival, stunning audience members. This was understandable, as he had been dead since 1996 and his virtual appearance had not been announced before his appearance. The hologram of Tupac performed with rap heavyweights Snoop Lion (formerly Snoop Dogg) and Dr. Dre. In 2014, Michael Jackson, in hologram form, appeared at the Billboard Music Awards and performed "Slave to the Rhythm," from *Xscape*, an album that was released after his death. If you think that is odd, you are not alone, as many people found the King of Pop's hologram appearance to be creepy, although many found it cool (France 2014). Frank Sinatra and Elvis Presley have also been reanimated as holograms to entertain the masses. Who's next? As a side note, the authors of this book plan on teaching and writing as holograms, long after their deaths. Give the public what it wants, we always say.

Virtual reality is especially important to individuals who seek to transcend the confines of ordinary reality in order to inhabit a fantasy world. In these fantasy worlds, participants can create whimsical versions of themselves through such mechanisms as avatars. The 2009 blockbuster film *Avatar* (the first film whose revenues cracked the $2 billion ceiling) was hugely popular because of its virtual reality special effects and the idea of transcendence they conveyed. In the escapist world of virtual reality, individuals can create a virtual self—an alter ego whose identity can be hidden from in the occupants of the real world. There are many virtual worlds to choose from, including "Second Life" (SL) and "World of Warcraft" (WoW). In these virtual worlds, gamers create an Avatar and navigate a 3-D world of fun, adventure, and danger. In 2014, there were more than 38 million registered residents of SL and eleven million monthly subscribers of WoW. Based on these two virtual worlds alone (and there are many more in cyberspace), it is apparent that humans enjoy escaping the real world as their virtual selves.

Lesson Learned: If we can live forever as holograms or avatars, virtual reality may be the Fountain of Youth.

Gamers and "Swatting": Gaming Defeats in the Virtual World Are Causing Havoc in the Real World

In the previous short story, we examined virtual reality and the desire of many people to escape ordinary reality. Video games represent one form of virtual reality, and many people, especially children and young people, spend a great deal of time playing video games. It may be understandable that young people play video games, as they have more free time than adults, who have jobs, family obligations, and household chores (mowing the lawn, shoveling the driveway, painting the house, and general upkeep) to occupy their time. It is estimated that 97 percent (99% of boys and 94% of girls) of American children play video games (ABC News 2014).

The most popular video games tend to incorporate violence. A 2011 study found that 71 percent of all games contained at least some mild violence, while 25 percent included intense violence, blood, and gore and that children ages seven to twelve routinely play games rated "M" for mature audiences—that is, the most violent and graphic games (Hicks 2013). Smith, Lachlan, and Tamborini (2003) found that in nearly all video games, violence goes unpunished and that in more than half of them the perpetrators of violence were rewarded for their aggressive actions; 78 percent of all violent interactions in the first ten minutes of game play featured lethal violence; in nearly 25 percent of the violent interactions in mature games, players perceived themselves as stalkers; almost half of all violent video game segments treated the violence as humorous; and only 10 percent of all video game protagonists possessed "good" or "prosocial" qualities.

Video games, like most games, provide players an opportunity to win a game. Typically, people who win are happy and those who lose are displeased, but because it's "just a game" it is relatively easy to move on with life. There has been a growing development of late, however, as some gamers, especially those who lose at "Mortal Kombat," engage in a phenomenon known as "swatting." We will discuss swatting in greater detail shortly, but for now it's worth stating that swatting refers to the practice of someone calling 911 and having emergency units dispatched to someone else's home based on a false report (Kovacs 2013). It is also important to note that swatting is not limited to video games.

Undoubtedly, a number of readers of this short story have played "Mortal Kombat." the American video game franchise series created by Ed Boon and John Tobias, and could describe this popular game better than we can, so we will keep our analysis limited to the basics. "Mortal Kombat," with its main character based on Jean Claude Van Damme, was originally released in 1992 on arcade machines, and later on home console and computer systems.

The "Mortal Kombat" series takes place in a fictional universe consisting of eighteen surviving realms created by the Elder Gods that serve as the homes of legendary heroes (Kung Lao, Johnny Cage). The object of the game is to conquer other realms, and to do so one must defeat the greatest warriors of the other realms in ten consecutive "Mortal Kombat" tournaments. The series is known for its high level of bloody violence, including its signature "fatalities"—finishing moves that require the gamer to push a sequence of buttons. For players of "Mortal Kombat" the thrill of the game is in the fatalities, which provide the gamer the chance to demonstrate his or her virtual skills.

As it pertains to video gamers, swatting occurs when an online player maliciously seeks personal information regarding another player, which the first player uses in filing a fake 911 emergency report. The reported emergency leads to emergency response teams appearing at the address of the targeted user, or victim of the vengeful gamer. The term *swatting* is derived from the tactical response typically generated by such calls, which may include dispatching SWAT. The vengeful gamer has, of sorts, performed a nonlethal, real-world "fatality."

Most gamers involved in swatting are participants in the games "Mortal Kombat," "Call of Duty," and "Counter-Strike." "Call of Duty" is a very popular violent video game that can be played as either a first-person or a third-person shooter. There are many variations of "Call of Duty," with the earlier ones consisting of World War II scenarios. "Counter-Strike" is a first-person shooter game involving terrorism and counterterrorism, in which the player takes on hostile combat teams all over the world. In August 2014, while Jordan Mattherson of Littleton, Colorado, was playing "Counter-Strike," he became involved in a swatting incident. As he recorded himself playing the game and live streaming his play, the camera caught the SWAT team entering his room to arrest him. One of the authors had a student in his Fall 2014 Introductory Sociology class who reported that he was watching the streamed video live and saw Mattherson get arrested.

Swatting has become increasingly popular beyond isolated incidents of an occasional upset gamer perpetrating a hoax. Swatters have turned swatting into a game in itself, by keeping track of the number of emergency response vehicles and personnel that respond. The swatting gamer with the highest number wins. The win, which might be enjoyed by no more than a small number of gamers, comes at a potentially great cost, as emergency crews responding to a false call are not available to respond to a real emergency. If swatting incidents were part of a game and restricted to the virtual world, law enforcement and the general public would not care, but because swatting impinges on the real world, it is a growing nuisance.

In April 2014, for example, a hoaxer (swatter) triggered a massive police response on New York's Long Island. Long Beach Police Commissioner Michael Tangney states, "It's a nationwide epidemic right now, where people play video games, and if you lose the video game, you try to develop information about the person you're playing, and then we send this army of police personnel out. In this bizarre world of swatting, you get points for the helicopters, police cars, the SWAT team, and the type of entry. It's very sophisticated, and unfortunately it's also very dangerous" (Stableford 2014). Tangney reported that dispatchers received a call from a person who identified himself as Rafael Castillo, a seventeen-year-old from Long Beach. Pretending to be Castillo, the swatter told the dispatcher, "I just killed my mother and I might shoot more people" (Stableford 2014). "The threat prompted Nassau County police to scramble helicopters and send a SWAT team to Castillo's home, leading to a 90-minute standoff that involved more than 60 officers, some with guns drawn" (Stableford 2014).

Castillo's mother was in the kitchen making coffee when the police arrived. Castillo was in his room playing "Call of Duty" with his headphones on and never heard the initial commotion. If this had been a hostile situation, Castillo would have been an easy real-life victim because he was so immersed in the virtual world and isolated from the real world by his headphones. A real soldier or "Mortal Kombat" hero would not be so dumb as to turn off the reality that surrounds him. But gamers like Castillo are not real soldiers. His brother, Jose, told the *New York Post*, "He didn't realize anything was going on—he couldn't hear anything. I told him, 'There's a bunch of cops outside that are looking for you'" (Stableford 2014). When Castillo, a high school junior, rejoined the real world, he realized that he was a swatting victim, "I right away had an idea what it was, because I've seen it on the news," Castillo said (Stableford 2014).

Swatting has been in the news quite a bit lately. As Stableford (2014) chronicles:

- The FBI reports that swatting cases have occurred since at least 2005; in 2008 the bureau issued an advisory on the "new phenomenon" of swatting.

- States such as California, Washington, Texas, and Colorado have seen a rise is swatting calls in recent years.

- In 2009, Matthew Weigman, a nineteen-year-old hacker from Massachusetts, was sentenced to eleven years in federal prison for years of phone-related conspiracies, including swatting.

- In 2012, police in Washington state reported that two teen gamers had been the victims of swatting. One, a thirteen-year-old from Rainier, was home alone playing on an Xbox when an anonymous 911 caller reported a hostage situation, triggering a police response. Police responded to another call in Washington stating that a father had shot his fourteen-year-old daughter after finding out she was pregnant.

In Los Angeles, swatters have called in emergencies allegedly occurring at celebrities' homes. Among the victimized celebrities are Rihanna, Miley Cyrus, Justin Timberlake, Ashton Kutcher, and Selena Gomez. In 2013, the LAPD announced that it would no longer issue press releases or immediately confirm instances of celebrity swatting, saying that intense media coverage seemed to fuel more incidents (Blankstein 2013). Cmdr. Andrew Smith (LAPD Media Relations Section) stated, "It's our belief that the perpetrators of these false police reports are motivated entirely by the publicity these calls receive. We intend to reduce or eliminate that motivation" (Blankstein 2013). In September 2013, in reaction to the number of swatting incidents in California, Governor Jerry Brown signed a new law that makes people convicted of making false emergency calls liable for the full cost of the response.

Swatting is occurring in Canada, too. A sixteen-year-old Ontario resident was arrested for a string of fraudulent calls to police, including a number of "swatting calls" that attempted to summon teams of heavily armed police to the target's home (Brandon 2014). Swatting incidents are increasing because of copycat gamers who want to gain attention in the cyberworld, as well as the militarization of police forces and the increased availability of trace-resistant phone services (Brandon 2014). Most swatters are under eighteen and do not mean to cause serious harm; they see swatting as a harmless prank, despite the potentially serious consequences. However, as one Ontario police officer stated, "These irresponsible incidents have created real fear in people, put public safety at risk, and disrupted entire communities where these events have occurred" (Brandon 2014).

Our final swatting story involves a desperate attempt by a man old enough to have secured a real life. Michael Adams, twenty-two, of Marple Township, Pennsylvania, was charged with reporting false alarms to an agency of public safety, falsely reporting weapons of mass destruction, and other charges in connection with a call made to 911 in which he told the 911 operator that he was being held hostage by a man with an AR-15 rifle and a bomb strapped to his chest (Kovacs 2013). In reality, Adams was self-swatting. He reported an incident and claimed to be the victim, all in one swoop. His self-swatted was an attempt to boost his reputation on hacking forums. "Detectives noted in court documents that Adams might have wanted to be equal to his peers, some of which had been swatted" (Kovacs 2013).

Swatting: the bridge between the made-up virtual world and the real world of the desperate gamer.

Lesson Learned: Only sore losers resort to swatting.

Video Games and Street Gangs: You Too Can be a Bad Ass Gang Leader

As stated in the previous story on swatting, gamers love violent video games. They enjoy the rush that "living on the edge" in the virtual world provides. Some people worry that children who play violent video games are likely to become desensitized to real-life violence and may view violence in a positive light when they become adults. The vast majority of gamers are not violent in the real world, however, and are unlikely to participate in behaviors such as swatting. In fact, people have been gaming so long that the stereotypical view of a gamer as a teenaged male slacker is badly outdated; instead, in 2014, only 29 percent of gamers were under eighteen years of age; 32 percent were 18 to 35 years old; and 39 percent were 36 years and older (*Statista* 2014). In addition, females now comprise 48 percent of gamers (*Statista* 2014; Wingfield 2014). Furthermore, of the 233 million active Internet users in the United States, it is estimated that more than half are active gamers (*Statista* 2014).

The cases of extreme violence in the real world that have been connected to gamers who played violent video games attract the attention of the traditional mass media and the masses. For example, Anders Behring Breivik, the Norwegian who slaughtered dozens of people at an island youth retreat (July 2011) before he was apprehended by police, told authorities that he sharpened his aim by playing the video game "Call of Duty: Modern Warfare" for hours on end. He also told an Oslo court that he took steroids to build his physical strength and meditated to "de-emotionalize" himself before the bombing and shooting rampage that left seventy-seven people dead (*The Post-Standard* 2012b). His lack of remorse and his matter-of-fact description of weapons and tactics—he even considered using a flame thrower—were deeply disturbing to the families of the victims. The "Call of Duty" game teaches gamers how to use military tactics, and Breivik took it to the extreme.

Despite cases such as Breivik's, studies attempting to link aggression, violence, and criminal behavior to video games are inconclusive. "Studies on whether violent video games lead to aggression in children have been mixed: some studies have found a strong connection, while others find no link" (Rettner 2014). It is worth mentioning here, again, that most gamers, although they enjoy the virtual worlds of violence and mayhem, and admire their own skills and ability to survive and move on to the next level of a game, will not engage in violent confrontations with others on the streets of reality. Real-life street violence entails random acts of violence, criminal organizations, and street gangs. Gamers, other than extremists such as Anders Behring Breivik, would not last much longer than a few minutes in certain gang-infested urban environments. In fact, many gamers might have a difficult time beating gang members in the virtual gaming world, as gangbangers also enjoy playing video games.

Game manufacturers have long realized that the real-life world of street gangs is filled with violence and mayhem and consequently would make a great backdrop for storylines in video games. Not surprisingly, then, there are numerous video games than include street gangs. Among the top street gang–based video games are "The Warriors" (2007) and

"The Warriors: Street Brawl" (2009), both based on the 1979 classic street gang film *The Warriors*. (The original movie was based on a 1965 novel by Sol Yorick, which itself was loosely based on the classic work *Anabasis* by the Ancient Greek writer Xenophon—a fascinating case of popular culture being influenced by high culture.) In the movie, the Warriors, a street gang from Coney Island, Brooklyn, has joined street gangs from all five of New York City's boroughs in an unarmed gang summit organized by Cyrus, the leader of the revered Gramercy Riffs gang. Cyrus has requested that every street gang in NYC send unarmed representatives to Van Cortlandt Park in the Bronx to discuss unification among all street gangs so that they can rule the city. Most of the gangs are in favor of the unification idea but Luther, leader of the Rogues, shoots Cyrus and frames Cleon, the leader of the Warriors. Cleon is jumped and his fate is unknown. With all the other street gangs after them, the Warriors try to get home to Coney Island.

The video game of "The Warriors," released in 2005 for PlayStation 2 and Xbox and in 2007 for PlayStation Portable, is based on the film and takes place in 1970s New York City, encompassing the five city boroughs. The game is about survival and relies heavily on violent brawls. The gamer participates in many gang-related activities, including spray painting graffiti to mark turf and disrespecting rivals. The follow-up "Warriors" game, "The Warriors Street Brawl," was released on Mac OS X, Microsoft Windows, and Xbox Live Arcade in 2009. Gamers participate in gang-related behaviors in 3-D. They can punch, kick, or use weapons (knives, wrenches, pipes, and bats). The punching is realistic and so too are the many impact sounds (from punching and the use of weapons) (Delaney 2014).

"Saints Row: The Third" is another popular video game featuring street gangs. It is an action/adventure-based game that was released in 2011 for Microsoft Windows, PlayStation 3, and Xbox 360. In this game, the player controls the leader of the Third Street Saints, a gang that operates in the fictional city of Steelport. The Saints are at war with three other gangs, the Morningstar, Deckers, and Luchadores. As the gamer progresses through a series of missions he or she earns in-game money, weapons, cars, and gang respect. The gamer who earns enough points can set off a gigantic bomb to demolish one of the enemy skyscrapers in the city. There are negative consequences to setting off the bomb, so gamers have to weigh the decision carefully.

In 2013, "Saints Row IV" was released for Microsoft Windows, PlayStation3, and Xbox 360. In this fourth installment, the player controls the leader of the Third Street Saints street gang, who has now become the president of the United States. The game takes place five years after the events of its predecessor, with the Saints in Steelport who now must fight off an alien invasion as well as rival street gang enemies from their past. Let the killing and maiming continue!

Perhaps the most popular video game featuring street gangs is the "Grand Theft Auto" series. In 2013, "Grand Theft Auto V" was released for PlayStation 3 and Xbox 360, and in 2014 for Microsoft Windows, PlayStation 4, and Xbox One. The game is played from a third-person perspective with the gamer following, either by foot or vehicle, three criminals and their efforts to commit heists within the setting of the fictional city of Los Santos (based on Los Angeles) and the open countryside of the state of San Andreas (based on Southern California). In online multiplayer mode, up to sixteen people can play at the same time in either cooperative or competitive game matches. The game has scenes depicting torture and is, by design, very violent. Within days of its release, the sales of "Grand Theft Auto V" exceeded more than $1 billion; by mid-May 2014, sales exceeded $2 billion (Forbes 2014).

Lesson Learned: It's safer fighting street gangs in video games than it is in real life.

Facebook and Friendship: Can You Be a "Virtual Friend?"

In Book VIII of his *Nichomachean Ethics*, Aristotle categorizes three types of friendship: friendships of utility, friendships of pleasure, and friendships of the good. Briefly, friendships of utility are those in which people are on cordial terms primarily because each person benefits from the other in some way. Business partnerships, relationships among co-workers, and classmate connections are examples. Friendships of pleasure are those where individuals seek out each other's company because of the joy it brings. Passionate love affairs, people who belong to the same hobby organization, and fishing buddies fall into this category. Most important of all are friendships of the good. These are friendships based upon mutual respect, admiration for each others' virtues, and a strong desire to aid and assist each other because one person recognizes an essential goodness in the other.

In Aristotle's view, the first two types of friendship are relatively fragile. When the purpose for which the relationship is formed somehow changes, the friendship tends to end. For instance, if the business partnership is dissolved, or one takes another job, or one graduates from school, it is more than likely that no ties will be maintained with the former friend of utility. Likewise, once the love affair cools, or one takes up a new hobby, or gives up fishing, the friends of pleasure will go their own ways.

Friendships of the good are those that are the most important. They tend to be lifelong, are often formed in childhood or adolescence, and will exist as long as the friends continue to remain virtuous in each other's eyes. To have more than a handful of such friends of the good, Aristotle states, is indeed a fortunate thing. Rare indeed are such friendships, for men of this kind are rare. Or as the Girl Scouts song goes, "Make new friends but keep the old, for one is silver and the other is gold." Such friendships of the good require time and intimacy—to truly know people's finest qualities you must have deep experiences with them, and close connections. "Many a Friendship doth want of intercourse destroy," Aristotle warns us.

And yet, for those of us living in the frenetic twenty-first century, it can be difficult to maintain such ties. Friendships of utility and pleasure come and go quickly as we move from job to job and relationship to relationship, but for Aristotle this need not be a tragedy. Since the interchanges of both are less intense and less permanent, their endings are not necessarily detrimental to one's self. But to lose a friend of the good—ah, there is tragedy indeed.

Facebook and other social media have added a new wrinkle to Aristotle's threefold schema. Thanks to these, and the wonders of the Internet in general, it is now easier than ever to stay in touch with people from throughout one's life. Old acquaintances, long forgotten, can be found relatively easily through Google searches and services such as "classmates. com," wherein you can, for a fee, track down old school chums you haven't spoken to in many a moon.

While Aristotle might have found such re-connections of broken ties problematic, they allow people to have friendship networks numbering in the hundreds, if not thousands. Even more fascinating, though, is the fact that many of these "friendships" involve people who have never even met face to face. They share similar likes and dislikes, have complementary traits, and feel strongly compatible with one another, yet, by Aristotle's criteria, they cannot truly be friends, since they have never had actual interactions with one another, but only virtual.

And yet, clearly there are countless individuals today who would argue that their "virtual" friends—with whom they often share their most intimate secrets and most private reflections—are closer to them in many ways than those they see on a regular basis in the "real" world. Since many of us spend an inordinate amount of time in cyberspace, and often assume personas online very different from the ones we manifest outwardly, it seems that new sorts of relationships are flourishing that could never be dreamed of previously.

Often, discussions of personal relationships in the cyber age dwell on the negative: the superficial connections, the dangers of identity theft, and the reality of information overload. Aristotle does warn that, at least where friendships of the good are concerned, there are limitations to how many it is feasible to handle. He writes, "To be a friend to many people in the way of the perfect Friendship, is not possible."

Perhaps Facebook *has* made it possible for friendships of all three categories to thrive and prosper in ways Aristotle could never have anticipated, and indeed has given us a new category to contemplate: virtual friendship.

Lesson Learned: Social media have given new meaning to the old phrase, "Can't we be friends?"

Bitcoins: Virtual Money Makes the World Go 'Round

Bitcoins are an increasingly popular form of digital currency, by which transactions take place "peer to peer," without the involvement of any bank or central authority. Devised in 2008 by a pseudonymous individual known only as "Satoshi Nakamoto" (thus a "virtual" personality—it may be either a human being or the name of a group of individuals), bitcoins are often referred to as "virtual cryptocurrencies," "digital cash," or "electronic currency." It is a medium of exchange which is not issued by, or backed up, by any government, nation, or international monetary authority, and yet more and more people are utilizing it as a means of payment. Libertarians, in particular, who have long been suspicious of any centralized authority, have advocated this as a potent means of peer-to-peer financial interaction, bypassing any middlemen or third sources.

Sophisticated software programs and computer networks make it possible for most people to make such transactions with ease. Bitcoin servers validate the transactions while maintaining the anonymity of those involved.

To capitalize on this new means of transaction, entrepreneurs are developing bitcoin ATMs, similar to the ones we have become used to over the past thirty years that are operated by traditional banking systems. One such is Robocoin, "the maker of automated teller machines that turn bitcoins, the growing virtual currency, into hard cash. The bitcoin ATMs, in the view of the start-up's founder, would challenge traditional money transfer services such as Western Union" (Snyder 2014). John Russell, the twenty-five-year-old founder of Robocoin, speaks in militaristic tones about his lofty ambitions. "Western Union is on our crosshairs big time. . . . The process of wire transfers, international wire transfers—we're going to smash them, we're going to crush them. We're going to totally disrupt that environment, and that's what I'm most excited about" (Snyder 2014). With thirty or so such ATMs presently in existence and more than eight hundred projected to be installed shortly, this could have a transformative impact on the way all of us use and distribute money.

The potential financial impact worldwide of the bitcoin revolution is causing traditional banking institutions and governments to take a long hard look at this phenomenon, which was almost completely unanticipated. They are trying to figure out the legal issues arising from this new form of financial transactions, as well as its implications for the world's increasingly interconnected economic system. Some claim that such free-floating types of transactions could ultimately cause a financial panic that would be even more catastrophic than the 2008 recession from which the world is only now emerging.

Another practical fear arising from the newfound interest in bitcoins is the danger of money laundering. As *Fortune* magazine points out: "Spend some time in the sketchy online marketplace for this currency and you'll find that Bitcoin users range from the common Iranian on the street, who is worried about inflation, to hit men and drug dealers, who prefer to be paid in an untraceable currency. If Bitcoin is able to stabilize its value on the international markets, it could eventually creep into the legitimate world of finance, threatening major profit centers for both the banks and payment operators like Visa and MasterCard" (Sanati 2012). Shady business deals, tax dodging, unscrupulous illegal drug sales, and even terrorist transactions are already difficult to monitor when traditional financial industries are involved, and almost all such industries have been fined for allowing such money laundering to occur. If this is the case, it seems even more likely that the use of bitcoins will only increase such illicit activities. Efforts are underway to regulate this nebulous industry, but given the anonymity and flexibility inherent in how it functions, how to do this remains a mystery.

As Nathaniel Popper points out, our own computers are vulnerable to kidnappers demanding bitcoins. He writes: "In a modern day version of a mob shakedown, hackers around the world have seized files on millions of computers, taken down public websites and even, in a few cases, threatened physical harm. The victims—who have included ordinary computer users, financial firms and police departments—are told that their only way out is through a bitcoin payment that is sometimes more than $20,000. . . . Criminals like the virtual currency because it can be held in a digital wallet that does not have to be registered with any government or financial authority—and because it can be easily exchanged for real money. A single bitcoin can be sold online or on the street for around $290" (Popper 2015).

So suspicion about the stability and legality of the bitcoin industry is a growing international concern.

But not everyone shares this sense of gloom and doom. Various mainstream websites such as WordPress, OKCupid, and Expedia have begun to accept bitcoins as valid currency. And the Electronic Frontier Foundation, an international not-for-profit digital rights group that defends online personal liberties, is also showing the way by agreeing to accept bitcoin donations.

For those who utilize bitcoins, the anonymity, ease of service, and speed of transactions seem to override traditional worries, although real concerns are being expressed as to whether this might be a short-term fad that will ultimately crash, much like previous Internet-related economic "bubbles." And economists caution that one should ignore grandiose claims and take a more wait-and-see attitude. Jerry Brito, director of George Mason University's Technology Policy Program, for instance, although himself a bitcoin user, states that it is unlikely that bitcoins will soon, if ever, replace government-controlled currencies. "I've always been not totally convinced by the argument that bitcoin is going to stand apart from banks," he said. "Bitcoin standing apart as a flat currency doesn't make sense to me" (Snyder 2014).

For those of us who've become used to online banking, credit card apps on our phones, and other types of virtual transactions, the bitcoin phenomenon seems more like a natural evolution than a radical leap forward. Its ease of transaction, and its connection with our growing reliance on online interactions in general, makes it increasingly likely that more and more of us will be making use of this new financial instrument on a regular basis.

Lesson Learned: "Virtual" money seems pretty real if you can buy what you like with it; but, who guarantees its value if the virtual system collapses?

Digital Assets: Virtual Reality after Death

As we've seen throughout this chapter, we are all spending more and more of our waking hours online. Checking Facebook, reading e-mail, tweeting friends, blogging about our daily activities, playing online videogames, watching sporting events, flirting on computer dating services—it's amazing that we have time to do anything in our nonvirtual lives. In addition, we are generating a huge amount of data about ourselves which is stored online. Our medical records are now digitized, as are our school and work information, as well as our social network connections. Many of us have our own websites and/or daily blogs, as well as countless numbers of photographs and videos stored on various Internet sites or in the "the cloud." But little thought has been given about what is going to happen to all these data when we're no longer around to retrieve them. The Internet may live forever, but not so all of us. Who will have access to this information when we're dead and gone?

Many of us have had the unnerving experience of receiving a Facebook greeting from a person who we know is no longer alive. Automatically generated "responses" meant to help facilitate communication can have the unanticipated effect of opening emotional wounds, or of being downright scary. One of the authors of this text, shortly after learning of the unexpected death of a friend, was startled to receive a few days later an e-mail from that person, with the tag line reading "important message." Feeling somewhat like a character in the old TV show *The Twilight Zone*, he hesitatingly opened the message, only to see that it had been sent by the friend's partner, using the friend's e-mail account, to let everyone know the time and place of the memorial service.

Receiving greetings from the dead is a new form of virtual horror, to be sure, but there is another, more pertinent issue facing all of us. When a loved one dies, who should be allowed access to that person's data, and how can this best be determined? Geoffrey Fowler of *The Wall Street Journal* writes of the sad case of Alison Atkins, a Toronto native who died of ulcerative colitis, a type of colon disease, at the tragically young age of sixteen. Her family wanted to retrieve the many photos and messages on her various password-protected sites. Her twenty-year-old sister Jaclyn remarked that "Alison had pictures, messages and poems written that we wanted to keep to remember her," but she and the other Atkins family members found that they were not allowed to retrieve any of Alison's passwords, due to the websites' terms of service. The reason given in each case was that not only would this violate the law, it would also violate the deceased person's privacy. Fowler writes that "families like the Atkinses can lose control of a process they feel is their right and obligation when the memories are stored online—encrypted, locked behind passwords, just beyond reach. One major cause is privacy law. Current laws, intending to protect the living, fail to address a separate question: Who should see or supervise our online legacy?" (Fowler 2013).

So-called digital assets are not treated by U.S. or Canadian laws as identical to physical assets that can be designated and distributed by wills or other legal documents. In most cases, the owner's consent must be given in order for service providers to release privileged information, including personal passwords. But what happens when the person is no longer alive? In some cases, the service terms state that, upon receiving notice of a person's death, all such data will be permanently deleted—a form of virtual death comparable to actual physical death. Since many of these providers are in business to sell data to advertisers, they want to delete accounts of the deceased as quickly as they can, whereas loved ones may well want to preserve or at least continue to have access to such information as a type of memorial for the deceased.

Jaclyn Atkins was ultimately able to get into her late sister's accounts thanks to the help of a technician friend who cracked the password codes. Once she had gained access, she was able to change the privacy settings and reopen the various closed accounts, as a means of alerting Alison's network of contacts to her untimely death, as well as to allow other family members to read her blogs and other messages as a way of achieving closure. But such methods are, to say the least, controversial. Fowler adds: "In the Atkins situation, no law-enforcement agency or company is suggesting it would press charges. Still 'there hasn't been a lot of case law on this,' says Jim Lamm, a Minnesota estate lawyer who focuses on digital issues. 'It's up to a prosecuting attorney whether to charge' a family member with a crime for accessing the accounts of the dead, he says, 'and that's not a risk that I would advise them to take'" (Fowler 2013).

In this particular case, it is understandable why grieving family members would resort to such methods in order to retrieve personal information. But such methods are not always benign or so easily defendable, and we should all give thought to which family members or friends we would want to have such assess when we are no longer around to okay it.

Not surprisingly, the law is finally starting to take this issue seriously, and various measures are being debated as to how best to regulate a deceased person's digital assets. "The Uniform Law Commission, whose members are appointed by state governments to help standardize state laws, has endorsed a plan to automatically give loved ones access to—but not control of—all digital accounts unless otherwise specified," reports Anne Flaherty of the Associated Press (Flaherty 2014). This would have to be ratified by each state's legislature in order to become a law. And while it is a rational way of trying to deal with the increasing number of frustrated family members who are unable to gain access such data legally, privacy advocates are concerned about the implications of this. Might there not be cases in which one would not want one's spouse or parents to retrieve such personal data? Ginger McCall, associate director of the Electronic Privacy Information Center of Washington State, for instance, strongly argues that, rather than being an automatic process that one would otherwise need to opt out of, such data should remain sealed unless a judge's approval is given. In her words, "The digital world is a different world" than the offline one, where we routinely shred and destroy a great deal of personal information we would prefer no one, including our loved ones, ever see. "No one," she adds, "would keep 10 years of every communication they ever had with dozens or even hundreds of other people under their beds" (Flaherty 2014).

Clearly, this is an issue that will continue to concern to all of us. Just as we should all have a medical and legal proxy who can speak on our behalf if we are incapacitated, and a will that details where our physical assets should be distributed after our death, so each and every one of us should think hard about who should have access to our digital assets upon our demise, and what sorts of information we are storing. Who do we want spending our bitcoins after we're gone?

Lesson Learned: In cyberspace, our virtual lives will go on and on.

13

Parting Thoughts

We hope we have demonstrated throughout this book the value of popular culture in society and its ability to teach us life lessons. Popular culture is the vernacular or people's culture that predominates in society at any given time. It engages those aspects of social life in which the public is most actively involved. As the culture of the people, popular culture both reflects and shapes the perceptions, values, and norms of society. Everyday activities of people are shaped by pop culture influences, including the latest fashions in clothing and hairstyles, fads and trends, the use of slang, greeting rituals, and especially the mass media—including film, television, radio, social media, music, newspapers, cartoons and comics, books, technology, sports, virtual reality, and ambassadors of popular culture. Popular culture invites large, heterogeneous masses of people to identify collectively; it serves an inclusionary role in society, because it affords people a framework in which they may unite in the latest forms of accepted behavior. Thus, by participating in popular culture, individuals become parts of the greater society.

American popular culture is influential in many parts of the world besides just the United States. Its influence is felt both positively and negatively. For instance, some governments (e.g., Islamic regimes in the Middle East) condemn American popular culture as a source of hedonism and the devil's work, while Western societies seemingly cannot get enough of it. We will restrict our parting thoughts to those who participate in the global consumption of U.S. popular culture.

"Global consumption of American popular culture" is a key phrase, as the entities, such as American television and the film and music industries, that are responsible for mass-producing the artifacts of popular culture are also aggressive pushers of consumerism. Popular culture does indeed reflect and influence the norms, values, and perceptions of the masses, and it also encompasses products that must be purchased by the masses. Producers of popular culture flood U.S. and global markets with marketing and advertising that encourage people to "shop and buy"—the battle cry of societies that rely on mass consumption of products. Citizens around the world have accepted the idea that the consumption of goods and services is desirable, and they participate in many aspects of popular culture, whether that entails movies, ballgames, video games, live or recorded music, or the latest technological devices (smart phones, laptops, or whatever "must-have" gizmos promise to make our lives better, easier, or more glamorous).

Considering the changes that have taken place in American industry, with an ever-growing number of manufacturers deserting the United States for cheaper labor markets overseas, there are those who wonder if we manufacture any products for export any longer. The answer is, of course, that we do. In fact, the United States still produces more goods than other country in the world—$1.6 trillion worth, according to the federal Bureau of Economic Analysis—and while some analysts predict that China will soon overtake the U.S. as the world's leading producer, America currently accounts for about 20 percent of all manufacturing output (*Parade* 2009; *Economics in Pictures* 2013; *National Association of Manufacturers* 2014). And although it is true that China and many other nations are nearing America's level of production of manufactured goods, few come near the United States in the exportation of popular culture. People around the world love our television programming, feature films, music, and fads and trends. Americans traveling abroad find many reminders of home, especially in the realm of popular culture.

For example, it is interesting to note that Broadway musicals, a distinctly American combination of popular culture and high culture, have found a second home in Seoul, South Korea—we might call this Way Off Broadway. Bearing an unavoidable pop culture influence, they are hugely popular with South Korean audiences, with ticket sales rising from $9 million in 2000 to $150 million in 2013 (*CBS News* 2014b). Women in their twenties make up nearly 40 percent of the audiences in Seoul. Among the popular productions in Seoul in 2014 were *Jersey Boys*, *Mamma Mia*, and *The Sound of Music.* Some shows that flopped on Broadway, such as *Jekyll and Hyde* and *Ghost*, have also done very well. Conversely, *The Lion King* which is still going strong in New York, with more than 6,800 performances (as of June 2014) put on since 1997 (Scott 2014), was not at all successful in Seoul. Another show, *The Wizard of Oz*, did not resonate with Korean audiences either, probably because they did not grow up with this pop culture film icon. On the other hand, *Wicked*, based on a novel that presented an "alternative" version of Oz, has enjoyed considerable success, possibly because the Korean production featured a Korean pop star in a leading role. Just as the Disney organization in the United States helped launch the careers of Britney Spears, Christina Aguilera, Selena Gomez, and Miley Cyrus, in Korea "K-pop," a highly commercialized Korean pop music genre has created musical celebrities such as Ock Joo-Hyun. Ock stars in the Seoul production of *Wicked*, and many in the audience show up just to watch her perform (*CBS News* 2014b). It's fair to predict that the success of Broadway shows in Seoul will serve as a stepping stone in spreading American influence throughout Asia in the years ahead.

The spread of American popular culture via television, film, music, and fads and trends amounts to a dissemination of core American values (Crothers 2007). As previously stated, this is a frightening thought to some regimes around the world. Nonetheless, much of the world has embraced American popular culture as enthusiastically as we have, here in the United States.

We leave you with this parting thought and life lesson, restating the comment made by *The Simpsons'* Krusty the Clown that we quoted in chapter 1: "Would it really be worth living in a world without popular culture? I think the survivors would envy the dead."

Lesson Learned: Popular culture: consume it, live it, enjoy it; there's plenty to go around.

References

A&E Television. 2014a. "Matt Groening Biography." (http://www.biography.com/people/matt-groening-9542573#recent-projects&awesm=~oGjQ7v3IfZ16GG).

———. 2014b. "Stanley Tookie Williams Biography." (http://www.biography.com/people/stanley-tookie-williams-476676#awesm=~oGlJuV7M3j7EWE).

ABC News. 2014. "Survey: Nearly Every American Kid Plays Video Games." (http://abcnews.go.com/Technology/story?id=5817835).

Advertising Age. 2014. "Who Bought What in Super Bowl XLVIII: From AB-InBev to Wonderful Pistachios, With Many, Many Marketers in Between." February 3. (http://adage.com/article/special-report-super-bowl/super-bowl-ad-chart-buying-super-bowl-2014/244024/).

Agence France-Presse. 2010. "Cartoonist Stands Firm After Police Foil Alleged Plot Against Paper." *Sydney Morning Herald*, December 31:6.

Alberge, Dalya. 2008. "Hans Christian Andersen's Visit No Fairy Tale for Charles Dickens." *The Australian,* May 2007. (http://www.theaustralian.com.au/archive/news/andersen-visit-no-dickens-fairytale/story-e6frg6to-1111116449165?nk=3bb5cba55f6fe71f27605e7173b34b2f).

Alexander, Heather. 2014. "Surfing Dogs to Become Annual Event at Galveston." *Houston Chronicle.* August 26. (http://www.chron.com/neighborhood/bayarea/news/article/Surfing-dogs-to-become-annual-event-at-Galveston-5713077.php).

American Experience. 2014. "The Development of Radio." (http://www.pbs.org/wgbh/amex/rescue/sfeature/radio.html).

Anderson, Kyle. 2014. "Tour de Fierce." *Entertainment Weekly*, Summer Double Issue:70.

Anderson, Taylor W., and M. L. Johnson. 2014. "'Slenderman' Creator Eric Knudsen Speaks Out on Wisconsin Stabbing." June 4. (http://www.huffingtonpost.com/2014/06/04/slenderman-creator-eric-knudsen-speaks-out_n_5449334.html?flv=1).

Associated Press. 2014. "Ice Bucket, Brazil Elections Popular on Facebook." As it appeared in *The Citizen*, December 10:A9.

———. 2015. "Girls to be Tried as Adults in Stabbing." As it appeared in *The Citizen*, March 14:A5.

Atkins, Hunter. 2014. "Festivus Poles. Close-Talker Mascot. Yada, Yada, Yada." *The New York Times*, July 6. (http://www.nytimes.com/2014/07/07/nyregion/brooklyn-cyclones-seinfeld-night-asserts-shows-wide-appeal.html?_r=0).

Banned Books and Authors. 2011. "Mississippi School District Bans Book on Censorship: *Fahrenheit 451* by Ray Bradbury." (www.banned-books.com/bbarti-cle-miss.html).

Barclay, Eliza. 2012. "How Many Calories Do Olympic Athletes Need? It Depends." *National Public Radio (NPR)*, July 25. (http://www.npr.org/blogs/thesalt/2012/07/24/157317262/how-many-calories-do-olympic-athletes-need-it-depends).

Bauder, David. 2011. "Smart Phones Foster Dumb Habits in Pedestrians." *The Citizen*, January 21:A9.

Beneke, Chris, and Arthur Remillard. 2014. "Is Religion Losing Ground to Sports?" *The Washington Post*, December 17. (http://www.washingtonpost.com/opinions/is-religion-losing-ground-to-sports/2014/01/31/6faa4d64-82bd-11e3-9dd4-e7278db80d86_story.html).

Berokowitz, Bill. 2012. "Are Conservative Documentary Films on the Rise?" *Buzzflash.com.* (http://www.truth-out.org/buzzflash/commentary/are-conservative-documentary-films-on-the-rise/11730-are-conservative-documentary-films-on-the-rise).

Bershadker, Matthew. "Why We Can't Forget Michael Vick's Dog-Fighting Past." *New York Post.* March 26. (http://nypost.com/2014/03/26/why-we-cant-forget-michael-vicks-dog-fighting-past/).

Beschloss, Michael. 2014. "Kahanamoku Helped Bring Aboard 50th State." *New York Times.* August 23:B11.

Bharucha, Jamshed. 2007. "A Space for Music: Mind over Music." *Tufts Magazine*, Winter 2007. (http://www.tufts.edu/alumni/magazine/winter2007/features/music-mind.html).

Biederharn, Isabella. 2015. "Found in a Box, A Seuss Discovery Rocks." *Entertainment Weekly.* August 7:65.

Biskind, Peter. 2013. *My Lunches with Orson: Conversations between Henry Jaglom and Orson Welles.* Edited and with an introduction by Peter Biskind. New York: Metropolitan Books.

Black Panther Party. 1999. "The FBI's War on the Black Panther Party's Southern California Chapter." (http://www.itsabouttimebbp.com/Chapter_History/FBI_War_LA_Chapter.html).

Blake, Meredith. 2014. "The Big Bang of Older TV Viewers." *The Los Angeles Times*, February 22. (http://www.latimes.com/entertainment/tv/showtracker/la-et-st-aging-tv-audience-20140223-story.html#page=1).

Blankstein, Andrew. 2013. "LAPD to Keep Quiet about Celebrity 'Swatting' Cases." *The Los Angeles Times*, April 11. (http://articles.latimes.com/2013/apr/11/local/la-me-swatting-20130412).

Bonsor, Kevin. 2014. "How Satellite Radio Works." *How Stuff Works.* (http://electronics.howstuffworks.com/satellite-radio.htm).

Boyer, Jeremy. 2010. "Which Comics Do You Like Best?" *The Citizen*, November 25:A4.

Brandon, Russell. 2014. "Canadian Teen Arrested For Making More Than 30 Swatting Calls." *The Verge*, May 12. (http://www.theverge.com/2014/5/12/5709270/canadian-teen-arrested-for-making-more-than-30-swatting-calls).

Brown, Douglas. 2005. "Manhug!" *The Denver Post*, May 22. (http://www.denverpost.com/style/ci_2740288/ci_2740289).

Brown, Ryan Lenora. 2013. "Sugar Man: Did the Oscar-Winning Documentary Mislead Viewers?" February 27. (http://www.csmonitor.com/World/Africa/Africa-Monitor/2013/0227/Sugar-Man-Did-the-Oscar-winning-documentary-mislead-viewers).

Browne, Ray B. 2005. "Folklore to Populore," pp. 24–27 in *Popular Culture Studies Across the Curriculum*, edited by R. B. Browne. London: McFarland.

Brummett, Barry. 1991. *Rhetorical Dimensions of Popular Culture*. Tuscaloosa, AL: University of Alabama Press.

Brunner, Borgna. 2013. "Banned Books: *From Harriet the Spy* to *The Catcher in the Rye*." *Infoplease*. (http://www.infoplease.com/spot/banned-kids-books.html).

Burton, Orville Vernon. 2007. *The Age of Lincoln*. New York: Hill and Wang.

Busbee, Jay. 2014. "2015 Super Bowl Ads will Cost $4.5 Million Apiece." *Yahoo! Sports*, June 3. (http://sports.yahoo.com/blogs/nfl-shutdown-corner/2015-super-bowl-ads-will-cost--4-5-million-apiece-135554114.html).

Buzz Feed Comics. 2014. "42 Web Comics You Need to Read." (http://www.buzzfeed.com/kevintang/42-web-comics-you-need-to-read).

Callow, Simon. 1997. *Orson Welles: Volume 1: The Road to Xanadu*. New York: Penguin Books.

CBS News. 2014a. "Is 'Digital Cloning' the Future of Movie Making?" News segment on *CBS This Morning*, June 2. (http://www.cbsnews.com/news/future-of-movies-digital-cloning-in-maleficent/).

———. 2014b. "Rise of Broadway Shows in S. Korea Is Only the Beginning." News segment on *CBS This Morning*, June 9. (http://www.cbsnews.com/news/rise-of-broadway-shows-in-south-korea/).

Celebrity Networth. 2014. "Jerry Seinfeld Net Worth." (http://www.celebritynetworth.com/richest-celebrities/richest-comedians/jerry-seinfeld-networth/).

Chambliss, William. 1993. "State Organized Crime," in *Making Law: The State, the Law, and Structural Contradictions*, edited by W. J. Chambliss and M. Zata. Bloomington, IN: Indiana State University Press.

CBC Sports. 2014. "Seinfeld-Themed Jerseys to Be Worn by Oilers." (http://www.cbc.ca/sports/hockey/seinfeld-themed-jerseys-to-be-worn-by-oilers-affiliate-1.2755624).

CNN Money. 2006. "Howard Stern & Co. Score $200M Payout." January 5. (http://money.cnn.com/2006/01/05/news/newsmakers/stern/index.htm).

Collodi, Carlo. 2008. *Pinocchio,* translated by Geoffrey Brock, with an introduction by Umberto Eco. New York: New York Review of Books Classic.

Consumer Reports. 2010. "Should You 'Buy This Now!' "? (http://www.consumerreports.org/cro/magazine-archive/2010/february/shopping/infomercial-products/overview/infomercial-products-ov.htm).

Creepypasta Wiki. 2014. "Welcome to the Creepypasta Wiki." (http://creepypasta.wikia.com/wiki/Creepypasta_Wiki).

Crothers, Lane. 2007. *Globalization and American Popular Culture.* Lanham, MD: Rowman and Littlefield.

Crupi, Anthony. 2015. "CBS's Moonves: Nest Year's Super Bowl Ads Will Get 'North of $5 Million.' " *Advertising Age,* February 12. (http://adage.com/article/special-report-super-bowl/cbs-s-moonves-super-bowl-ads-north-5-million/297128/).

Daily Finance. 2014. "Top 25 Celebrity Spokespeople of All-Time." (http://www.dailyfinance.com/photos/top-25-celebrity-spokespeople/).

Dale, Renee.2014. "Night Fright." *New York Times Book Review,* November 23:20.

Deadline. 2013. " 'Sharknado!' Gets Midnight Screening Treatment Via Regal." July 26. (http://www.deadline.com/2013/07/sharknado-gets-midnight-screening-treatment-via-regal/).

Delaney, Tim. 2006. *Seinology: The Sociology of Seinfeld.* Amherst, NY: Prometheus.

———. 2008. *Shameful Behaviors.* Lanham, MD: University Press of America.

———. 2010. Personal E-mail Correspondence with Jeremy Boyer. November 26.

———. 2012a. *Connecting Sociology to Our Lives.* Boulder, CO: Paradigm.

———. 2012b. "Georg Simmel's *Flirting* and *Secrecy* and Its Application to the Facebook Relationship Status—"It's Complicated." *Journal of Journalism and Mass Communication* 2(5):637–47.

———. 2014a. *Classical and Contemporary Social Theory: Investigation and Application.* Upper Saddle River, NJ: Pearson.

———. 2014b. *American Street Gangs, Second Edition.* Upper Saddle River, NJ: Pearson.

———. forthcoming. "Infomercials," in *The Wiley Blackwell Encyclopedia of Consumption and Consumer Studies,* edited by D. T. Cook and J. M. Ryan.

———, and Tim Madigan. 2015. *The Sociology of Sport: An Introduction,* Second Edition. Jefferson, NC: McFarland.

Diamond, Dan. 2014. "Ok, the Ice Bucket Challenge Worked. Now Where Will the Dollars Go?" *Forbes.* August 18. (http://www.forbes.com/sites/dandiamond/2014/08/18/ok-the-ice-bucket-challenge-worked-now-where-will-the-dollars-go/).

Dictionary.com. 2014. "Slang." (http://dictionary.reference.com/browse/slang).

Dugdale, Addy. 2010. "New Jersey Police to Shame Drunk Drivers on Facebook." *Fast Company,* August 13. (http://www.fastcompany.com/1681227/new-jersey-police-shame-drunk-drivers-facebook).

Eames, Tom. 2014. "*The Big Bang Theory*: 7 Reasons It's the Biggest Show on TV." *Digital Spy,* March 14. (http://www.digitalspy.com/tv/s217/the-big-bang-theory/feature/a557647/the-big-bang-theory-7-reasons-its-the-biggest-show-on-tv.html#~oFQzkk2Y2J7OB3).

Easley, Jason. 2014. "Jon Stewart Is Now More Trusted Than MSNBC to Provide Accurate Information." PoliticsUSA.com. June 10. (http://www.politicususa.com/2014/06/10/jon-stewart-daily-show-trusted-msnbc-news.html).

Ebert, Roger. 1986. Review of *Star Trek: The Journey Home*. November 26. (http://www.rogerebert.com/reviews/star-trek-iv-the-voyage-home-1986).

———. 2014. Review of *Searching for Sugar Man*. August 8. (http://www.rogerebert.com/reviews/searching-for-sugar-man-2012).

Economics in Picture. 2013. "Changing Top Manufacturing Countries (1980–2010)." January 8. (http://www.economicsinpictures.com/2013/01/changing-top-manufacturing-countries.html).

Egelko, Bob. 2004. "Shaming Ok'd as Part of Sentence. Court Upholds Thief's Wearing 'I Stole Mail' Sign." *San Francisco Chronicle*, August 10:B4.

Ellis, Ralph, and Sara Sidner. 2014. "Rampage in College Town Began with Stabbings." *CNN*, May 24. (http://www.click2houston.com/news/Rampage-in-college-town-began-with-stabbings/26153616).

Empire News. 2014. "Actress Betty White, 92, Dyes Peacefully in Her Los Angeles Home." September 3. (http://empirenews.net/actress-betty-white-92-dyes-peacefully-in-her-los-angeles-home).

Entertainment Weekly. 2014. "The Bullseye." June 20:70.

———. 2014. "Casey Kasem, 1932–2014: The Voice of Pop." June 27:20.

Erion, Gerald. 2007. "Amusing Ourselves to Death with Television News: Jon Stewart, Neil Postman, and the Huxleyan Warning." Pp. 5–15 in *The Daily Show and Philosophy*, edited by J. Holt. Malden, MA/Oxford, UK: Blackwell.

ESPN.com. 2005. "The 25 Best Sports Movies." (http://sports.espn.go.com/espn/espn25/story?page=listranker/bestmoviesresult).

Estren, Mark James. 1993. *A History of Underground Comics*. Berkeley, CA: Ronin.

Fact Monster. 2014. "A Decade-by-Decade Look at Fashion in the United States." (http://www.factmonster.com/ipka/A0878570.html).

Fantasy Sports Trade Association. 2015. "Industry Demographics." (http://www.fsta.org/?page=demographics).

Federal Communications Commission (FCC). 1984. "Public Law 98-549—Oct. 30, 1984." (http://transition.fcc.gov/Bureaus/OSEC/library/legislative_histories/1286.pdf).

———. 2014. "The Dangers of Texting While Driving." (http://www.fcc.gov/guides/texting-while-driving).

Feifer, Jason. 2013. "Obama's Funeral Selfie Is a Fitting End to My Tumblr—Selfies at Funerals." *The Guardian*. December 11. (http://www.theguardian.com/commentisfree/2013/dec/11/obama-funeral-selfie-tumblr-mandela-teens).

Finney, Ben, and James D. Houston. 1996. *Surfing: A History of the Ancient Hawaiian Sport*. Petaluma, CA: Pomegranate Communications.

Flaherty, Anne. 2014. "What About Digital Assets After Death?" *The Post-Standard*, July 17:A-12.

Flanigan, Patrick. 2003. "Neighborhood Mum on Gang." *Rochester Democrat and Chronicle*, December 23:1A.

Forbes. 2013. "The World's Happiest (And Saddest) Countries." (http://www.forbes.com/pictures/mef45ejmi/the-worlds-happiest-and-saddest-countries-2/).

———. 2013b. "Jerry Seinfeld Tops Highest-Earning Comedians of 2013 List." July 11. (http://www.forbes.com/sites/vannale/2013/07/11/jerry-seinfeld-tops-list-of-the-highest-earning-comedians/).

———. "'Grand Auto Theft 5' Has Sold Nearly $2 Billion." May 13. (http://www.forbes.com/sites/davidthier/2014/05/13/grand-theft-auto-5-has-sold-nearly-2-billion-at-retail/).

Fox, Margalit. 2015. "Gary Dahl, the Inventor of the Pet Rock, Is Dead at 78." *New York Times*, April 1:B10.

Fox News. 2008. "Michael Phelps' 12,000 Calorie-a-day Diet Is not for Everyone." August 13. (http://www.foxnews.com/story/2008/08/14/michael-phelps-12000-calorie-day-diet-not-for-everyone/).

Fowler, Geoffrey. 2013. "Life and Death Online: Who Controls a Digital Legacy?" *The Wall Street Journal.* January 5. (http://online.wsj.com/news/articles/SB10001424127887324677204578188220364231346).

France, Lisa Respers, 2014. "Michael Jackson's Hologram: Creepy or Cool?" *CNN Entertainment*, May 19. (http://www.cnn.com/2014/05/19/showbiz/michael-jackson-hologram-billboard-awards/).

Frost, Greg. 2006. "Extra Credit." *The Boston College Chronicle*. March 30, Vol. 14 (14).

Gabler, Neil. 1998. *Life: The Movie.* New York: Vintage Books.

Glazer, Andrew. 2006. "Authorities Say Gangs Using Internet." *The Washington Post*, July 6. (http://www.washingtonpost.com/wp-dyn/content/article/2006/07/06/AR20006070600886.html).

Glyn, Andrew. 2006. *Capitalism Unleashed: Finance Globalization and Welfare.* New York: Oxford University Press.

Gorman, Siobhan. 2014. "Iran-based Cyberspies Targeting U.S. Officials, Report Alleges." *The Wall Street Journal*, May 20. (http://online.wsj.com/articles/iran-based-cyberspies-targeting-u-s-officials-report-alleges-1401335072?tesla=y&mg=reno64-wsj&url=http://online.wsj.com/article/SB10001424052702303633604579590492758580048.html).

Gospel of Reason. 2014. "George Carlin, 'The Planet is Fine.'" (https://gospelofreason.wordpress.com/2007/05/24/george-carlin-the-planet-is-fine/).

Graff, Amy. 2014. "Long Lost Collection of Dr. Seuss Stories Hits Bookstores." September 9. "The Mommy Files." (http://blog.sfgate.com/sfmoms/2014/09/09/long-lost-collection-of-dr-seuss-stories-hits-bookstores-today/#26562101=0).

Grammarphobia. 2013. "Is Go Viral Going Viral?" May 20. (http://www.grammarphobia.com/blog/2013/05/go-viral.html).

Griffith, Janelle. 2014. "'Dancing with the Stars' 2014 Winners: Meryl Davis, NJ's Maksim Chmerkovskiy." NJ.com. (http://www.nj.com/entertainment/tv/index.ssf/2014/05/dancing_with_the_stars_2014_winner_meryl_davis_maksim_chmerkovskiy.html).

Grossman, Lev. 2010. "Mark Zuckerberg," *Time*, December 15. (http://www.time.com/time/specials/packages/article/0,28804,2036683_2037183_2037185,00.html).

Gruber, William. 2012. "PSY's 'Gangnam Style' Video Hits 1 Billion Views, Unprecedented Milestone." *Billboard Biz*, December 21. (http://www.billboard.com/biz/articles/news/1483733/psys-gangnam-style-video-hits-1-billion-views-unprecedented-milestone).

Hanson, David J. 2014. "Driving While Texting Six Times More Dangerous Than Driving While Drunk." Alcohol Problems and Solutions. (http://www2.potsdam.edu/alcohol/files/Driving-while-Texting-Six-Times-More-Dangerous-than-Driving-while-Drunk.html#.U5Ygo2lOWM8).

Happy Planet Index. 2013. "HPI Map." (http://www.happyplanetindex.org/data/).

Hawthorne, Tim. 1993. "As Seen on TV: The New World of Infomercials." *DM News*, July19. (http://www.hawthornedirect.com/tim_hawthorne_articles/?post=as_seen_on_tv_the_new_world_of_infomercials).

Hernandez, Brian Anthony. 2011. "Twitter Now Let's 'X Factor' Viewers Vote via DMs." (http://mashable.com/2011/10/26/xfactor-twitter-vote-dm-direct-messages/).

Herszenhorn, David M. 1995. "Wolfman Jack, Raspy Voice of the Radio, Is Dead at 57." *The New York Times*, July 2. (http://www.nytimes.com/1995/07/02/obituaries/wolfman-jack-raspy-voice-of-the-radio-is-dead-at-57.html).

Hiblen, Carolyn. 2014. "It Was Only a Matter of Time! Undisputed Queen of the Selfie Kim Kardashian to Release 352-page Hardcover Photo Book Aptly Titled *Selfish*." MailOnline.Com. August 8. (http://www.dailymail.co.uk/tvshowbiz/article-2720320/Undisputed-Queen-Selfie-Kim-Kardashian-release-352-page-hardcover-photo-book-aptly-titled-Selfish.html).

Hicks, Marybeth. 2013. "Violent Video Games Create Unhealthy Emotions." (http://www.washingtontimes.com/news/2013/apr/30/hicks-violent-video-games-create-unhealthy-emotion/print/).

Higgins, Matt. 2005. "Endless Winter: A Surfing Paradise Not for the Faint of Heart." *The New York Times*, November 19:B21.

Holt, Douglas B. 2004. *How Brands Become Icons: The Principles of Cultural Bonding*. Boston, MA: Harvard Business School Press.

IMDb. 2014a. "Garry Trudeau Biography." (http://www.imdb.com/name/nm0874034/bio).

———. 2014b. "Dave Chappelle." (http://www.imdb.com/name/nm0152638/).

Jenkins, Holman W. 2015. "When Robo-Cars Crash, It's Your Fault." *Wall Street Journal*, June 10:A13.

Jennings, Angel. 2014. "Compton Shifts Tune on Dr. Dre." *Los Angeles Times*, July 8:A1, A9.

Jet. 2005. "Stanley 'Tookie' Williams Receives Presidential Award for Good Deeds." September 5. (http://findarticles.com/p/articles/mi_m1355/is_10_108/ai_n15655319/).

Jones, Brian. 1991. *The Beatles' Liverpool: The Complete Guide*. Liverpool: Liverpool History Press.

Kastrenakes, Jacob. 2014. "Stephen Colbert Is a Casualty in Amazon's War with Hachette, and He's Mad About It." *The Verge Newsletter*, June 5. (http://www.theverge.com/2014/6/5/5782184/colbert-skewers-amazon-war-with-hachette).

Katz, Elihu, and Paul Felix Lazarsfeld. 1955. *Personal Influence: The Part Played by People in the Flow of Mass Communications.* Glencoe, IL: Free Press.

Kaufman, Donna. 2014. "10 Celebrity Spokespeople Who Will Pretty Much Endorse Anything—No Matter How Weird." *iVillage*, August 1. (http://www.ivillage.com/10-celebrity-spokespeople-who-will-pretty-much-endorse-anything/1-a-543037).

Kelton Research and Support. 2008. "News & Information." (http://sev.prnewswire.com/computer-electronics).

Keyes, Cheryl. 2002. *Rap Music and Street Consciousness.* Urbana, IL: University of Illinois Press.

Kharif, Olga. 2008. "The FCC Approves the XM-Sirius Merger." *Bloomberg Businessweek,* July 25. (http://www.businessweek.com/stories/2008-07-25/the-fcc-approves-the-xm-sirius-mergerbusinessweek-business-news-stock-market-and-financial-advice).

King, Stephen. 2014. "Sounds Off on Amazon." *Entertainment Weekly*, June 13:18.

Knapp, Alex. 2013. "Five Banned Books That You Should Read (That You Probably Haven't." *Forbes,* September 23. (http://www.forbes.com/sites/alexknapp/2013/09/23/five-banned-books-that-you-should-read-that-you-probably-havent/).

Kovacs, Eduard. 2013. "Man Tries to Get Himself Swatted to Boost Reputation on Hacking Forums." November 14. (http://news.softpedia.com/news/Man-Tries-to-Get-Himself-Swatted-to-Boost-Reputation-on-Hacking-Forums-400220.shtml).

Krug, Gary. 2005. *Communication, Technology, and Cultural Change.* Thousand Oaks, CA: Sage.

Laird, Sam. 2012. "Is Social Media Destroying Real-World Relationships?" June 14. (http://mashable.com/2012/06/14/social-media-real-world-infographic/).

Lamont, Tom, and Robert Muchamore. 2014. "Should Celebrities Stop Writing Children's Books?" *The Guardian*, April 5. (http://www.theguardian.com/commentisfree/2014/apr/05/celebrities-writing-childrens-books-debate).

Lansky, Sam. 2014. "Taradise Lost: Tara Reid's Sharknado Comeback." July 30. (http://time.com/3056050/tara-reid-sharknado-2/).

Lavoie, Denise. 2009. "Jury Orders Student to Pay $675,000 for Illegally Downloading Music." *ABC News.* (http://abcnews.go.com/Business/story?id=8226751).

Le Nevez, Catherine. "Where Irish Eyes are Surfing." *BBC Travel*, February 13. (http://www.bbc.com/travel/feature/20140204-where-irish-eyes-are-surfing).

Lee, Stephan. 2014. "Jason Segel Pens Spooky Children's Book." *Entertainment Weekly.* Summer Double Issue:24.

Leiner, Barry M., Vinton G. Cerf, David D. Clark, Robert E. Kahn, Leonard Kleinrock, Daniel C. Lynch, Jon Postel, Larry G. Roberts, and Stephen Wolff.

2014. "Brief History of the Internet." *Internet Society*. (http://www.internet-society.org/internet/what-internet/history-internet/brief-history-internet).

Levitin, Daniel J. 2007. *This Is Your Brain on Music: The Science of a Human Obsession*. New York: Plume Books.

Liautaud, Alexa. 2014. "Driverless Cars: Who Is Responsible When Something Goes Wrong?" *Chicago Tribune*, September 5. (http://www.chicagotribune.com/classified/automotive/sns-wp-blm-news-bc-driverless04-20140904-story.html).

Los Angeles Times. 2014. "Facebook's Lab Rats." July 1:A14.

Machir, Troy. 1994. "Yankees Fan Caught Sleeping on TV Sues ESPN, MLB for $10 Million." *Sporting News*, July 8. (http://www.sportingnews.com/mlb/story/2014-07-07/yankees-fan-caught-sleeping-on-tv-suing-espn-for-10-million-andrew-robert-rector-dan-schulman-john-kruk-mlb-video).

Mannen, Amanda. 2013. "6 Famous Documentaries That Were Shockingly Full of Crap." *Cracked*, August 12. (http://www.cracked.com/article_20585_6-famous-documentaries-that-were-shockingly-full-crap.html).

Mantyla, Kyle. 2010. "Christian Coalition Wants 'Twilight' Books Banned." *People for the American Way*, July 7. (http://www.rightwingwatch.org/content/christian-coalition-wants-twilight-books-banned).

Mashable. 2014. "13 Silly Shamings To Make Your Dog Feel Better." (http://mashable.com/2013/10/24/fish-shaming/).

McCullough, David. 1992. *Brave Companions: Portraits in History*. New York: Simon and Schuster.

Melkonyan, Robert. 2009. "History of the Infomercial." (http://ezinearticles.com/?History-of-the-Infomercial&id=2407073).

Merriam-Webster Dictionary. 2014. "A Sample of New Dictionary Words for 2014." (http://www.merriam-webster.com/new-words/2014-update.htm).

Michaelis, David. *Schulz and Peanuts: A Biography*. 2007. New York: HarperCollins.

Mitovich, Matt Webb. 2014. "NBC Wins the 2013–14 TV Season, for First Time in 10 Years; CBS Is Still Most Watched Network." *TV Line*. (http://tvline.com/2014/05/20/ratings-nbc-wins-2013-2014-tv-season/).

Moir, Alan. 2011. "Drawn and Quartered." *The Sydney Morning Herald*, January 1–2:8.

Mollod, Phineas, and Jason Tesauro. 2002. *The Modern Gentleman: A Guide to Essential Manners, Savvy, and Vice*. Berkeley, CA: Ten Speed Press.

Mongelli, Lorena, David K Li, and Bruce Golding. 2014. "Yankee Fan Caught Sleeping Suing ESPN for $10 million." *New York Post*, July 7. (http://nypost.com/2014/07/07/yankees-fan-caught-sleeping-suing-espn-for-10-million/).

Morrison, Patt. 2014. "Is Public Shaming Fair Punishment?" Op-ed column in *The Los Angeles Times*, May 24. (http://www.latimes.com/opinion/op-ed/la-oe-0525-morrison-sentencing-shame-judges-20140525-column.html).

MTV News. 2013. "Miley Cyrus Twerks, Gives Robin Thicke Some Tongue at VMAs." August 25. (http://www.mtv.com/news/1713017/miley-cyrus-robin-thicke-vma-twerk/).

National Association of Manufacturers. 2014. "Facts about Manufacturing in the United States." (http://www.nam.org/Statistics-And-Data/Facts-About-Manufacturing/Landing.aspx).

National Gang Intelligence Center. 2011. "2011 National Gang Threat Assessment—Emerging Trends and the Internet." (http://ilookbothways.com/2011/11/07/2011-national-gang-threat-assessment-%E2%80%93-emerging-trends-and-the-internet/).

Nielsen. 2014. "Super Bowl XLVIII Draws 111.5 Million Viewers, 25.3 Million Tweets." February 3. (http://www.nielsen.com/us/en/newswire/2014/super-bowl-xlviii-draws-111-5-million-viewers-25-3-million-tweets.html).

Nudd, Tim. 2014. "Pamela Anderson Declines Ice Bucket Challenge, Citing ALS Animal Testing." *People*, August 22. (http://www.people.com/article/pamela-anderson-ice-bucket-challenge).

Orlin, Jon. "It's 2012 Already, So Where Are All the Jetsons' Flying Cars?" TechChrunch.com. January 1. (http://techcrunch.com/2012/01/01/its-2012-already-so-where-are-all-the-jetsons-flying-cars/).

Oxford Dictionaries. 2013. "The Oxford Dictionaries Word of the Year 2013 is . . . Selfie." (http://blog.oxforddictionaries.com/2013/11/word-of-the-year-2013-winner/).

Parade. 2009. "Intelligence Report: What's Made in the USA." April 19:10.

Paul, Mark. 2012. " 'The Big Bang Theory' Draws Highest Ratings Yet: Why Its Popularity Is Growing." *Yahoo News.* (https://tv.yahoo.com/news/big-bang-theory-draws-highest-ratings-yet-why-184500803.html).

Pearce, Matt. 2014. "A Violation, or Social Media as Usual?" *Los Angeles Times,* July 6:A10.

Petracca, Michael, and Madeleine Sorapure, editors. 1998. *Common Culture*, 2nd edition. Upper Saddle River, NJ: Prentice-Hall.

PoliceOne.com. 2014. "Gangs Find New Home on the Internet." January 12. (http://www.policeone.com/gangs/articles/6732469-Gangs-find-new-home-on-the-Internet/).

Pond, Neil. 2011. "History of Comic Strips." *American Profile.* (http://american-profile.com/articles/history-of-comic-strips/).

Pooley, Jefferson, and Michael J. Socolow. 2013. "The Myth of *The War of the Worlds* Panic." *Slate,* October 28. (http://www.slate.com/articles/arts/history/2013/10/orson_welles_war_of_the_worlds_panic_myth_the_infamous_radio_broadcast_did.html).

Popper, Nathaniel. 2015. "Hackers Skip the Cash, Ask for Bitcoin Ransom." *The Star Tribune.* July 26:A1.

Pressler, Charles, and Fabio Dasilua. 1996. *Sociology and Interpretation: From Weber to Habermas.* Albany, NY: State University of New York Press.

Pritchard, Justin. 2014. "Look Ma, No Hands: Prototype of a Truly Driverless Car in the Works." *The Post Standard*, May 29:A2.

Public Broadcasting Service (PBS). 2011. "Political Cartoons." (http://www.pbs.org/opb/historydetectives/feature/political-cartoons/).

———. 2012. "The 25 'Greatest' Documentaries of All Time." December 3. (http://www.pbs.org/pov/blog/2012/12/the-25-greatest-documentaries-of-all-time/17/#top).

Pyle, Richard. 2000. "Batch of New Words for Dictionary." *CBS News*, June 27. (http://www.cbsnews.com/news/batch-of-new-words-for-dictionary/).

Raymond, Adam K. 2014. "Why Are 23.4 Million People Watching *The Big Bang Theory*?" *New York Magazine*, May 5. (http://www.vulture.com/2014/05/big-bang-theory-ratings.html).

Recording Industry Association of America (RIAA). 2014. "For Students Doing Reports." RIAA Homepage. (http://www.riaa.com/faq.php).

Redhage, Rick. 2006. "County Tries to Deter DUIs with Ads: Mug Shots of Offenders Will Go Up on Internet Site." *The Tribune* (Mesa, AZ), December 14.

Rensin, Emmett. 2014. "The Great Satirical-News Scam of 2014." June 5. (http://www.newrepublic.com/article/118013/satire-news-websites-are-cashing-gullible-outraged-readers).

Rettner, Rachael. 2014. "Do Violent Video Games Boost Aggression? Study Adds Fire to Debate." *Live Science*, March 25. (http://www.foxnews.com/tech/2014/03/25/do-violent-games-boost-aggression/).

Robinson, Byran. 2005. "Tookie Williams: Gang Founder Versus Nobel-Nominated Peacemaker." *ABC News*, December 8. (http://abcnews.go.com/US/LegalCenter/story?id=1377890).

Rolling Stone Music. 2014. "500 Greatest Songs of All Time." (http://www.rollingstone.com/music/lists/the-500-greatest-songs-of-all-time-20110407).

Ross, Shmuel. 2007. "Comics Timeline." *Infoplease*. (http://www.infoplease.com/spot/comicstimeline.html).

Rouse, Margaret. 2005. "Display." *WhatIs.com*. (http://whatis.techtarget.com/definition/display).

Ryder, Tarin. 2014. "Kim Kardashian Is Releasing a Book of Selfies." *Yahoo Celebrity!* August 8. (https://celebrity.yahoo.com/blogs/celeb-news/kim-kardashian-is-releasing-a-book-of-selfies-214434245.html).

Sanati, Cyrus. 2012. "Bitcoin Looks Primed for Money Laundering." December 18. (http://fortune.com/2012/12/18/bitcoin-looks-primed-for-money-laundering/).

Sanchick, Myra. 2015. "Testimony Wraps Up in Hearing for Anissa Weier, Charged in 'Slenderman' Stabbling." Fox6News, May 27. (http://fox6now.com/2015/05/27/hearing-resumes-for-anissa-weier-charged-in-slenderman-stabbing/).

Schuessler, Jennifer. 2014. "Still No Flying Cars? Debating Technology's Future." *New York Times*, September 22:C3.

Schulz, Charles. 2008. *The Complete Peanuts: 1967–1968*. New York: Fantagraphics Press.

Science Daily. 2013. "Study Explores Gang Activity on the Internet." March 26. (http://www.sciencedaily.com/releases/2013/03/130326101525.htm).

Scott, Walter. 2014. "Personality." *Parade*, June 15:2.

————. 2014b. "Personality." *Parade*, July 6:2.

Seinfeld. 1992. "The Pitch." First air date, September 16.

————. 1993. "The Puffy Shirt." First air date, September 23.

————. 1993. "The Lip Reader." First air date: October 28.

————. 1995. "The Sponge." First air date: December 7.

————. 1996. "The Bizarro Jerry." First air date, October 3.

————. 1997. "The Yada, Yada." First air date, April 24.

————. 1997. "The Strike." First air date, December 18.

Sentencing Law and Policy. 2013. "New Commentary Calls 'Creative' Shaming Punishments 'Terrible' (on Curious Grounds)." September 6. (http://sentencing.typepad.com/sentencing_law_and_policy/2013/09/new-commentary-calls-creative-shaming-punishments-terrible-on-curious-grounds.html).

Sevenson, Lucky. 2001. "Nobel Peace Nominee." *Religion and Ethics*, February 16. (http://www.pbs.org/wnet/religionandethics/week425/cover.html).

Shaer, Matthew. 2009. "English Gets Millionth Word, Site Says." *Asia Times Online*, December 3. (http://www.csmonitor.com/Innovation/Horizons/2009/0610/english-language-gets-its-one-millionth-word-website-says).

Sherwell, Philip. 2014. "Four Long-lost Dr. Seuss Stories Published in New Collection." *The Telegraph*, September 9. (http://www.telegraph.co.uk/culture/books/booknews/11085031/Four-long-lost-Dr-Seuss-stories-published-in-new-collection.html).

Shipman, Tim. 2006. "A Public Shaming For Child Support Dodgers." *The Daily Mail*, December 11:20.

SiriusXM. 2013. "Investor Relations." (http://investor.siriusxm.com/releasedetail.cfm?ReleaseID=775739).

Smith, Catharine. 2011. "Facebook Study Finds Narcissistic Users Spend Most Time on Site. (http://www.huffingtonpost.com/2010/08/25/facebook-study-finds-narc_n_693719.html).

Smith, Craig. 2014. "By the Numbers: 105 Amazing Facebook User Statistics." March 13. (http://expandedramblings.com/index.php/by-the-numbers-17-amazing-facebook-stats/#.U4dD5GlOWM8).

Smith, Stacy L., Ken Lachlan, and Ron Tamborini. 2003. "Popular Video Games: Quantifying the Presentation of Violence and its Context." *Journal of Broadcasting and Electronic Media* 47(1):58–76.

Snyder, Riley. 2014. "Lofty Ambitions for Bitcoin ATMs." *Los Angeles Times,* July 5.

Social Media Defined. 2014. "What Is Social Media?" (http://www.socialmediadefined.com/what-is-social-media/).

Space Foundation. 2002. "Satellite Radio Technology." (http://www.spacefoundation.org/programs/space-technology-hall-fame/inducted-technologies/satellite-radio-technology).

Sports Illustrated. 2014A. "Head Start: A New Car Allows Hands-Free Driving." June 2:20.

————. 2014B. "Bucket List." August 18:18.

Stableford, Dylan. 2014. "New York Teen Gamer Latest Victim of 'Swatting,' Police Say." *Yahoo News*, April 23. (http://news.yahoo.com/call-of-duty-swat-long-island-131101346.html).

Statista. 2014. "Age Breakdown of Video Game players in the United States in 2014." (http://www.statista.com/statistics/189582/age-of-us-video-game-players-since-2010/).

————. 2015. "Number of Monthly Active Facebook Users Worldwide as of 1st Quarter 2015 (in Millions)." (http://www.statista.com/statistics/264810/number-of-monthly-active-facebook-users-worldwide/).

Statistic Brain. 2014a. "Facebook Statistics." July 1. (http://www.statisticbrain.com/facebook-statistics/).

————. 2014b. "Twitter Statistics." July 11. (http://www.statisticbrain.com/twitter-statistics/).

Steel, Emily. 2014. "A Series of Icy Baths Going Viral, for Charity." *New York Times*. August 18:B8.

Steinmetz, Katy. 2014. "#Selfie, Steampunk, Catfish: See This Year's New Dictionary Words." *Time*, May 19. (http://time.com/103503/merriam-webster-dictionary-selfie-catfish/).

Stelter, Brian. 2012. "Nielsen Reports a Decline in Television Viewing." *The New York Times*, May 3.(http://mediadecoder.blogs.nytimes.com/2012/05/03/nielsen-reports-a-decline-in-television-viewing/?_r=0).

Subramanian, Pras. 2013. "5 Surprising Stats About Fantasy Sports." *Yahoo Finance*, September 4. (http://finance.yahoo.com/blogs/breakout/5-surprising-stats-fantasy-sports-154356461.html).

Swartz, Jon. 2014. "McCartney Hits It Out of Candlestick Park: Ex-Beatle Returns for Stadium's Swan Song." *USA Today*, August 16:7B.

Tait, Simon. 2008. "A Tale of Two Writers." *The Independent*, May 26. (http://www.independent.co.uk/arts-entertainment/books/features/a-tale-of-two-writers-6145401.html).

The Beatles: 50ᵗʰ Anniversary Collector's Edition. 2014. Liverpool: The Daily Mirror Collection.

The Citizen. 2009. "Jury Awards $675K in Music Downloading Case." August 1:A5.

————. 2010. "What Drove Girls to Stabbing?" June 4:A6.

————. 2014. "Technology: Frustration Over Passwords Growing." June 27: A6.

————. 2014. "'Wimpy Kid' Author Opening Bookstore." May 31:A2.

The Economist. 2006. "Ingenious Punishments: Their Object All Sublime." October 14:31.

The Guardian. 2014. "Just How New are the Merriam-Webster Dictionary's New Words?" (http://www.theguardian.com/science/shortcuts/2014/may/20/how-new-are-merriam-webster-new-words).

The Moore Collection. 2014. "Underground Comix." (http://lib.calpoly.edu/spec_coll/comix/).

The Post-Standard. 2009. "Jury Rules Against Woman in Music Downloading Case." June 19:A-15.

―――. 2010. "Reporter Brenda Starr Is Leaving the Biz." October 12:A-1.

―――. 2012a. "Social Media: Facebook by the Numbers." February 4:A-1.

―――. 2012b. "Killer Sharpened Aim by Playing Video Game." April 20:A-11.

―――. 2014. "'Sharknado 2' Whipped Up Storm of Viewers, Tweets." August 3:A-2.

―――. 2014. "When Your Best Friends Become the Boogeyman: 12-Year-Old Didn't Know Sleepover Plans Included Her Murder to Impress Slenderman." June 8:B-1, B-3.

The Simpsons. 1995. "Sideshow Bob's Last Gleaming" (#3F08). First air date, November 26.

―――. 2008. "Any Given Sundance" (KABF11). First air date, May 4.

Tobak, Steve. 2013. "10 Dumb Things People Do with Smartphones." Fox Business. September 27. (http://www.foxbusiness.com/technology/2013/09/27/10-dumb-things-people-do-with-smartphones/).

Toomer, Jessica. 2014. "'The Big Bang Theory' Blasts China." The Huffington Post, May 7. (http://www.huffingtonpost.com/2014/05/07/big-bang-theory-china-an_n_5282030.html).

Top Web Comics. 2014. "Comic Rankings." (http://topwebcomics.com/).

Trejos, Nancy. 2014. "Deal Them Out: Apps Could Replace Hotel Key Cards." USA Today, June 30:B1.

TV Guide. 2004. "Together Again? Get Out!" November 21–27.

Twitter.com. 2014. "FAQs About Retweets (RT)." (https://support.twitter.com/articles/77606-faqs-about-retweets-rt#).

Twitter Athletes. 2014. "Top 10 Twitter Athletes." (http://twitter-athletes.com/TopAthletes.cfm).

Twitter Counter. 2014. "Twitter Top 100." (http://twittercounter.com/pages/100).

Tyson, Jeff, and Carmen Carmack. 2014. "How Computer Monitors Work." HowStuffWorks.com. (http://computer.howstuffworks.com/monitor1.htm).

Urban Dictionary. 2014. "Hater." (http://www.urbandictionary.com/define.php?term=hater&page=7).

―――. 2014b. "Twerking." (http://www.urbandictionary.com/define.php?term=twerking).

―――. 2014c. "Locomotion." (http://www.urbandictionary.com/define.php?term=Locomotion).

United States Military. 2012. "The Hip Hop Music History of Boot Camp Clik." Boot Camps. (http://www.usmilitarymuscle.com/the-hip-hop-music-history-ofboot-camp-clik.php).

USA Today. 2004. "Shame Works, So Use It." September 1:14A.

Valby, Karen. 2014. "A Battle by the Books." Entertainment Weekly, June 13:17–18.

Villarreal, Yvonne. 2014. "'Sharknado 2' nabs 3.9 Million Viewers, Millions More Than Original." Los Angeles Times, July 31. (http://www.latimes.com/entertainment/tv/showtracker/la-et-st-sharknado-2-viewers-20140731-story. html).

Walker, Sam. 2006. *Fantasyland: A Season on Baseball's Lunatic Fringe.* New York: Viking.

Ward, John William. 1966. "Afterword." In Harriet Beecher Stowe, *Uncle Tom's Cabin.* New York: Signet Classic.

Ward, Kat. 2014. "Chart Attack: Top Broadcast-TV Shows Week Ending Sept. 28." *Entertainment Weekly,* October 17:25.

Warhol, Andy. 1975. *The Philosophy of Andy Warhol (From A to B and Back Again).* New York: Harvest Books.

Watson, Stephanie. 2012. "Top Ten Most Popular Infomercials." How Stuff Works: A Discovery Company. (http://money.howstuffworks.com/10-most-popular-infomercials.htm).

Watts, Duncan J., and Peter Sheridan Dodds. 2007. "Influentials, Networks, and Public Opinion Formation." *Journal of Consumer Research* 34 (Dec.):441–58.

Waxman, Sharon. 2004. "The Political 'Fahrenheit' Sets Record at Box Office." *The New York Times,* June 28. (http://www.nytimes.com/2004/06/28/movies/28BOX.html).

Weber, Bruce. 2014. "Malik Bendjelloul, Oscar Winner for 'Sugar Man' Film, Dies at 36." *The New York Times,* May 13. (http://www.nytimes.com/2014/05/14/movies/malik-Bendjelloul-36-dies-directed-sugar-man-movie.html?_r=0).

Weisbaum, Herb. 2014. "Cell Phone Thefts Soar as Advocates Hail 'Kill Switch.'" *CNBC,* April 18. (http://www.cnbc.com/id/101589854).

Williams, Randy. 2006. *Sports Cinema 100 Movies.* Pompton Plain, NJ: Limelight Editions.

Williams, Stanley Tookie. 1997a. "Tookie's Corner: My Letter to Incarcerated Youth, No. 1." (http://networkforyouthintransition.org/forum/topics/tookies-corner).

———. 1997b. "Tookie's Corner: The Apology." (http://networkforyouthintransition.org/forum/topics/tookies-corner).

Wingfield, Nick. 2014. "E-Sports at College, with Stars and Scholarships." *The New York Times,* December 8. (http://www.nytimes.com/2014/12/09/technology/esports-colleges-breeding-grounds-professional-gaming.html).

Worland, Justin. 2014. "Here's What's Happening with the Ice Bucket Challenge Money." *Time,* November 4. (http://time.com/3556217/ice-bucket-challenge-als-money/).

Wyatt, Susan. 2014. "Sir Mix-A-Lot Performs 'Baby Got Back' With Seattle Symphony." *USA Today Network,* June 9. (http://www.usatoday.com/story/news/nation-now/2014/06/09/sir-mix-a-lot-seattle-symphony/10222125/).

Yardley, Jim. "In His Focus on Rich and Poor, Pope Admits to Overlooking the Middle Class." *New York Times.* July 14:A7.

Yarm, Mark. 2014. "Inside the Celebrity-Lust Gaming Boom." *Rolling Stone,* August 28:13.

Index